Your First Parenting Journey

How to Have A Worry-Free Pregnancy, How Baby Sleep Training Works and How to Succeed In Your Baby's First Year

By:

Harley Carr

professional before attempting any techniques outlined in this book.

By reading this document, the reader agrees that under no circumstances is the author responsible for any losses, direct or indirect, that are incurred as a result of the use of the information contained within this document, including, but not limited to, errors, omissions, or inaccuracies.

Having a baby is one of the most exciting and life-changing experiences you can have. You've probably dreamed of the special moments you'll have with your new baby. But have you thought about how you want to give birth to your little bundle of joy? And on how you will help your newborn establish a consistent sleep pattern by making routines for your baby's daily activities? And how you will document your baby's milestones, not only to capture their magical moments, but also for medical reasons?

We have made several products that can help you to be more prepared and starting from your pregnancy all the way to end of your baby's first year.

My Birth plan - ensures that you and your partner are on the same page as your doctors and nurses when it comes to issues like pain meds, people allowed in the delivery room, episiotomies, cord-cutting, etc.

Baby Schedule Tracker- Track your baby's daily schedule for feeding, sleeping, crying and changing diapers. Once those patterns begin to form, you can help your baby settle into a daily routine and sleep pattern. In this way you can get back your sleep as well.

Baby's Milestones Journal- It's also easy to miss an important baby's milestones in the chaos of new parenthood. So, we've compiled a list of suggestions on how to document baby's first year and which milestones are worth documenting. This printable Baby's Milestones Journal is available in both "Baby Girl" and "Baby Boy" version.

Get them all for free in PDF format by going to the link below:

https://harleycarrparenting.com/your-first-parenting-journey-book/

Or

Scan the QR code

Print all the 3 documents and start to make your own birth plan, track your baby's daily activities and record your baby's important milestones and events.

Let´s get started ...

Enjoy and best wishes to your pregnancy and parenting journey!

Harley Carr

Table of Contents

Part 1: A Worry-Free Pregnancy for First Time Parents

How to Be Stress-Free and Feel Secure Throughout Your Pregnancy Journey for Baby's and Mom's Optimal Health

Introduction

Pregnancy is an ongoing journey that can be full of first-time experiences for all parents alike. It is normal to feel unprepared and uneducated about the journey. If you have never gone through it before, or if you are just particularly nervous, finding out that you are pregnant can be a stressful experience whether you were trying to become pregnant or not. As parents, you are about to take on the responsibility of caring for another human life. It is natural to feel like you need all the help you can get. With the use of this guide, you are going to learn everything that you need to know about being a great parent. From maintaining a healthy pregnancy to having a relaxed delivery, there is plenty that you can do to ensure that having your baby can be the happiest and easiest experience possible.

Caring for a baby is a lot more than changing diapers and getting up throughout the night for feedings; it takes instinct and intuition. The only way to become great at this is to get rid of your fear and insecurity. Nobody knows what they are doing in the beginning, and that is okay. Remember that all parenting must start somewhere. Also, keep in mind that the level of difficulty you experience in your pregnancy does not indicate the level of difficulty you will face as a parent. All pregnancies are unique, and there are just certain aspects that you cannot control. Let go of this desire to control things, and fully experience your pregnancy.

You are a parent the moment you realize that you have life growing inside of you. Each choice that you make from that moment on is going to directly impact your baby. This is why your lifestyle plays such an important role in your pregnancy. There are plenty of people who realize that they are expecting, so they must change their lifestyle in order to accommodate a baby. This can mean anything from cutting down on spending to cutting down on partying. By using your common sense, you are going to allow your parental instincts to kick in. You know what is going to be best for your baby, so listen to these thoughts and feelings that develop.

Pregnancy has the ability to bring a couple closer together. While only one individual is going to be experiencing the pregnancy first-hand, you are both going through it together. Every decision that you make should be made with excellent communication and your baby's wellbeing in mind. This can often put stress on the relationship because so many important decisions must be made in only a few months. Know that it is okay to take some time to breathe before rushing into decisions. Discuss things openly with your partner, and try to be mindful of both opinions. Even though the father isn't going to be physically carrying the child, he is still going to have valuable insight into what he believes is best for the baby.

By learning steps that you can apply to your real life, you are going to feel comfortable and prepared for what is to come. Starting from the very beginning, you are going to learn how to care for your baby from inside the womb. Every mother should know what it means to be healthy during pregnancy, and that is exactly what you are going to learn. From finding out which foods you are able to eat to decide on how much exercise you can manage, all of these decisions are things that will impact your baby. If you are taking good care of yourself, then you are taking good care of your child.

As your pregnancy progresses, you will learn about the important signs and symptoms that all parents should be aware of. By discovering what is normal and what is abnormal, you will know when you need to seek medical attention and when you simply need an easy remedy. Pregnancy can cause you to feel things that you have never felt before, and this can be a scary experience. By taking away some of the fear, you will be able to have a better idea of how to handle these experiences and turn them into lessons. Not all pain is bad pain, but all pain can be managed if you know how to identify it.

Through delivery, having a guide that teaches you about what to expect is important because it will allow you to be more relaxed. A relaxed mother is thought to have a better labor and a higher chance of being able to deliver the baby naturally. While not all mothers can deliver this way, the guide is still going to be able to teach you techniques that will get you through your peak times of labor and allow for the safest possible delivery for your baby. Delivery preparation, no matter what kind of pregnancy you are having, is exactly what you will learn from this guide.

After birth, a different type of care will begin. You are going to learn the best ways to care for your newborn to ensure that they have a healthy start in their life. All of the decisions that you made before your baby was born will prepare you for the moment that you must start making them in-person. Much like pregnancy, parenting can also be full of trial and error. This is normal and expected, so make the most of the experience. Enjoy everything that you learn, and if you make a mistake, use that as an example of what not to do again in the future. Since no one is perfect, you should not have to put pressure on yourself to be society's idea of the "perfect" parent.

As a mother of three, I have experienced several different types of pregnancies. Beginning with my first-born son, the process was as smooth as can be. I had four-hour labor and was able to deliver naturally. It truly encouraged my abilities as a mother, as well as my ability to carry another child again in the future. Two years later, and my daughter was born. This pregnancy showed me the other side of being pregnant. From difficult symptoms to an emergency C-section delivery, I was shaken to my core. It was with the help of my partner, my midwife, and my resilience as a mother that I got through it and delivered a healthy baby.

Admittedly, this experience discouraged me from having more children. Though my partner and I wanted to have another baby, I was fearful that my next pregnancy would be as difficult as my last. Five years after our daughter was born, we found out that I was pregnant again. This was unplanned, but it automatically jump-started my adrenaline. It was a race to prepare for our third baby, and I hoped that my body would cooperate. My symptoms were difficult again, and finally, it came time for the delivery. Through meditation and breathing techniques that I had learned through the years, I powered through the pain. The labor was long and intense, but I didn't let this discourage me. I was able to give birth naturally once again, and although it was more difficult than my first, it allowed me to birth a healthy baby boy.

I learned that there is always going to be more to learn. No matter how prepared I thought I was there was always something to throw me for a loop. I learned how to love this aspect of pregnancy and parenting in general. Through letting go of my own unfair expectations of myself, I was able to just enjoy being a mom to my three children. And in doing so, my spouse was also able to do the same. When there are two people embarking on this journey together, it is so important that they are both on the same page. Through including my partner on my decisions throughout the pregnancy, we were

17

able to form a great team and be great providers to our children.

The experiences that I've had in the last couple of decades have inspired me to write a guide that can help all expecting parents. While you might not be able to control exactly what goes on during your pregnancy, you can certainly do your best to make sure that you are prepared for anything. If there is one thing that I found to be important as a pregnant woman, it was the ability to expect the unexpected. Getting rid of all the imaginary standards I had about a symptom-free pregnancy with a quick and natural delivery allowed me to just enjoy everything that was happening to me. I saw each of my pregnancies as an important and valuable experience.

By reading this guide, you are going to be mastering the following experiences that many expecting parents are faced with:

- Noticing your pregnancy symptoms from the beginning and knowing when to take an at-home pregnancy test
- How to choose the right doctor for you
- What to expect and what questions to ask during your first prenatal checkup
- Deciding if any changes in your lifestyle that must be made after finding out you are pregnant
- Learning how rapidly your baby is growing inside the womb

- Learning about how your body is changing
- Knowing how to care for yourself if you get sick while being pregnant
- Caring for your skin if it begins to break out
- Dealing with your swollen feet and aching back
- How to properly nourish yourself through the nausea
- Becoming educated on how much coffee and wine you can drink
- Learning about how safe it is to eat fish and deli meat
- Deciding how long you will be able to work and knowing what maternity leave options your job provides
- Forming opinions on whether you'd like to have a gender reveal party or a 4-D ultrasound
- Traveling when you are pregnant
- Having sex while you are pregnant
- Determining how much you can work out
- Choosing your birthing option (water birth, home birth, traditional hospital birth, etc.)
- Knowing the signs of going into labor

All of the above topics will be covered in detail so you can feel as prepared as possible. No matter what kind of pregnancy you are experiencing, even if you are expecting more than one child, there will be a topic to answer your questions and find solutions for your problems. While most pregnancy guides only focus on the mother-to-be, this one will also include information that expecting fathers must know. By having both parents feeling as though they are prepared, the overall experience is going to be better and safer. There is no such thing as too much education when it comes to the topic of pregnancy. All of the knowledge that you gain during your pregnancy is going to be useful to you for the rest of your life.

After you are through reading this guide, you are going to feel informed and empowered. While there might be difficulties along the way, you are going to have all the tools you need in order to make the most of your pregnancy and deliver a healthy and happy baby. Regardless of how far along you are or even if you are simply considering having a baby, this guide is going to teach you everything you need to know. Many parents have utilized these methods over the last several years because they work so well. They will give you the confidence you need in order to be the very best parents you can be.

If you currently don't know what to do after finding out you are pregnant or finding out that you want to become pregnant, take the first step toward action by reading this guide. The sooner you are able to read this information and learn everything you need to know, the sooner you will feel ready to be a parent. Any questions you have, this book is going to not only answer, but also offer solutions. There will be no details spared as you navigate through each chapter of this guide. While there is no such thing as a perfect parent, there is such a thing as a perfectly prepared parent. This preparation truly pays off!

"Make preparations in advance. You will never have trouble if you are prepared for it." -Theodore Roosevelt

Chapter 1: What Are the Early Signs and Symptoms?

There is nothing to fear when you realize that you might be pregnant. While your body is about to undergo changes, accept that your body is going to know exactly what to do throughout your pregnancy. It is up to you to listen to these signs and symptoms in order to determine how to make yourself feel the best you can. Finding out you are pregnant can be one of the most exciting times in your life, so knowing how to read the signs are incredibly important. In this chapter, all of the symptoms you need to be aware of are going to be covered. From the ones you have probably heard of to other rarities, you will be very familiar with your body and what it is trying to tell you.

Most of the time, what you are experiencing is completely normal, even if you have never felt it before. Even as early as a few weeks into a pregnancy, many mothers agree that they were able to tell that something was different. If you have any sort of feeling like this, take a closer look at exactly what you are experiencing. Often, the symptoms in the very beginning can be so subtle that they are overlooked. It is only when looking back on these things do some realize that these were the pregnancy symptoms that they needed to be paying attention to.

The Most Common Early Signs and Symptoms

These are the classic symptoms of pregnancy that most women experience. While they might not experience these things at the exact same stage in their pregnancies, it is likely that they will at some point. Examine the following symptoms, and see how many you can resonate with:

- Missed Period: This one is pretty self-explanatory - a missed period is normally one of the earliest indications of pregnancy. When you become pregnant, you stop menstruating, so it is natural that a missed period would lead you to believe that you are pregnant. For some, this can be a misleading symptom because not all women have regulated periods. Some experience missed periods even when they are not pregnant, so keep this in mind. Compared to your normal menstruation schedule, determine if your missed period is a symptom or simply your period being sporadic. If you need further confirmation, you can consult your doctor.

- Tender and Swollen Breasts: Changes in your breasts are going to be felt early on in your pregnancy. This can feel similar to what you would experience right before you start your period. Not only will your breasts feel more tender and potentially even heavy, but they might also begin to change color around the areola and nipple. This happens because your progesterone levels are rising. You might notice this symptom as early as 1-2 weeks after conception. It will normally last for a while, often well into your first trimester of pregnancy.

- Nausea With or Without Vomiting: What most women picture when they find out they are pregnant is the rush to the toilet in order to vomit. Morning sickness is not a myth, but the way it is experienced among pregnant women can greatly vary. When you are pregnant, feeling nauseous is normal. This does not necessarily mean that you are going to vomit, though. Certain smells or sights can trigger this nausea, so pay attention to any moments where you are feeling this way.

- Increased Urination: Being pregnant puts a big strain on your bladder. As your baby grows and develops, your body must make room on the inside for this expansion. A fascinating process when you study it, all of your internal organs, even your ribcage, will expand or contract to make way for the growing baby. Since your baby is in your uterus, this happens to be very close to your bladder. This added pressure can cause you to urinate more frequently. If you notice that you feel the need to go more often, then this might be an indication that you are pregnant.

- Fatigue: Soon after conception, it is normal to feel a wave of tiredness crash over you. Certain tasks that are normally part of your daily routine can begin to feel draining. This is one of the symptoms that is commonly felt by nearly all pregnant women in the beginning. This also happens due to your progesterone levels increase. A spike in progesterone can make you feel very sleepy. Don't be alarmed if you feel like napping throughout the day because your body is simply trying to prepare itself for what is happening.

Whether you have all or one of the symptoms listed above, it can still be hard to determine if you truly are pregnant or not. By only listening to your body, you are solely operating on instinct. While it is great to try and predict this for yourself, the best way to find out if you really are pregnant happens after a visit to your doctor. Your doctor is going to be able to run the most accurate testing in order to confirm your pregnancy. While experiencing the symptoms can be exciting if you are trying to get pregnant, know that a visit to the doctor is always going to be the smartest thing for you to do.

Before you see your doctor, you can take an at-home pregnancy test. Most of the time, an at-home test is taken and then a doctor's appointment is scheduled soon after. A lot of tests that are available for purchase have increased accuracy ratings nowadays. Some even promise to give you results as early as five days after your missed period. Make sure that you keep in mind that no at-home test is going to be 100% accurate, but nonetheless, the process is still exciting. Seeing a positive reading is enough to change your entire life.

This is a very exciting time for a couple to go through together. A positive reading is when the idea of parenting becomes very real. Knowing that you are probably going to have a baby in less than a year's time is an incredibly special moment to share with your significant other. From that reading onward, you must come together as a team in order to do your best for your child. From visits to the doctor to picking out items for the nursery, you are both about to start this journey together.

Sometimes, you might have many symptoms of pregnancy, but find out that you are not pregnant. Do not let this discourage you if you are trying to get pregnant. Know that not every single mother got pregnant on the first try. Just as exciting as a positive pregnancy test reading can be, a negative reading can truly tear you down. Try not to let this hinder your desire to try again. Fertility takes a mixture of biology and luck. While there are ways that you can try to make yourself more fertile, know that you will become pregnant when the time is right.

Make sure that you are leaning on your significant other for support during this time. Whether you find out you are pregnant or you find out that it hasn't happened yet, you both need one another for support. This is a journey you are both taking, and while your partner might not be physically carrying the child, they are still a valid part of the entire process. Acknowledge this and express your appreciation often. Small things like this will keep a relationship strong.

Know that your pregnancy journey is not something that you have to share with the world right away. In fact, most couples do not announce a pregnancy until the end of the first trimester. This is usually for health reasons as well as privacy. Once a mother has reached the end of the third month, this is normally a sign of a healthy pregnancy. This also gives both parents the chance to decide who they would like to tell first and how they'd like to make the announcement. A lot of couples have been opting for gender reveal parties in order to break the news to their loved ones. No matter what you decide to do, take the first 13 weeks as your time to make these plans with your partner. Remember, there is no right or wrong way because this is your pregnancy.

A lot of new parents, especially mothers, feel pressure in the beginning to do what others are advising them. While certain tips and recommendations can be very helpful, know that you are the one who is going to be going through the pregnancy. Therefore, you have every right to deviate from "normal" plans and do what feels right. By listening to your symptoms and your body from the moment after conception, you are going to be on the right track to making the best decisions possible throughout your pregnancy and as a parent.

Less Obvious Signs and Symptoms

What most expecting mothers don't know is that there are several other symptoms of pregnancy that can occur during the first trimester that isn't as common as the ones that have been mentioned above. While these symptoms are not abnormal, you should be aware of them in order to understand what your body is going through. Some of these symptoms are less obvious because they are simply overlooked as normal daily functions. Make sure to be aware of these symptoms as well:

- Moodiness: When you are pregnant, you are going to experience a wide range of emotions. This can sometimes even occur over short spans of time. These feelings might cause you to believe you are unstable or overly emotional, but this is a normal pregnancy symptom. All of the hormones that are flooding through your body can cause you to feel moody. One minute you might be laughing with a friend, and the next you might feel like crying. This can be a rollercoaster of a symptom to experience.

- Bloating: We all feel bloated from time to time. It can happen after eating too much of a certain food, or just eating too much in general. There is also PMS which causes you to feel bloated sometimes. This is why bloating is often an overlooked pregnancy symptom.

Thinking about it in the bigger picture, it seems obvious that bloating would be a symptom, but at the moment it can be easy to ignore. When you feel this way, it should feel exactly like the way that PMS bloating causes you to feel. It is the kind of pressure that doesn't go away even after eating an antacid.

- Light Spotting: Many women who are trying to get pregnant or trying to determine if they are pregnant see spotting as a bad sign. This usually means that your period is about to begin, or worse, that you are having a miscarriage. Know that light spotting is actually a normal and healthy pregnancy symptom. If you experience this, there is no need to panic. This bleeding is known as "implantation bleeding" and it actually happens because the fertilized egg is attaching to the lining of the uterus. This bleeding will usually occur about a week and a half to two weeks after conception. Around this time is when you would normally start your period.

- Cramping: As a woman, you are likely very used to the experience of abdominal cramping. Each month, cramping is one of the main symptoms that you will feel before you start your period. It is an indication that your uterus is beginning to shed its lining. Even when you become pregnant, this cramping can still occur because your uterus is working hard. Many expecting mothers say that they experienced mild cramping during the first trimester of their pregnancy.

- Constipation: Naturally, this is a symptom that can be easily overlooked because it is part of normal bodily function. Constipation can actually happen when you are pregnant due to hormones. This usually goes overlooked because anyone can experience constipation, some experience it regularly. The hormonal changes that you experience when you become pregnant can impact your digestive system, and this is why you can experience constipation. There does not necessarily have to be a change in diet to feel this way because the hormones are changing so rapidly.

- Food Aversions: When you become sickened at the thought of eating certain foods, it is likely that you are being impacted by the odor. Hormonal sensitivity is typically the reason for any food aversions you develop when you become pregnant. Any changes in appetite are usually overlooked because our tastes change constantly. You might decide that you are just being more picky than usual, but for a pregnant woman, there is a deeper reason behind it.

- Nasal Congestion: This is something that is hardly associated with pregnancy because it can seem entirely unrelated. Of course, feeling nasal congestion is going to lead you to believe that you are getting sick. This is typically something that you will try to treat with cold medicine or allergy medicine. When you become pregnant, your hormones and blood production can actually cause your nose to swell or dry out causing you to experience nosebleeds.

The same advice can be given if you notice these symptoms, much like the above symptoms. A visit to your doctor is still going to be the best way to confirm if you are truly pregnant. Being aware of your body is something you are going to become great at as soon as you suspect you are pregnant. Know that sometimes your body is just going through a lot of changes, so it is going to feel different. This feeling that you can't describe can drive you crazy if you let it. Your pregnancy symptoms are all normal, and you do not need to define each one in order to confirm this. Trust that your body knows what it is doing.

Talk to your partner about how you are feeling. This is the best way to gauge your symptoms. Though you know your body well, your partner is also going to be able to provide you with some additional input. Ask them if they notice anything different, and pay attention to even the smallest details. Most women who find out that they are pregnant agree that a lot of the signs were subtle or easily missed. A lot of women expect the symptoms to be way different than anything they have felt before, but they normally feel a lot like PMS symptoms.

In order to manage your symptoms, try to get as much rest as possible. A good night's sleep is highly underrated, and you are going to need a lot more of it the further along you get into your pregnancy. Also, make sure that you are eating properly. Well-balanced meals and plain foods are essential for any pregnant woman. On the days that nausea or food aversion is just too strong, you can opt for something simple, like plain bread or crackers. Getting something in your stomach is important, even when you don't feel like eating. Sleep and food are what fuel you. Hydration is also essential. Water is the very best thing for you to drink during your pregnancy. Since you are likely going to be feeling weak already, staying hydrated with water is going to replenish you.

If you need to leave the house for long periods at a time, keep in mind that you might be feeling your symptoms more than usual. Being on your feet for a while or moving around can intensify these things. Also, being out in public can lead you to encounter different scents that make you feel sick. Always be sure to bring a snack with you if you know you are going to be out for a while. If you are hit with a sudden bout of weakness or fatigue, you can get some quick nourishment by having a snack. Never travel without water on hand, either.

Ensure that you are taking a prenatal vitamin. This is going to keep your immune system and body strong as you begin your pregnancy journey. A great vitamin is one that includes plenty of B6, folic acid, iron, and calcium. Not only is this going to keep you strong, but it is also going to protect your developing baby. Allow your pregnancy symptoms to motivate you to stay healthy. If you start feeling bad, eating junk food and keeping an unbalanced sleep schedule isn't going to help. Think of your body as a safe home for your baby. Only bring good things into this home to ensure that your baby stays healthy.

Chapter 2: Healthy Options

There are many ways that you can ensure you are being healthy during your pregnancy. This does not only include eating plenty of fruits and vegetables. A pregnant woman has a lot to consider, and health should definitely become a priority. As the baby is growing, he/she is going to be receiving their nutrients directly from you. This means that anything you put into your body or do to your body will be felt by your baby. Providing you with the motivation to be healthier overall, it often takes a lifestyle change to make sure you are doing what is best for your baby and your health.

Healthy Eating Habits

As soon as you find out you are pregnant, you should be making all of the necessary changes in your lifestyle to maintain a diet that is healthy and nutritious. While the pregnancy cravings might be hard to avoid at times, your daily diet needs to be balanced and reasonable. Remember, you are eating for two, and anything that you eat is what your baby is also going to eat.

Pregnancy Diet

While there is no standardized diet that should be eaten during pregnancy, there are a few things you can do to become healthier. Typically, you will need to increase your caloric intake the further along you get into the pregnancy. In total, you will likely need to add around 300 extra calories to your regular diet. Aim to eat 2-4 servings of fruits each day and 4+ servings of vegetables. Carbs are actually essential to a pregnant woman. You are going to be receiving a lot of your energy from good carbs. Feel free to eat plenty of bread and grains. Protein is important, too. Eating meat, poultry, eggs, and beans will ease your fatigue and give you enough energy to get through your days. Since calcium is also a necessity, you should eat around 4 servings of dairy each day.

Daily Menu Sample

Breakfast: Oatmeal cereal with 1 sliced banana, 1 piece whole-wheat toast, 2tsp jam, 1 cup skim milk

Morning Snack: Yogurt and grapes

Lunch: Warm turkey sandwich with cheese on whole wheat bread, potato chips, 1 pear, 1 cup skim milk

Afternoon Snack: Raw veggies and dip

Dinner: 4-ounce chicken breast, 1 cup wild rice, 1 cup veggies, 1 cup skim milk

Nighttime Snack: Fresh fruit or yogurt

Seafood

A common question that comes up regarding pregnancy is if seafood is safe to eat. While the answer might surprise you, the FDA actually recommends that pregnant women eat more fish during their pregnancy. What is important is the kind of fish that is consumed. By eating fish, you are able to get a lot of valuable Omega-3 fatty acids and vitamins B12, B6, and D. These are all very important in a pregnant woman's diet. Fish that are known to be low in mercury and safest for pregnant women to eat are crawfish, Atlantic mackerel, salmon, sardines, scallops, shrimp, and tilapia. It is thought that a pregnant woman could eat around 36 ounces of fish each week.

In the past, it was thought that fish was entirely off-limits during pregnancy. Many women feared mercury poisoning, but through the newest research, you will find that certain fish are actually great for you to eat during your pregnancy. As long as your portions are monitored, you should be fine to eat fish as a source of protein. Some brands even take extra care to test their fish for safety in order to reassure pregnant women. Take a look around your local grocery store to see what your options are.

The fish that you need to avoid are bigeye tuna (common in sushi), king mackerel, marlin, and swordfish. These all contain high levels of mercury. Remember that eating fish during pregnancy should be a careful process, but you must also consider how much you are eating if you decide to breastfeed after the baby is born. While the baby is breastfeeding, they are still going to be receiving nutrition straight from you, so what you put into your body is still going to matter until they are weaned.

Nutrition

When you are eating healthy, your baby has a better chance for healthy brain development. Eating poor quality food is not only bad for your body, but it also limits your baby's ability to grow properly. Birth weight is important, too. When you are properly nourished during your pregnancy, you are more likely to give birth to a baby with a healthy weight. Once your baby is born, their birth weight becomes their first few months of development. This transition can be hard on a baby who is under-nourished and underweight.

If you are having a hard time with your pregnancy symptoms, your diet can help alleviate your pain. It can also help decrease your mood swings, improve your morning sickness, and give you easier labor and delivery. With all of the benefits that a good diet provides, it makes sense to prioritize it during your pregnancy. While you are naturally going to be gaining weight, you need to make sure that you are gaining the right kind of weight that will benefit your baby. Junk food might be satisfying every now and then, but it isn't going to support your baby's development in the way that healthier foods will.

Vitamins for You and Baby

As stated, taking vitamins when you find out you are pregnant is essential. While you can make sure that you are maintaining a healthy diet, you are still going to need an extra boost of vitamins and minerals to keep you feeling your best. Prenatal vitamins are designed for expectant women. They combine all of the essentials into one pill so you can ensure that you aren't missing anything. Not only do vitamins keep you healthy, but they also keep your immune system healthy. This is important because getting sick when you are pregnant can be a miserable and risky experience. If you aren't strong enough to fight the illness, it can begin to have negative impacts on your baby, as well.

Types of Prenatal Vitamins

Much like regular vitamins, prenatal vitamins usually come as pills or in a gummy. There are many different brands available on the market for you to choose from, so how can you determine which one is going to best suit your needs? Organic and vegan vitamins normally offer the best health benefits because they are not filled with any unnecessary low-quality fillers. These vitamins are only made with the best ingredients to ensure that you are getting exactly what you need from them. Normally made in a dry capsule instead of a gel capsule, it might be slightly more difficult for you to swallow. While gelatin makes for a smoother vitamin, it is an unnecessary animal byproduct that doesn't benefit your health.

If you want to stick with an organic or vegan vitamin, but you need something easier to swallow, look for veggie capsules. As they sound, the capsules are actually made from vegetables so they are easier to swallow and easier for you to digest, as well. If you choose, you can have your doctor write you a prescription for the vitamin that they believe is going to work best for you. While a prescription prenatal isn't mandatory, some women prefer this because they appreciate their doctor's opinion. If you decide to go with a more traditional, over-the-counter vitamin, make sure that you at least avoid the ones with added salts and synthetic materials. Doing some research on the top brands can help you make your decision.

Why is Vitamin D Important?

Technically speaking, Vitamin D is actually a steroid vitamin that supports your immune system, keeps your cell division healthy, and makes sure that your bones remain strong. These are all very important for people, in general, but especially for pregnant women. Most prenatal vitamins do not supply you with the recommended amount of vitamin D necessary to support your pregnancy. Try to find one that offers 4,000 IU of vitamin D each day, or else find a supplement that will give you the remainder of what you need.

Vitamin D can be absorbed by your body as well as taken in a pill form or through various foods. Know that sunshine and a glass of milk isn't going to be enough vitamin D for any pregnant woman. Ensuring that you are taking your prenatal each day, with or without a supplement, is going to protect you from cancers, autoimmune disorders, neurological issues, and cardiovascular diseases. The area in which you live also plays a role in how much vitamin D you need. If you are in an area that experiences little sunshine, then you might need to consult with your doctor to ensure that 4,000 IU of vitamin D daily is going to be enough during your pregnancy.

Natural Sources of Vitamin B6 and Why It Is Important

Another vitamin that is important to your baby's brain development and immune function is vitamin B6. Along with folic acid, which is necessary for developing your baby's neural tube in the early stages, vitamin B6 has been known as another essential vitamin for an expecting mother. Vitamin B6 helps with early development, and you will want to provide your baby with all the nutrients possible in the beginning. Another great benefit of taking vitamin B6 is that some studies have shown that it can reduce nausea and vomiting for pregnant women. Those who are particularly sensitive to these symptoms have found great relief by increasing their vitamin B6 intake. The recommended amount to take is around 1.9 milligrams per day. Unless otherwise prescribed by your doctor, you should not exceed 100 milligrams in a single day. While an overdose of vitamin B6 isn't going to be particularly dangerous, it will make you feel sick or lead you to experience indigestion if you aren't careful.

If you are looking for natural ways to get B6, eat plenty of chicken, salmon, potatoes, spinach, hazelnuts, bananas, cereals, and vegetable juice. These are all great foods to include in your pregnancy diet, and they will also benefit you by getting your B6 levels where they need to be. Getting enough B6 isn't hard if you are being mindful of it. As long as you are eating a well-balanced diet, it is likely that you are indeed getting the amount you need. Talk to your doctor if you are ever unsure if you need to add a supplement to your vitamin regimen. Each pregnant woman is going to have different needs. Even if you are taking the recommended amount, yet you still feel that you are weak or experiencing bad nausea, you can always talk to your doctor about increasing your dosage.

How to Treat Illness When Pregnant

Getting sick when you are pregnant can be a scary feeling. Not only are you going to be battling your illness, but you are also going to be worrying over your baby's health and development. It is no secret that a weakened immune system is not good for a growing baby during pregnancy, but there is no need to panic. We all get sick sometimes, no matter how careful we are. By taking extra precautions as an expecting mother, you will be able to combat your colds in no time.

Starting from the beginning, avoid situations that could potentially get you sick. For example, if you know that your friend is sick, do not spend time around them until they are feeling better. Limiting your exposure to other people and other germs is going to help your immune system tremendously. If you begin to feel your immune system crashing, get some probiotics into your body. These are live microorganisms that provide you with health benefits. They eat away at the bacteria and make you stronger and better able to maintain your health. You can either consume them in liquid form, pill form, or through certain foods such as yogurt. Probiotics have also been known to help your digestion, too.

Get plenty of rest, and take some time to incorporate physical activity into your daily routine. While you do not need to have a cardio-focused workout each time, you should still make sure that you are up and moving as much as possible without overworking yourself. While melatonin is a known sleep aid, it has not been proven safe to use while you are pregnant. Do your best to regulate your sleep schedule naturally by getting to bed at a decent hour, taking naps when necessary, and winding down before you are ready to go to bed.

One of the very best steps you can take to avoid getting sick is to wash your hands frequently. After you go out in public, wash your hands as soon as you can. Being around a lot of germs and bacteria is going to increase your chances of getting sick, so washing your hands a lot never hurts. Make sure that you use anti-bacterial wipes around the house on doorknobs, cabinet fixtures, the toilet flusher, and any other surfaces that are touched frequently.

What is Safe to Take?

If you do end up getting sick, you might need medicine to help you fully recover. Along with getting plenty of rest, staying hydrated, and taking your prenatal vitamins, you need to know which medicines are safe for you to take during your pregnancy. If you are in pain, acetaminophen (Tylenol) is a known drug that is safe to take. While most doctors recommend avoiding ibuprofen (Advil or Motrin) during the third trimester, it is safe to take in moderation during the first two trimesters if necessary. These drugs have been tested by the FDA in terms of how safe they are for pregnant women to take. But the safest pain reliever by far is acetaminophen. Aspirin should be avoided at all costs; it is known to be among the most harmful to an expecting mother.

If you are experiencing a cold, it is suggested that you avoid taking any cold medicine until you are at least 12 weeks along. This is to minimize any risks that are to be experienced. If you must take cold medicine, some safe options for you are Vicks, Robitussin, cough expectorant (day), and a cough suppressant (night). While Sudafed is another popular cold medicine, it has actually not been tested by the FDA for safety during pregnancy. If you'd like to take Sudafed for your cold, consult with your doctor first.

Heartburn and indigestion are something that pregnant women experience often. Sometimes, these symptoms get so bad that the mother needs to regularly take medicine in order to alleviate the pain. Over-the-counter antacids are almost always safe to take. Look for ones that contain magnesium, calcium, aluminum, and alginic acid. Some examples include Tums, Mylanta, Pepcid, and Maalox. If the heartburn is more severe, you might need to discuss some other options with your doctor. Zantac and Tagamet are two that are known to be prescribed by doctors to pregnant women.

Allergies can make your pregnancy very difficult. They cause you to feel sick without actually experiencing a cold. If you need some allergy relief during your pregnancy, you can safely take Benadryl, Claritin, Alavert, Zyrtec, and Chlor-Trimeton. These are considered safe for any light to mild allergy sufferers. If your allergies are too much for any of these medications to handle, ask your doctor is you can take Rhinocort, Flonase, and Nasonex. The summer months can cause your allergies to become more severe because of all the pollen floating around. Keeping your house clean and your windows closed can help limit your exposure to these allergens.

As mentioned, constipation is an often overlooked symptom of pregnancy. While you are normally going to be able to let it pass on its own, there are times when you could benefit from some medicine to help you stay comfortable. Stool softeners and laxatives are mainly known for being safe during pregnancy, but this is something you should consult your doctor before taking one. If drinking more water and adding more fiber to your diet doesn't provide enough relief, you can ask your doctor about taking Colace, Surfak, Dulcolax, or Senokot.

Chapter 3: What is Safe and what is Not?

Finding out you are pregnant can change a lot in your life. Aside from preparing for the arrival of your new baby, you must also ensure that your old habits do not create conflict with your desire to have a healthy pregnancy. By becoming smarter and more aware of the dangers of the things you might already do, you are going to be protecting your baby from the very beginning. While there are some things you might need to give up, you should never feel ashamed. A lot of parents, both mothers, and fathers alike find that the pregnancy stage is when they were most motivated to make lifestyle changes. Keeping your baby in mind, consider if anything you are currently doing is going to be dangerous or harmful to your baby's development.

In this chapter, you will learn how to give up your vices by replacing them with healthier options. Once you have mastered this willpower, you are going to feel rightfully proud of your accomplishments. Through becoming better at doing research and reading labels carefully, you are going to be able to spot dangers to your health and to your baby's health before being told by your doctor. Then, you are going to learn how to listen to your body and know when it is the right time to give yourself the necessary rest and relaxation. While there are plenty of places to go and things to do, know that pregnancy is going to temporarily limit these for you. In the end, it is all going to be worth it as you have a successful pregnancy and an effortless delivery to a healthy baby.

Caffeine, Alcohol, and Tobacco

Drinking coffee, consuming alcohol, and smoking tobacco are the top 3 most common vices that anybody can have. After finding out you are pregnant, if you participate in any of these things, then you must make some immediate changes in order to ensure that your baby is protected from these actions. If you cannot get through your day without a cup of coffee, the good news is that you don't have to when you are pregnant! It is actually okay for a pregnant woman to drink around 200mg of caffeine each day - that is about 2 cups. A common myth that has been circulated for years is that you must give up coffee as soon as you find out that you are pregnant. While you don't want to overdo it, as long as you are monitoring your intake, caffeine is actually not going to be harmful to your baby.

Alcohol, on the other hand, has very negative impacts on the health of a pregnancy and even on the health of your baby if you drink while you are still breastfeeding. Because all that you consume is going directly to your baby, even a single drink is going to be impacting your child. The alcohol will cross from the bloodstream into the placenta, and your baby will have no choice but to consume it as well. This can lead to many damaging long-term effects such as learning disorders, malformation of the heart, damage to other organs, and birth defects. If you are trying to become pregnant, it is best to give up alcohol before conception. This can be a tough habit to kick, but it will terribly damage your baby's health if you end up drinking while pregnant or breastfeeding.

Understandably, smoking is a common coping mechanism for stress. It is very easy to become addicted to tobacco products, and when you become pregnant, quitting can be a nightmare. Quitting anything cold turkey is going to cause you to experience withdrawal symptoms, so quit before you become pregnant if you can help it. Cigarettes are filled with toxins that are going to enter your baby's bloodstream the same way that alcohol will. Nicotine of any kind is extremely harmful to your baby, and it can narrow the umbilical cord. This can mean that your baby's oxygen supply is reduced. Simply smoking less isn't going to be a healthy option during your pregnancy; you must kick the habit entirely. If you cannot give up smoking, then you need to evaluate your desire to become a parent. Your baby's health must come before any coping mechanisms or vices that you are holding on to.

Surviving Pregnancy without Vices

Though getting rid of your vices is going to be a difficult process, it is one that is worth every second. Think about how much healthier your baby is going to be when you can lead a healthy lifestyle. Your lifestyle not only matters during your pregnancy but before and after it as well. Starting by cutting down on your coffee intake, you can then find other ways to gain energy throughout the day. Changing the way you eat is one way to accomplish this. If you eat several small meals throughout the day instead of 3 big ones, you are going to have more energy distributed throughout your body at any given time. For a pregnant mother, having extra energy is very important. Exercise can also give you a boost in energy. While it might make you tired at the moment, the endorphins that you feel afterward are enough to keep you going.

Practicing yoga can be a great way to assist you with quitting cigarettes. If you are trying to get pregnant, begin taking yoga classes right away to assist with your breathing. Yoga is helpful for quitting smoking because it teaches you other ways to breathe deeply without needing to rely on nicotine. If you are able to quit smoking for the duration of your pregnancy, there is no need for you to pick up another cigarette again. These eight to nine months that you spend smoke-free should show you how great you can feel without having to rely on this vice. Not to mention, secondhand smoke is extremely harmful to babies and children. You wouldn't want to pick up a cigarette immediately after you give birth because your baby is still going to feel its impacts by being around you.

Drinking alcohol is normally picked up as a social habit. A lot of people enjoy having a drink with friends as a form of relaxation and a way to unwind. As you know, excessive alcohol consumption is terrible for your liver and heart. When you are pregnant, if you drink, all of these negative impacts are going to be passed straight down to your baby. If you would still like to experience the fun of going out without drinking, you can feel free to hang out with your friends as much as you want. Order seltzer water so you can still have something to sip on without drinking alcohol. Sometimes, the feeling of having a drink in your hand can be enough to supplement the fact that you aren't drinking.

Why You Must Beware of Deli Meats

Many pregnant women believe that they need to avoid eating deli meat. A lot of these meats are filled with nitrates and additives that are harmful in general. They are high in saturated fats and sodium, which need to be consumed in moderation while you are pregnant. If you decide to eat deli meat, you must make sure that it is properly stored and heated up to 165°F. There are 3 basic types of deli meat: whole cuts that are cooked and sliced, reconstructed pieces of several different types of meat that are put together, and processed meat. You should only eat the first type of deli meat because it is going to be least harmful to you.

Understandably, cravings happen while you are pregnant. You

might get intense cravings to eat deli meat, and this is okay, as long as you are mindful of its quality. The following are the safest to eat during your pregnancy:

- Turkey Breast: This is a low-calorie option with a lot of protein. Turkey can help to lower your cholesterol and blood sugar.
- Deli Sliced Ham: It is another protein-packed option that also provides you with plenty of calories. Ham sandwiches with lettuce are great to eat to satisfy your deli meat craving.
- Chicken Breast: This is the healthiest option for you to consume during your pregnancy. It is actually recommended that you eat plenty of chicken breasts in order to keep a balanced diet.
- Grilled Pork Slices: Pork is something that will keep you satiated. It is more filling than a lot of other deli meat, and it is a great source of calcium and protein.

A general rule for what to avoid should be anything that is cured in salt. This is going to contain too much sodium, plus it is going to be filled with nitrates. If you consume too much salt during your pregnancy, you could experience hypertension and edema. Also, nitrates are carcinogenic. While a few bites of these meats won't be enough to create long-term impacts, you should definitely be opting for the healthier deli meat overall.

Much like fish, there is more of a misconception that you must not eat any deli meat at all. As long as you are eating it in moderation, you will be doing what you can to ensure you are being safe. The type of meat matters more than the frequency in which you decide to eat it. If you are ever unsure about the deli meat you are consuming, consult your doctor for a better recommendation to satisfy your craving.

Reading Content Labels

The easiest way to determine if something is safe for you to eat or use during your pregnancy is to become familiar with its content label. When you are looking at food labels, pay attention to the serving size. This is going to provide you with a guideline for how to read the contents. As you know, when you are pregnant, you need to increase your caloric intake. If something is high in calories, this does not necessarily mean that you need to avoid it. What you need to observe next is the amount of trans fat and saturated fat. These fats are the kind that isn't going to provide you with nutritional benefits.

Cholesterol comes from animal products. Small amounts of cholesterol are okay for pregnant women, but too much can lead to health problems. Much like cholesterol, sodium is also something that needs to be closely monitored. One teaspoon of salt is the recommended amount each day. Anything higher is going to lead to high blood pressure and cause you to remain bloated. Carbohydrates are generally good for you.

When you eat plenty of bread and grains, you are going to be gaining energy while staying full. If you consume too much, then you are going to raise your blood glucose level.

As you know, fiber is great for pregnant women. If you are experiencing constipation, adding more fiber to your diet is going to be helpful. In order to determine if something has a healthy amount of fiber in it, start with foods that have more than five grams of fiber and subtract half from the total amount of carbohydrates. If you can aim for around 25-30 grams of fiber each day, you will be in a good range. Sugar must be eaten in moderation, but this is something that you can likely monitor if you are aware of what you are eating.

There isn't really such thing as eating too much protein when you are pregnant. Any protein that your body gets goes straight to your body and to your energy level. The better you feel, the better your baby is going to develop. It is thought that pregnant women who consume a lot of protein give birth to healthier babies with fewer illnesses in the future. As long as you can stay strong, then your baby is likely going to be strong as well.

Reading content labels does not have to be a complicated experience. As long as you know how to seek out the benefits you are looking for, you should not have a problem with determining which foods are going to benefit you during pregnancy. If you are ever unsure about whether or not it would be good to eat something, you can keep in mind the various ratios of its calories, carbohydrates, sodium, fiber, sugar, and protein to see if you would be receiving any nutritional value from consuming the specific food.

Traveling While Pregnant

Most pregnant women are able to travel safely until they reach the 36-week mark. The best time to travel is during your second trimester. Specifically, you should plan to travel when you are 14-28 weeks pregnant. This is because most of your symptoms should be manageable by this point, and you will not be too close to your due date. There are a few conditions that will limit your ability to travel, and these include preeclampsia, pre-labor rupture of membranes, and preterm labor. Also, if you are carrying more than one baby, this makes travel riskier. While you might have the urge to get away, as a pregnant woman, you will need to consider all of the potential risks involved.

In terms of where you can travel, you can go just about anywhere you want. The only areas that should definitely be avoided are those known for Zika outbreaks. The Zika virus is very harmful to unborn babies, causing potential birth defects and developmental problems. Zika virus is spread by mosquitoes, and it is not the only disease they carry. Malaria should be another concern when you plan on traveling. To keep track of these dangerous areas, you can do some research online to see which countries are currently experiencing the viruses.

Before you go on any trip, it is a good idea to visit your doctor to make sure that everything is looking alright. Mention the trip and get an honest, professional opinion on whether or not your doctor believes you are suited to travel. Bring plenty of over-the-counter medications with you in order to treat your basic symptoms, and keep in mind when your due date is in case you do need to seek medical attention while away. Medical professionals are going to need to know what you are taking and when you are due in order to treat you. Ensure that you are up to date with your vaccines, and be cautious in general. Travel insurance is a good option to consider in case you are forced to cancel your trip for any reason relating to your pregnancy. Otherwise, you should still be able to experience the joys of traveling until getting closer to your due date.

When to Take Bed Rest

At a certain point in your pregnancy, it might benefit you to take bed rest. This is just as it sounds, and it is meant to alleviate your symptoms near the end of your pregnancy. Before you go into labor, symptoms can become intensified. The level of bed rest you need is going to depend on how much difficulty you are having. This can range from as simple as resting periodically in your own bed at home to becoming hospitalized and monitored for your safety. If this happens to you, know that many pregnant women go through periods of time where they must be on bed rest, too. It can become a normal part of your pregnancy journey.

Your doctor will usually be the one to tell you to take bed rest, but you also should be aware of the signs that you need it. These signs include vaginal bleeding, high blood pressure, premature labor, gestational diabetes, cervical effacement, poor fetal development, placenta complications, and history of pregnancy loss. Bed rest is meant to take the stress off your body so your baby can continue to grow at a healthy rate.

The main benefit of bed rest is simply that you get the chance to relax. When there is too much going on in your life, this can cause stress and complications in your pregnancy. Whether you are working too much or doing too much physical activity, bed rest gives your body the chance to reset. The best position for bed rest is being on your side with your knees bent and a pillow between them to make the position more comfortable. You can also rest on your back with a pillow to support your hips/legs so they are elevated above your shoulders. If you still feel discomfort while on bed rest, try squeezing stress balls and turning your wrists/feet in circles.

Chapter 4: Pregnancy Fears and Reasons Not to Worry

There are plenty of "what ifs" that will likely be running through your head as you enter your pregnancy journey. For all of the things that can go wrong, it can be difficult to reassure yourself that everything is going to be alright. Worrying is one of the main causes of illness, and if you can help it, you must do your best to set the worries aside in order to preserve your health. The following are some fears that many pregnant women encounter. As you will experience, there are always going to be solutions and options for you.

- Fear of Miscarrying: Statistically, less than 20% of pregnancies end in miscarriage. Once you have gotten past your first few weeks of pregnancy, then you are likely going to carry a healthy baby to term. Once your doctor can see and hear a heartbeat (at the 6-8 week mark), then your risk of miscarriage drops to below 5%.
- Being Too Sick: Many women worry that morning sickness takes away the nutrition that is supposed to be going to your baby. If you are going through a spell of frequent vomiting, as long as you are still taking your prenatal vitamins regularly, then your baby is still going to be getting nutrition. Do your best to eat smaller meals, more frequently, to ease the sickness.

Babies have the ability to absorb nutrients very well, so even when you feel that you can't keep anything down; know that your baby is still eating.

- Worrying About Birth Defects: While your baby can be tested for all of the different birth defects that are known, it is still natural to worry that your baby is going to be born with one. The risk of having a baby with a birth defect, without any clear indicators, is only 4%. This statistic includes serious birth defects as well as small ones that can improve as the baby grows up.

Nausea and Morning Sickness

Feeling nauseous is one of the most common pregnancy symptoms that you will experience as a pregnant woman. Up to 70% of expecting mothers can identify with this feeling. Most nausea and morning sickness tends to occur during the earlier months of your pregnancy. Though it is common in your first trimester, sometimes, it can last longer. The exact link between nausea and pregnancy is not definitively known. Many medical professionals believe that there is a link between nausea and the pregnancy hormone known as HCG. Morning sickness and nausea tend to peak at the same time as your HCG levels.

Your nausea will normally begin around 8 weeks, and it can last until your 14th week, or in some cases, even longer. The only true way to combat nausea is by practicing self-care. It is not something that can be avoided or necessarily controlled, but there are ways you can make it easier on yourself. Drinks that include ginger are great for limiting nausea. When you start feeling sick, a glass of ginger ale can do a lot for you. Plain crackers are also very helpful. Keep them close to your bed for times when you feel like you need something in your stomach, yet you cannot keep much down.

Lemons are also great for helping your nausea. Simply smelling a lemon can lessen your chances of vomiting. When all else fails, try to keep your meals as plain as possible. While you might be craving certain flavors, it is better to keep things plain instead of having to vomit later on after eating something with too many ingredients. If certain smells begin to trigger you during your pregnancy, fresh air is very helpful. Step outside when you can, and take some deep breaths to regulate your body.

Listening to your physical symptoms is a smart idea. When you become fatigued, your body is going to be much more prone to vomiting and get sick easily. If you start to feel tired, then give yourself a chance to rest. Just because you used to be able to do certain things before you got pregnant does not mean that you will be able to do all of them during your pregnancy. Your body is going through a lot during this time, so make sure that you are being mindful of this. Even if you do not sleep or nap, lying down can be helpful.

If it ever becomes too much for you to handle, your doctor can prescribe you with anti-nausea pills that will get you through the bad spells that you experience. Some women are just more prone to morning sickness than others. If the at-home remedies do not seem to help you, then you can consult your doctor for something else. Most of the time, these at-home remedies are actually highly effective. Know that it is going to get better, and this nausea isn't going to last forever.

Prenatal Screening and Testing

Throughout your pregnancy, you are going to be guided through many screening and testing sessions to monitor the health of your baby. There are three main prenatal tests that you will go through during each of your trimesters. The purpose of these tests is to identify your baby's blood type, spot any health concerns, and determine the baby's size/gender/position. You are likely most familiar with the test that is done to identify a baby's gender. This is a very commonly awaited test that many parents look forward to. While some prefer to keep the gender a surprise, it has become popular to host a gender reveal party to make a surprise announcement about the gender of your baby. No matter what you choose to do, you can tell the ultrasound technician whether you would like to know the gender or whether you would rather keep it a mystery.

The main difference between screening and diagnostic testing is the depth of the information you can find out. In screenings, you can be presented with the possibility of a problem or health concern. During diagnostic testing, however, you are going to get a more concrete answer. This is going to be a more accurate way for you to find out exactly what is going on with your child in the womb. Your OB-GYN is going to recommend which of these tests and screenings you should have depending on how your pregnancy is going.

Some screenings are recommended for all pregnant women, as they are a routine part of your regular check-ups. You do have the right to refuse a test or a screening if you feel that it isn't going to benefit you. These are all optional, but your OB-GYN should make it clear which tests are routine and beneficial. If you have a certain circumstance surrounding your pregnancy, you might be offered other tests. This usually happens during teen pregnancies, pregnancies with women who are over 35, those with high blood pressure, those with heart or kidney disease, or those prone to asthma.

To decide which tests are right for you, consider the following:

- How accurate is the test?
- What information will it give you?
- Is the procedure painful?
- Will it be dangerous for you or the baby?
- When will you get the results?
- How much does it cost?

- Will your insurance cover it?
- Is there any preparation necessary for the test?

When you gather all of the above information, you will be able to make an educated decision on whether you'd like to go through the process or skip it. This combined with your doctor's advice is how you should be making all medical decisions that pertain to your pregnancy. Since you are going to be offered several tests that you are likely unfamiliar with, it is always best to do your own research before making your final decision.

How to Choose an OB-GYN

There are a few ways that you can go about making your selection, but it is worth asking your current gynecologist if they also practice obstetrics. Since you are already familiar and comfortable with your gynecologist, it makes sense that you might want to use them during your pregnancy, too. If you do not want to use the same doctor, or if you do not have a gynecologist that you visit on a regular basis, there are a few ways to find an OB-GYN. The first is to consult your current healthcare provider. They will normally have a list that you can choose from and they can narrow down the ones that are in your area. This is probably the most helpful way to make your selection.

The reviews matter. You wouldn't want to see an OB-GYN that

is known for being rude and untimely, so ensure that you take your time to read the reviews. It is also worth it to ask your friends and family members if they can make any recommendations for you. Hearing real opinions from loved ones that you already trust can become a big influence in your decision-making process. If neither of the above options provides you with any results, you can consult the College of Obstetricians and Gynecologists' website to do a search in your local area.

Only you are going to be able to know who is right for you, but there are some other criteria that you can consider while making your decision. If you have any chronic illnesses or preexisting conditions, you might need to see a specialist who is familiar with these conditions. These OB-GYNs are going to be known for handling high-risk pregnancies. You must also consider each doctor's outlook and methodology that is used in their practice. Each OB-GYN is going to follow a different philosophy and set of techniques, and you need to make sure that these all fall in line with what you want for yourself and your baby.

When you are seeing a new doctor for the first time, think about the appointment as your trial period. See if you feel comfortable in the office and speaking with the doctor and their staff. You must be able to ask questions if necessary, so an office that dismisses your questions is not going to be a great choice for you. During your pregnancy, you are going to be experiencing many things for the first time, so being able to ask all the questions you have is a must. You should never feel like your questions are dumb or excessive. It is your right as the mother to know what is going on with your baby and your body during pregnancy. Make sure that your doctor is going to respect your wishes, even if your opinions do not exactly match theirs.

Common Pregnancy Problems and Solutions

The last thing you want to hear as an expecting mother is that there is a problem. Know that, like everything else in life, pregnancy can be unpredictable. Even if you go through all of the preparation necessary to ensure you have a smooth pregnancy, there is always going to be something that happens that you weren't expecting. Making yourself aware of these common problems is going to help you get through them if they become a part of your pregnancy journey. Knowing that there are solutions for all of these problems should help you to feel at ease.

1. Bleeding Gums: It is likely that you aren't going to expect trouble with your mouth during your pregnancy, but this is something that can happen. The same hormones that can cause your sinuses to act up can also cause your gums to bleed. While this is normal, you can

help ease the pain by ensuring you are getting plenty of calcium and cutting out some of the sugar in your diet. If you must go to the dentist, remind them that you are pregnant so they do not perform any procedures that will be harmful to the baby.

2. Vaginal Discharge: Just because your periods have stopped during pregnancy does not mean your vagina is going to stop producing discharge. This discharge is usually white and has a mild smell. While there is nothing you can do to prevent the discharge, you can wear panty liners if it begins to bother you. Consult your doctor if you notice it is a yellow or green color with a strong odor, as this can be a sign of an infection.

3. Leg Cramps: Because of the extra weight you are carrying, it is likely that you will encounter cramped legs. While the feeling is unpleasant, you normally have nothing to worry about. By stretching your legs frequently, you can lessen the risk of cramping. Cold compresses are also very helpful. If your pain lasts for a long period of time accompanied by redness, consult your doctor because this could be due to a blood clot.

4. Hemorrhoids: A lot of expectant mothers are shocked to discover that hemorrhoids can be a normal part of pregnancy. While they are very uncomfortable to deal with, Kegel exercises and over-the-counter medication can soothe the area. Another way to treat existing ones

is to try soaking a cotton pad in witch hazel and gently rubbing the area.

5. Itchy and Leaking Nipples: During your pregnancy, your breasts are going through the process of producing milk to feed your baby. While they are growing larger during this process, they can become itchy and potentially start to leak. Using nipple cream can soothe the discomfort. You can also place nursing pads inside your bra to prevent your breast milk from leaking through your shirt.

Working Until You Deliver

You can continue working while you are pregnant until you feel that your symptoms are making it too difficult to complete your normal workday. Legally, an American mother can take up to 12 weeks of maternity leave while having job security. Not all employers pay during this time, so this can vary depending on where you work. Planning on when you are going to take your maternity leave is a very important aspect of your pregnancy. While you might still be able to work a full day, toward the end of your pregnancy you should not be over-exerting yourself. It is better to be cautious than to push yourself and end up getting sick.

If your place of employment does not have an official system for women who need to take maternity leave, you can opt to use the Family and Medical Leave Act. In order to qualify for this, you must work for a covered employer for at least 1 year or longer. You must also work at a location that has 50+ employees within 75 miles. This is the only law that exists in America to cover you for any type of pregnancy-related leave. Although you will not have to utilize the act as a guarantee, you should still know that it is available for you to use if you meet the qualifications. In an ideal situation, your place of employment will already have a maternity leave system worked out.

At around 15 weeks until your due date, you should give your notice of maternity leave. You can do so by putting it in writing. Much like any major change in your life, you would likely need to inform your boss the same way. Once your notice has been turned in, your boss is going to let you know how much time you are going to be allowed off and if it will or will not be paid. Keeping your rights in mind, know that you can always negotiate at this point. Be reasonable, but also do not settle for something that you find unfair. Having a baby should not be a reason to receive any kind of poor treatment from your superiors at work.

Listen to your body. While there are typical time frames for when expecting mothers usually take maternity leave, you cannot guarantee that your pregnancy is going to allow you the same time frame. You might have different needs or other conditions that cause you to become unable to work a lot sooner than most people. If this applies to your pregnancy, be sure to discuss it with your boss as soon as you can. Remember, there is no reason that you need to overwork yourself during your pregnancy. Not only does it put stress on you, but it puts stress on the baby.

Chapter 5: The First Trimester (1 - 3 Months)

During the first three months of your pregnancy, you are going to experience a lot of new things. Not only are you going to be feeling the symptoms for the first time, but you are also going to be getting into a new routine of regular check-ups and accommodating the changes that your body is experiencing. While it can be easy to feel overwhelmed, having an idea of exactly what is going on during each stage of your pregnancy is going to put you at ease.

The First Month

Your Baby and Your Body

At this stage in your pregnancy, your body isn't likely to go through any visible changes. Since conception has just happened, your baby is a tiny embryo and is still developing. You won't be able to find out any additional details until you are further along, but this does not mean you need to hold back any of your excitement.

The one thing you might notice is that your pregnancy hormones have begun to kick in. This can mean that you will start to experience some pregnancy signs and symptoms that were discussed in the earlier chapter. Whether you have a sudden recognition of particular odors or you feel too emotional for your own good, these are all normal parts of being in your first month of pregnancy.

A slight pressure in your lower abdomen might be noticeable, but it is so slight that it likely won't do anything to change your outward appearance just yet. Some women experience a metallic taste in their mouth during the first month. This is normal, as your taste buds begin to adjust as they will throughout your entire pregnancy. Make sure you are taking your prenatal vitamins so you can keep your vitamin C and Iron levels high enough. Keep your fluid levels high to remain hydrated.

What to Expect at This Check-Up

During your first appointment, you can expect a lot of standard procedures that would happen during normal doctor appointments. You will be weighed, and your blood pressure will be taken. Then, you are going to provide your doctor with a urine sample so they can test your protein and sugar levels. You will also need to provide blood so your doctor can test for anemia and your HCG levels. It is possible that your doctor will also perform a pap smear, a standard procedure that you are likely already used to from your typical visit to the gynecologist. This is going to allow them to spot any abnormalities.

Your Rh can also be tested at this point. This is the protein carried by your red blood cells. You can either be Rh positive (have proteins) or Rh negative (do not have proteins). Why this matters is because your baby is also going to either be Rh positive or negative. If the two of you are not a match, this can become a reason for additional treatment to ensure that your baby is still developing properly.

The first appointment should not include much more than the above. Since it is still too early on to measure your baby and your body, your doctor's main concern is going to be focusing on your physical health and spotting any abnormalities. These appointments typically go by very quickly, and you will not have anything to worry about. The ultrasounds that you are likely looking forward to will not occur until you are around 12 weeks pregnant.

Questions to Ask Your Doctor

Remember, there is no right or wrong way to ask your doctor questions. If you have any questions at all, be vocal about them! It is your doctor's job to inform you of anything you are unsure of. As your body is about to undergo many changes, you will feel better when you can be aware of what exactly is happening and what you are feeling.

You can ask if your doctor has a nurse line that you can call in case you have any questions in the future. This will be helpful if you have a question that cannot wait until your next appointment. Also, ask your doctor what would be considered an emergency. Many expecting mothers do not know what qualifies, and knowing what to look for regarding whether or not to go to the hospital is essential. During this time, you can discuss any changes in your habits or lifestyle that must be made. If you have any questions about the testing, bring them up to your doctor. Ask them which tests they recommend to you at this point in your pregnancy and why.

How to Pamper Yourself During Pregnancy

Staying off your feet is one of the main ways that you can give yourself a break when you are pregnant. Even in your first month of pregnancy, you are naturally going to feel more fatigued than you usually would. Think about the way you feel when you are PMSing. Simple activities such as running errands and even doing simple chores around the house can feel like a big deal. Kicking your feet up for a few moments at a time can help to lessen this exhaustion.

Massages are safe during your first month of pregnancy. Whether you choose to receive one from your significant other or a spa professional, they can help to relax your muscles. As your body begins this significant change, you are going to experience new kinds of aches and pains. Massages help to keep your body loose and relaxed during your pregnancy.

Allow yourself to go shopping for a comfortable pair of pajamas and slippers. Whether you prefer to wear nightgowns or you'd like to opt for a top/bottom set, get a pair that is comfortable. When you can allow yourself to fully relax, your body is going to naturally recharge to the best of its ability.

The Second Month

Your Baby and Your Body

During your 8th week of pregnancy, your baby should be about the size of a raspberry. Compared to only one month ago, this is a huge development from a simple embryo. At this time, your baby's essential organs have begun to develop. With a heart rate of around 150-170 beats per minute, your baby's heart is beating nearly twice as fast as yours. Though you won't be able to feel any of their movements just yet, know that they are becoming more active. Spontaneous twitches start happening in the second month of pregnancy.

Though you might not be showing yet, your clothes are likely going to feel tighter in the second month around the abdomen. This happens because your uterus is also expanding in order to accommodate your baby. It is going to be around the size of a large grapefruit at this point. Morning sickness is likely to become a common occurrence during your second month. It can feel hard to keep anything down at all. Do your best to consume plenty of fruit. Not only is it healthy for you, but it will also provide you with the necessary vitamins and minerals that you need while you are pregnant. If you can't keep anything down, you are going to be losing a lot of these vitamins.

What to Expect at This Check-Up

Your next appointment is likely going to mirror your first. You will go through the same basic procedures such as blood testing and checking your blood pressure. During your first trimester, you are only going to be seeing your OB-GYN once per month, unless you have certain circumstances that would require you to go more frequently. Unfortunately, you still won't be able to see or hear anything at this appointment, but you are getting closer to being able to have an ultrasound.

Until this happens, your doctor's main concern is going to be ensuring that your pregnancy is still following a healthy path. Since this is still early on in the pregnancy, there is a good chance that they would be able to catch any abnormalities if some were to develop. Think about this appointment as yet another chance to become informed. Take notes of your symptoms and discuss them with your doctor if you feel inclined.

Questions to Ask Your Doctor

Aside from any symptoms that you'd like to discuss, you can bring up your preferences for your upcoming ultrasound. A lot of expecting mothers normally have an idea of whether they would like to have a traditional ultrasound or 3D or even 4D ultrasound. As we go more in-depth in later chapters, you will be able to decide if a 4D ultrasound is something that you'd like to do. As much as women do enjoy being able to see their baby at such a high definition and see movements, it requires different equipment. Most insurance will not cover it, as well. Don't forget, there is also a 3D method that will show your baby in 3D without the movement that the 4D ultrasound offers.

If you have any questions about your baby's rate of development, this is when you should ask your doctor. Finding out that your baby is growing at a normal rate can feel very reassuring, even when you didn't suspect that anything was wrong in the first place. It is nice to hear it directly from your doctor at the moment. Allow the doctor to reassure you about anything that you have been wondering about in the last couple of months.

Weight Gain

In the upcoming months of your pregnancy, people are going to comment on your weight gain. Whether they believe that you have barely gained any weight or if they feel that you are noticeably larger, it has become very common for others to remark about a pregnant woman's weight. This is something that you might not be used to at first, especially if you are particularly sensitive about the topic. Know that most people do not realize that this can come off as rude or an invasion of personal comfort. No matter how much you prepare for your body to undergo this change, the hardest part can be getting used to the comments that you hear from others.

On average, you are only going to gain around 25-35lbs of pregnancy weight. Of course, this can greatly vary due to your natural stature and the size of your baby. Thinking about it in these terms, the number isn't that large at all. The reason why it is more noticeable is that it is almost all going directly to your belly. You should feel proud of this weight that you have gained. It is a sign that you are carrying a healthy baby inside, and if you didn't gain any weight, your baby would not have adequate room to develop.

During your first trimester, you probably aren't going to gain more than 5lbs. This just shows how quickly the rest of the weight is gained. Aside from making room inside your belly for your baby, your body is going to distribute the rest of the weight in a few other places. You'll notice that your breasts are going to get larger, and your overall fluid levels are going to increase. This can add weight to your entire body in a subtle, yet noticeable, way. There are some fluids, and even an organ, that didn't exist before you became pregnant! The placenta develops as your baby grows, and this can account for around 1-2lbs on its own. As you begin gaining more weight, you can think of it as a way that your body is becoming stronger to carry your baby.

The Third Month

Your Baby and Your Body

As you enter your third month of pregnancy, your baby is going to be around the size of a lime. Your baby has already begun producing hormones of their own. Their bone marrow is creating white blood cells so they will be able to defend against any germs or bacteria that are encountered. Your baby can be anywhere from 2 - 2 ¼ inches long at this point. While all of this growth has been occurring on the inside, it shouldn't be surprising if you still aren't really showing on the outside. Don't worry because it is going to happen very soon.

Your uterus has likely begun its migration. Normally situated at the bottom of your pelvis, it will move to the front and center of your abdomen. If you had been experiencing frequent urination in the past months, this symptom should be lessened as your uterus migrates because it is taking some of the pressure off of your bladder. Now that you are approaching your second trimester, your nausea and tender breasts should be easing up as well. In general, many of your early pregnancy symptoms should be alleviated very soon. As nice as this can be, your symptoms can be replaced with a new one - dizzy spells. Feeling lightheaded is a common symptom that tends to appear during the second trimester.

What to Expect at This Check-Up

You will finally get to hear your baby's heartbeat at this check-up! This is the moment you and your significant other has been long awaiting, the one that makes everything feel so much more real. Getting to hear your baby's heartbeat is a special moment that you will never forget. It is likely to be the highlight of your 3rd appointment. Much like the other 2 appointments you have been to, the same testing will be completed to ensure that your baby is still developing as normal.

By request, it is at this appointment that you can ask your doctor for the NTD test. This is the one that can identify Down syndrome in your child. Through blood tests, your doctor will be able to provide you with more information. Since it is an optional test with additional blood work to be done, know that you do not have to opt-in. The decision is purely personal, and it will not impact the development of the Down syndrome gene in your baby either way. It is solely available for informational purposes. Another additional test you can ask your doctor for is Amniocentesis. This is another diagnostic test that can screen for many genetic diseases. Again, this is not mandatory, so do not feel pressured to get it done.

Questions to Ask Your Doctor

As you approach your delivery, it is great to be as prepared as possible. Training your muscles to work with you during this process is going to help the ease of your delivery when the time comes. Ask your doctor about different Kegel exercises you can practice in order to strengthen the core muscles that you will need to use. Kegels can even shorten the amount of time you spend in labor and speed up your post-birth recovery time. Overall, they are great to do at any stage of your pregnancy. Making them a regular part of your routine during your third month will give you plenty of time to perfect them.

Just as you would at any other appointment, you can discuss any symptoms that you have been experiencing lately. If anything has been particularly bothersome to you during the last few months, mention it to your doctor. There might be a medication or technique that will help make things more bearable. Consider mentioning to your doctor if you would like to know the gender of your baby. The timing for this is quickly approaching, so it helps to give your doctor an idea of your preference. It is something that you have probably been thinking about during your entire first trimester, and it is important.

Figuring Out Your Due Date

There are several different methods of figuring out your due date. The following are a few that you can utilize if you'd like to know when you can expect your little bundle of joy to arrive. While your doctor will be able to provide a more accurate date during your next appointment, these are some things you can do in the meantime to calculate it on your own:

- First Day of Last Period: Since a typical pregnancy lasts for 40 weeks, you can use the first day of your last period as a guide. By adding 40 weeks, or 280 days, to this date, you will be able to figure out an estimate.

- Conception Date: If you know your exact date of conception, a similar method can be applied. Taking this date, simply add 266 days to this date in order to figure out your due date. Many people do not know of their exact conception date, so don't be discouraged if you don't remember yours either.

- Online Calculators: With all of the resources that are available online, there are certainly ways that you can check what your due date will be by using a method like this. Some websites make it super easy to input minimal information that will automatically be calculated for you.

Chapter 6: The Second Trimester

During your second trimester, you will likely notice the most physical changes in your body. From not showing very much to showing a significant amount, you are truly going to be feeling all of the physical aspects of being pregnant. This is normally a time when a pregnancy announcement is made, so you will be able to share this news you have been keeping a secret with your friends and family. It is a very exciting time to experience as a couple and as an expecting mother.

The Fourth Month

Your Baby and Your Body

Though your baby's eyes are still closed, they are developed and able to make small side-to-side movements. The size of an avocado now, your baby's heart can pump around 25 quarts of blood each day. Amazingly, at the 16-week mark, your baby can already develop a thumb-sucking habit. This reflex develops very early on, and it is crazy to think that your little one might already be sucking their thumb from inside the womb.

Your bump is likely going to be pretty apparent at this point. You will notice that some of your clothes don't fit the way they used to. This might call for a maternity shopping spree. Make sure you buy loose-fitting clothing that is comfortable because comfort should be your main priority at this point in your pregnancy. Your breasts are also going to continue growing. They might be feeling especially sore or tender at this point. Remember, they are growing in order to support the milk production that will eventually feed your baby if you choose to breastfeed.

What to Expect at This Check-Up

At this appointment, you will get to listen to your baby's heartbeat again. You will also get to know more about the size and development of your little one. At this point, you will have the option to schedule an ultrasound. This is a very exciting moment in your pregnancy because you will finally get to see your baby. Though your baby will show up on the scan fairly clearly, the external genitalia might not be very visible at this point. Don't worry too much because you should be able to find out about your baby's gender very soon.

If your doctor can't determine the gender at this appointment, they might be able to do so in a few more weeks. It can be hard to stay patient, but if you want accurate information, this patience is a must. Enjoy the moments of being able to see your child and rest assured that your doctor is checking for any and all abnormalities during your pregnancy so far.

Questions to Ask Your Doctor

One of the main questions you will want to ask your doctor about is your baby's gender. Whether you would like to know, would like to keep it a surprise until delivery, or would like to have the results placed in an envelope for a gender reveal party, you should ask your doctor about your options now. You can also ask about your weight gain if you are curious. A lot of women like to know where they fall on the scale in terms of average weight gain for this point of pregnancy.

If you are curious about additional testing, you can ask your doctor if they have any recommendations for you. At this point in your pregnancy, your doctor is going to have a pretty good idea of what you should and should not do. It doesn't hurt to ask for some advice if you are unsure if you should endure any additional testing. Even if you decide to continue on without doing another test, you can at least feel reassured that you asked for your doctor's opinion.

How to Safely Work Out

While you might not be able to work out the way you used to before you got pregnant, exercise is still going to be beneficial for both yourself and the baby. Swimming is a great and safe way to get some exercise without overworking yourself. It allows you to experience a little bit of cardio mixed with a fun way to spend your time. If you decide to exercise in a more traditional way, ensure that you are keeping everything low-impact. You can still lift weights, but make sure they are no more than 5-10lbs. The last thing that you need is to strain your body on top of all the pregnancy symptoms you are experiencing.

No matter what you decide to do, keeping the exercise to around 30 minutes each day is about the average amount you should be getting. Whether you take 3 10-minute walks per day or swim for 30 minutes straight, it is up to you how you'd like to distribute this time.

Gender Reveal

If you decide that you'd like to find out your baby's gender, there are a few ways you can go about doing this. Some couples prefer to find out in private at the doctor's office, and then they will come up with ways to tell their loved ones the great news. In more recent popularity, couples have been holding gender reveal parties. This happens even when the couple does not know the results yet, and then they hold a party where the gender is revealed to all.

A lot of people will give the results to a bakery, and then the bakery will make a cake with either pink or blue inside to signify the gender. Upon cutting into the cake at the party, everyone gets to find out the gender at the same time. No matter what you decide to do, know that your decision is valid. Even if you'd like to keep the gender a surprise until birth, there is nothing wrong with that. Ultimately, the choice is up to the parents.

The Fifth Month

Your Baby and Your Body

This is a big week for development. Your baby should now be able to kick and punch, so this means that you will likely be feeling a lot of this on the inside as your baby goes through phases of being active. The size of a sweet potato now, you should definitely be able to find out the gender if you haven't been able to already. As your baby continues to grow even bigger and stronger, know that there is still plenty of room inside for this process to happen.

At this point, you are over the halfway point in your pregnancy! With only four months left to go, your baby's reproductive organs have formed. If you are carrying a girl, your baby already has a uterus that is fully formed. For a boy, his testicles are going to be developed and soon to descend. You should be showing a considerable amount at this point, and you will truly feel as though you are eating for two. Remember that heartburn can also follow, so make sure you keep some antacids nearby. Your hair and nails might be experiencing a surge in growth, and you will be delighted to know that they are stronger and healthier than ever. This is one of the many perks that come along with being pregnant.

What to Expect at This Check-Up

As mentioned, if you haven't been able to get sure confirmation of what you are having, then at this appointment, you will likely be able to find out the gender. Otherwise, the appointment is going to follow the same structure as your typical appointments have in the past. This is a point when you can decide on what kind of ultrasound photo you would like. A traditional 2D ultrasound is performed by placing the wand directly over the gel that is placed on your belly. This helps the scanner pick up the image. This is the most traditional type of ultrasound photo that is chosen by parents.

If you would like a 3D or 4D ultrasound, this process is going to be trickier. In order to capture such an image, you will need to keep in mind that these ultrasounds can heat up your tissues. In some cases, this can create pockets of gas or other bodily fluids, which the impacts are still unknown. It is something that is not necessary to expose your baby to, yet it is understandable why parents opt for these stunning, high-quality images of their little ones. Think carefully about your decision and about all the risks involved. Because there isn't as much information available about the impacts of the technology, many parents choose to stick to their 2D ultrasounds.

Questions to Ask Your Doctor

Aside from any normal questions about your current symptoms, you can ask your doctor their opinion on the various ultrasound options that you have available. While taking a more cutting-edge approach isn't necessary, some parents truly do value having the image that it can capture. Your doctor is going to be able to put your worries at ease and guide you toward the best decision for your personal beliefs.

Remember, you can always change your mind. If you opt for a 2D ultrasound at first, you can consider if you'd like to have a 3D or 4D in the future. Keep this idea in mind when you undergo your first scan. Your doctor should always be there to answer all of your questions about the different processes and the pros and cons of each one.

Now would also be the time to bring up any questions you may have regarding your diet. If you have noticed a spike in your hunger, you are probably eating more than you were in the past. Consult your doctor on whether you are getting enough vitamins and nutrients in your current diet. They will be able to tell you if you need to make any adjustments or if you need any supplements.

Sex during Pregnancy

This far along in your pregnancy, you are probably wondering if sex is going to be safe for the baby. It is no secret that your pregnancy hormones are going to have you feeling frisky toward your partner. Some expecting mothers have stated that their hormones had them feeling more turned on than ever. This can be very overwhelming, especially when you are worried about doing anything that will be damaging to the baby. To put any myths to rest, having sex with penetration is not going to harm or damage your baby.

The only thing to worry about during sex while pregnant is finding a position that is comfortable for you. You might have to try out several new positions with your partner that allow you to take the pressure off of your stomach. Consider lying on your side with your partner behind you. This tends to be a fairly comfortable position for women at this stage of pregnancy. If you can't find any positions that allow you to stay comfortable during penetrative sex, know that oral sex is also going to feel great at this point in your pregnancy. This can allow you to lie on your back with the help of some pillows to prop you up.

The Sixth Month

Your Baby and Your Body

You are nearly there! Now as big as a pomegranate, your baby should be putting on a lot more weight. Aside from accumulating more fat, your baby is also going to be gaining muscle mass. Any hair, from the head to the eyelashes, should still be white and transparent. Since their auditory system is forming rapidly, you might notice that your baby will have a music preference and will enjoy hearing the sound of your voice. You can tell by the way that they respond in the womb. Now at around 11-inches long, your baby likely weighs 1lb.

The biggest change you'll probably notice, other than your ever-growing belly, is the shape of your belly button. If you formerly had an innie, it should now resemble an outie. This is going to return to normal after you give birth. Some new symptoms you might become familiar with are swollen wrists and fingers. This can cause a feeling of numbness, and it can get in the way of your daily routine as well as your work, depending on what you do for a living. Your palms might even begin to itch. Expect to feel an increase in headaches and blurry vision, as well. These are all normal symptoms to experience in your sixth month.

What to Expect at This Check-Up

During this check-up, your doctor is likely to go over your birth plan. Even if you don't know exactly what you'd like that to be just yet, you will be encouraged to decide as the time is quickly approaching. Many expecting mothers do not know what they would like their birth plan to be at this point, but it is smart to begin thinking about it sooner rather than later. Consider where you would feel most comfortable with giving birth and what method you would like to aim for. Know that, even with a detailed birth plan, your birth can happen in an entirely different way depending on the circumstances involved with your labor. You can ask your doctor about what all of the different options are.

Aside from the normal testing that you will go through, your doctor will likely want to run a glucose test on you at this point. This involves drinking a special liquid that will allow doctors to see clearer results. They will likely give you the drink to take home, and then you will be instructed when to drink it and when to come back to get your blood drawn. Other than this, there should not be anything new or unfamiliar during your check-up.

Questions to Ask Your Doctor

The main questions you should be asking your doctor at this appointment should revolve around your birth plan. Whether you have done extensive research on your own or no research yet, your doctor is going to be able to inform you about all of the different ways that a woman can choose to give birth. Keep in mind that not everyone decides to give birth in a hospital. Some women prefer to be in the comfort of their own homes. While this can present risks, as long as you are having a typical course of pregnancy, there is no reason why you shouldn't be able to have a home birth as well. Your doctor will be able to confirm or deny this for you.

There is also the option to have your baby in a birthing center rather than a hospital. This involves guidance from a doula or midwife in a setting that is less clinical than a traditional medical facility. Your doctor will likely be able to tell you about the risks of this as well as recommend a center that is close to your area. Another thing to consider is whether or not you'd like the epidural. While there are risks and complications involved, many mothers still opt for the epidural because the pain becomes too unbearable. You aren't necessarily going to be able to predict your level of pain tolerance until you are giving birth, but your doctor can explain the process of getting the epidural and what it involves.

Childbirth Education

Consider taking some childbirth classes with your partner at this point in your pregnancy. These classes are meant to teach you about everything you need to know before, during, and after your delivery. For first-time parents, it can be helpful to walk through each step that is going to happen when the time comes. Not only will you be more informed on *how* to deliver your baby, but you are also going to feel more confident in your ability to do so.

Your instructor will be able to go over various breathing and relaxation techniques with you that can either be performed solo or with the help of your partner. They will show you how you can get through the delivery while relying on the support and help of your partner, too. Some classes even include a tour of the birthing facility of your choosing. Becoming familiar with it beforehand can do a lot to put you at ease when you go into labor. These classes create a special bond between you and your significant other. They will show you how to prepare for the miraculous experience to come.

Chapter 7: The Third Trimester

You have finally made it into the last trimester! This is the final stretch, and before you know it, you will be holding your baby in your arms. As you approach your due date, you should be feeling confident and prepared. You have likely already begun to arrange the nursery in your home that your baby will soon inhabit. These are the last few things you must know before you deliver your newborn.

The Seventh Month

Your Baby and Your Body

Now as big as a head of lettuce, your baby can experience the REM cycle. This series of rapid eye movements indicate that your baby is able to fall into a deep pattern of sleep. There is also a high likelihood that your baby can dream! At this point, your baby will be able to open and close their eyes and blink too. A baby in the womb at this point can also make faces and stick out their tongue. Doctors don't know exactly why they do this, but some believe it is because the baby is tasting the amniotic fluid.

Since your baby is getting settled into the proper position to be delivered, you are likely going to be feeling a lot of pressure in your lower region. You are likely to feel more uncomfortable at this point in your pregnancy because of this new pressure and your baby's ability to move freely, kicking and squirming often. Your feet might be swollen more, and you might notice that your back is continuously aching. Make sure that you are paying attention to your body and staying off your feet as much as possible. Since your uterus is much enlarged at this point, it is possible you will feel shooting pains down your spine known as sciatica. This is nerve pain that happens due to the pressure being put on the lower nerve in your spine.

What to Expect at This Check-Up

In your third trimester, you are going to possibly be introduced to a new test. An NST, or non-stress test, is actually not stressful at all. It is done to examine your baby's heart rate and movement. Not all women receive this test, but if you do, this does not necessarily indicate that anything is wrong. Some women with smaller babies receive it by default. It only takes around 20-40 minutes to perform. A belt monitor will be placed around your belly, and during this time, you will be given a button to press each time you feel your baby move. This gives your doctor an idea of how active your baby is and how reactive they are.

Your doctor will also likely do a vaginal exam, which includes feeling the position of your baby. It is important to know how your baby is sitting at this point because this is going to be an indication of whether you can have a natural birth or whether you might be forced to have a C-section. While it is still early to claim either of these things for sure, your doctor will have some kind of idea of how your baby is going to continue to drop and which way they will be facing.

Questions to Ask Your Doctor

This appointment will be a great time to ask about where your baby is currently located and what position they are in. You can ask if this is an ideal position, or if your doctor thinks that the baby is going to be moving in a way that is going to make the delivery a little bit more complicated. Of course, your doctor won't always be able to predict exactly what position your baby will be in as you go into labor, but the patterns that are currently forming will provide them with a good indication of what to expect.

Keep in mind that you might have to deviate from your original birth plan, as mentioned before. Talk to your doctor about the process of changing the birth plan mid-delivery. When you can feel prepared for this, it becomes less scary to think about the possibility. Your doctor and the entire staff present during your delivery are going to know what the safest option is for your baby and yourself at the moment. Having this trust in them comes from being able to ask all of your questions and express any concerns that you might have. If you are still uncertain about some aspects of your birth plan, this would be an excellent time to lock them in with your doctor.

How to Sleep

Getting enough sleep when you are uncomfortable can be difficult. As a pregnant woman, you are going to learn about several different things that can assist you with staying comfortable and getting enough rest. When you wake up cranky and exhausted, your pregnancy symptoms can feel amplified. A lot of women experience insomnia during pregnancy, and some even experience RLS (Restless Leg Syndrome). These two factors alone can completely destroy your sleep schedule.

While there is no magic pill that can fix these things, you can make sure that you are sticking to bedtime that is reasonable. If you plan what time you'd like to sleep and when you'd like to wake up, this allows you to have somewhat of a sleep schedule. You can also try sleeping on your left side. This is known to allow the most relief for a pregnant woman, and it can feel incredibly comfortable compared to most other sleep positions.

Make sure that you are drinking enough fluids throughout the day. Being dehydrated is only going to promote exhaustion. Drinking more is going to mean peeing more, but this is healthy for you. Put a night light in your bathroom to avoid having to turn on the light and completely wake yourself up. The night light will be less harsh on your eyes.

Easing Labor Pain

As you approach your delivery date, you are likely going to be anticipating the contractions and pain that you will endure. While it can vary based on your pregnancy and individual pain tolerance, the following are some tips to get you through it:

- Rhythmic Breathing: The way that you breathe is going to be your main form of control during contractions. Breathing techniques that you learn during classes, or on your own, will help to soothe the pain. By focusing on your breathing, you will be able to release tension. Taking a quick breath every 2-3 seconds can help to alleviate what you are feeling.

- Heat: A hot water bottle can feel nice on your lower back when you are experiencing labor pains. This heat is going to loosen your muscles, further prepping your body for the delivery. Because of all the tension, your pain sensors are going to be heightened. Allow yourself to relax into the heat.

- Movement: Sometimes, getting up and walking can help take your mind off the pain. When you are in labor, you do not necessarily need to be bedridden. The staff at the hospital will likely encourage you to get up and walk around your room if you want to!

- Gentle Massage: A gentle hand massage or back massage can do a lot to ease your nerves. Having your partner or doula massage you every so often will keep you in the relaxed state of mind for an easy birth.

The Eighth Month

Your Baby and Your Body

Right now, all of your baby's organs are fully formed except for their lungs. Your baby is still going to be inhaling amniotic fluid for practice using their lungs. Their skin is now opaque, and they are about as big as a cantaloupe! At around 4lbs and 16 inches, delivery is going to happen very soon.

Because your body is so close to having to deliver, you might start to experience what are known as Braxton Hicks contractions. This occurs when you notice your uterus tightening or hardening every so often. A lot of women mistake these contractions for labor contractions. Think about them as a rehearsal for what your body is about to do.

At nighttime, you are probably experiencing more leg cramping and tightness. The feeling of dizziness is also likely going to increase. As your breasts continue to grow in size, you might experience some leakage. This is normal, and the fluid leaking out is known as colostrum, which is what your breasts produce before breast milk.

What to Expect at This Check-Up

This visit should be routine for the most part. The same

normal procedures will take place in order to monitor your health and the health of your baby. Your doctor might have you do a vaginal/rectal culture which is used for the purpose of testing for Group B Strep. This can be harmful to your baby if it is present during the time of your delivery, so your doctor will likely check for it sometime around this appointment, if not the next one.

Questions to Ask Your Doctor

Now is the time to go over any additional details of your birth plan that you wish to discuss with your doctor. You don't have much time until your due date, so many unanswered questions should be taken care of at this appointment. A lot of women deliver early, so it is a good idea to have all of this information locked down well ahead of time. As usual, you can also discuss any symptoms that you have been having recently with your doctor. The discomfort is likely going to be increasing due to your size, and your doctor might have some advice on how you can stay comfortable.

Breastfeeding

Breastfeeding is a highly beneficial choice to make for your baby. Since your body is naturally producing this milk, it makes sense that it will have all of the nutrients that your newborn needs. If you are undecided on whether you would like to breastfeed, consider the following benefits that come with it:

- Protection Against Allergies and Eczema: Certain proteins in cow's milk and soy milk formula can stimulate an allergic reaction in your newborn. These proteins can be harder for your baby to digest, therefore creating a higher likelihood of certain allergies and even eczema.

- Less Stomach Upset: As mentioned, your breast milk is going to contain everything that your baby needs in terms of nutrients, so naturally, they are going to be able to easily digest it. A newborn's stomach is very sensitive, so this can help them transition into drinking cow's milk or formula in the future.

- Reduces Risk of Viruses: Through infant nutrition research, it has been shown that breastfed babies are less likely to get sick during their infant months. The statistics actually show that babies who are not breastfed are three times more likely to get ear infections than those who breastfeed. They can even be five times more likely to get pneumonia (Lucla, C. A., Hartshorn, J., n. d.).

- Makes Vaccines More Effective: As your baby grows up, they are going to be receiving vaccinations of your choosing. A breastfed baby is known to have antibodies that are more responsive to these vaccines as opposed to a baby who was never breastfed.

- Lose Pregnancy Weight: Your baby is not the only one who will benefit from breastfeeding. While it is a wonderful bonding experience for a mother to have with her child, it can also be a way for you to begin your weight loss after pregnancy. Producing breast milk actually burns around 300-500 calories each day!

The Ninth Month

Your Baby and Your Body

At this point in the pregnancy, your baby has done most of the in-womb growing already. The growth is going to slow down, and you will feel your baby dropping lower in order to get into a proper delivery position. As big as a bundle of kale now, your baby's hearing is going to be extra sharp during this final month of pregnancy.

You will notice that your walk has changed quite a bit during this final stretch of pregnancy. This occurs because your hips are widening and your baby is dropping. This is a natural occurrence and it is your body's way of showing you that it is ready to deliver the baby. During this time, it is normal to experience pain in your pelvic region. Expect a lot of bloating, cramping, and even passing of gas or burping.

What to Expect at This Check-Up

During this appointment, you are likely going to receive your pre-registration paperwork from your doctor to the hospital or birthing center of your choice. Your weight and blood pressure will be checked, as it normally is, and the baby's statistics will also be checked. You will be asked for a urine sample in order to check your sugar and protein levels. Your doctor will also likely ask you about your baby's movements since last time. Then, the height of your uterus will be measured in order to track just how much the baby has grown.

At this point, your doctor will likely inform you about all of the signs you need to be aware of to determine if you are going into labor. Keeping in mind that you might give birth before your due date, it is important that you know what to look for. Your urinary habits might also be discussed. It is common for women to leak slightly when they cough or laugh because of all the pressure being put on the bladder.

Questions to Ask Your Doctor

You can ask your doctor about your mobility from this point onward. A lot of women are advised not to travel too far from home or the hospital in case they were to go into labor. You can also ask about what you should do if you believe that you are going into preterm labor. At this stage in the pregnancy, a lot can happen very quickly, so you will want to make sure that you are prepared to give birth at any moment. Your doctor can go over the process with you for what happens after your water breaks and you realize that you are ready to give birth.

No matter where you are or what you are doing, this can be an exhilarating experience. You are about to meet your little one, yet you want to do it safely. Make sure you have a clear understanding of what you need to do when you see the signs.

Pre-Labor, False Labor, and Real Labor

Pre-Labor: Before you are about to go into labor, you will begin having contractions. This is your body's way of warning you that it is almost time to give birth. Before you actually go into labor, the contractions will be short and irregular. A day or so before you give birth you might notice a discharge that appears bloody. This is likely your mucus plug, and it is normal to lose this around this time in the pregnancy. It is not always noticed, but if you do see something like this, it should be a pinkish color that is the texture of mucus.

False Labor: While contractions are a big indication that you are going into labor, their frequency will ultimately be able to tell you if you are in real labor or false labor. In the latter, the contractions are going to be irregular and without progression. They will feel like a general period cramp.

Real Labor: When your water breaks, this is a big sign that labor has begun. Do not panic if yours does not break on its own because some women need assistance at the hospital to have theirs broken. Your contractions will now feel strong, starting from your lower back and extending down to your abdomen and groin. They will be progressively longer and stronger. Signs of active labor will mean that you are having contractions that last for around 45-60 seconds and are 3-4 minutes apart. When you notice this kind of regularity and frequency, then it is time for you to get to the hospital and get ready for delivery. Some women only stay in labor for a few hours, while others can stay in labor for a few days. Each pregnancy is going to be different, but your doctor is going to be there to guide you through the process.

Chapter 8: Labor and Delivery

The moment has finally arrived, and it is time to deliver your baby! This process is normally a mixture of a whirlwind and a waiting game. While you are going to be very excited to meet your new baby, there are a few steps that you must go through in order to have a safe and successful delivery. From knowing what to bring with you to the hospital to figuring out how to manage your pain, this chapter is going to teach you everything you need to know in order to give birth.

How to Pack

While there are some essentials that you will need with you at the hospital, you also need to make sure that you are going to be comfortable. Likely, you will be in the hospital for a couple of days, so make sure that you pack enough to last you for your entire stay. If you need help deciding what to bring, this sample list can help you make sure that you aren't forgetting anything:

- Your birth plan/maternity notes
- Something comfortable to wear during labor
- Something to wear home from the hospital
- A few changes of clothes
- A robe
- Slippers
- Socks

- Snacks and drinks
- Entertainment (books, magazines, phone, tablet, laptop)
- Lip balm
- Your favorite pillow
- Hair ties
- Massage oil or lotion
- Toiletries

What you pack is mainly going to keep you busy. Since you might be in labor for a long time before you actually begin pushing or delivering your child, having several different ways to pass the time is going to help you. Make sure that you do not run out of things to do that you can easily accomplish from your hospital bed. If you do decide you'd like to get up and walk around, hospitals can be chilly. This is why bringing a robe/socks/slippers is important.

Ideally, you will want to pack all of this stuff several days before you anticipate going into labor. It is never a good idea to leave the packing until the last minute. The bag should be packed and waiting in your closet until the time comes. With everything that you need inside, you can simply have your partner grab the bag so you can be out the door quickly. Plus, when you pack ahead of time, you can ensure that you aren't forgetting anything.

Remember that your partner should also pack a bag. While

you are the only one going into labor, your partner is likely going to be in the hospital for the same amount of time. While they will have the ability to leave if necessary, it is still better to ensure that they pack for a few days as well. Many couples prepare the mother, and when the time comes, the significant other is left scrambling to stuff clothing into a bag. Keep both bags packed well ahead of time and you will both be prepared.

Labor and Numbness

While you are probably already familiar with the epidural, you should also know about a pudendal block. This is something that is given as a shot vaginally before delivery. It will numb your vaginal area entirely but know that it is not going to stop the pain from contractions like the epidural will. This is a quick-acting fix and it will make your vagina feel numb. For some women, this is a happy medium between no pain relief and an epidural. The choice is up to you, but it is always good to know all of your options ahead of time.

If you are thinking about having something that is more cohesive to the pain that you will be experiencing, you might want to consider a spinal or epidural. Both of these options are used in order to numb certain parts of your body to assist you with pain relief. The spinal is a single shot of medicine that is best for short-term delivery situations. This type of pain relief is usually given to women who are having C-sections. The epidural stays in your back through a catheter. This allows the doctor to provide you with more medicine if necessary. When the doctor does not know how long the labor is going to last, this is likely the option that is going to be offered.

Whether you choose one of the above options or none, this does not make you a bad mother or an unfit mother. We all experience pain differently, and this process should be as calm for you as possible. When you are calm, the baby stays calm. A mother who is in distress can end up with a baby who is in distress. As you think about the options that are available, know that you might also change your mind during active labor. While having a plan is great and recommended, feeling your labor pains at the moment will tell you what is going to work best for you.

Epidural or Epidural-Free?

The decision to get an epidural is one that you are going to encounter as you enter active labor. Plenty of women opt for the epidural in order to better manage their pain, yet a lot of mothers do not wish to utilize any kind of pain drug during labor because they feel it is better for the baby. There can often be a stigma surrounding whether or not you get the epidural, but at the end of the day, this is your decision to make. As mentioned, everyone has a different pain tolerance and belief about the safety of the epidural.

Having a natural birth does not make you a better or more

capable mother. If you decide you need the epidural, then you need to do what is best for you and what is best for the baby. Remember that the more stress you experience, the more stress the baby is going to feel. This can impact your ease of delivery when it comes time to push. These are a few things that you must keep in mind when you are making your decision.

To make a more educated decision, it helps to know the pros and cons of getting an epidural:

Pros

- Painless delivery
- Better for prolonged labor
- Potentially lowered blood pressure
- Can speed up delivery
- Useful in case of a C-section because the mother is still alert

Cons

- Back pain/soreness
- Persistent bleeding at the puncture site
- Fever
- Difficulty breathing
- Potential dangerous drop in blood pressure

Much like your birth plan, you are going to probably have your choice in mind before you go into labor. Know that this plan can change at any point in time once you are getting ready to deliver your baby, and that is okay. The risks associated with getting the epidural, come from the idea that, since the mother can't feel everything that is going on, this can lead to complications. While this isn't always the case, it is something to keep in mind. Another reason why mothers choose to deliver naturally is that they do not want their newborn being exposed to any medication that comes through getting the epidural. There is no right or wrong decision, though; you need to do what feels best.

Beyond Pain Relief

Going into your delivery while being fearful of the pain is only going to stress you out. No matter what medication you decide to take or to pass on, the most important thing for you to do is to remain calm. This is something that you should be practicing in the months leading up to your delivery. Working on communicating with your partner is going to help you when the moment finally arrives.

As long as you can remember to breathe and feel that you can rely on your partner for support, you are going to be just fine while you deliver your baby. Having distractions can be a great way to pass the time when you first enter labor. The process can take a long time, and having someone to talk to is going to help you get through it. Talking to your partner or a loved one is a way to remain calm while also focusing on something else at the moment.

As your contractions come and go you need to keep your body as loose as possible. If you tense up each time, your body is only going to feel more stressed as they get more intense. Remember that this is a happy and amazing time; it will all be worth it once you can hold your baby in your arms for the first time. There is already going to be a lot of adrenaline pumping through your system, and this can act as a medication in itself. Your body knows what to do, so you just need to make sure that you are allowing it to happen in the calmest way you can.

Cesarean Delivery (Pros and Cons)

Pros

- The birth will be more predictable
- It gives mothers who cannot give birth vaginally another option
- The C-section can be scheduled
- Labor will likely be much shorter

Cons

- A longer hospital stay after giving birth
- Increased risk of blood loss
- Longer recovery period
- A scar on the lower abdomen
- Baby is at higher risk of developing breathing problems

With a C-section, sometimes it is necessary to have one due to the position of your baby. Other times, women request them. No matter the case, the process is generally fairly simple. The mother will get an IV for fluids. A catheter is placed inside the bladder to remove any urine. The doctor will make a single horizontal incision in the lower abdomen, and this will normally serve the dual purpose of rupturing the amniotic sac. Once this has been ruptured, the baby will be removed by the doctor from the uterus.

Sometimes, the doctor can simply pull the baby out by hand, but other times, tools like forceps are necessary. The surgery can take anywhere from 1-2 hours, and the mother remains awake for it. A surgical tarp is normally put up so the woman cannot see what is going on below her torso in order to keep her calm. Some hospitals offer the chance to watch the procedure from a monitor if the mother chooses to see exactly what is happening. Once the baby is out, there is the same option to cut the umbilical cord yourself.

Recovery can take around 6 weeks, with 2-4 additional days spent in the hospital as compared to those who deliver vaginally. Even if you do plan to have a vaginal delivery, if your labor is too prolonged, your doctor is likely going to recommend that you get a C-section for the health of your baby and yourself. It is a faster way to get the baby out, and the doctor can perform any necessary check-ups to ensure that your baby is healthy and that everything is functional.

Home Birth (Pros and Cons)

Giving birth in the comfort of your own home might sound like an amazing alternative to sitting in the hospital for a few days. It is a less clinical setting that a lot of mothers prefer. Naturally, there are going to be risks involved because there will not be a staff of trained medical professionals in your home to assist you if you are having any difficulties, are in need of an emergency C-section, or if the baby is born with complications.

Typically a midwife or doula is going to be present, so you do not have to go through the entire process alone, but keep in mind that they are mainly going to be there for your own moral support. You will not have the option to get an epidural that they would offer in a hospital. Those who know ahead of time that they do not wish to use pain medication have no problem with choosing home birth. There is something incredibly special about giving birthright from the comfort of your own home, and that is something that a lot of people desire. Naturally, you might be scared to go with this option during your first pregnancy since you do not know what to expect.

Talk to your doctor about this option. They are going to be able to give you a realistic answer as to whether or not it is a good idea for you and your baby. Some pregnancies are naturally going to be higher risk than others, and for those, home birth is likely not going to be the best option.

Water Birth (Pros and Cons)

Waterbirth is exactly as it sounds, and it can actually happen from home or in a participating hospital. When you go into labor, you would enter a small, shallow pool of water and give birth to your baby inside of it. If you plan on doing this from home, you can do it in your bathtub, but getting a proper birthing pool is recommended. It will allow you more room to move around, and you will likely feel more comfortable. A lot of women find the idea of wading in a pool of water to be comforting, and it can provide an alternative birthing position from the typical one that is encouraged in the hospital. Giving birth on your back might not be right for you, so water birth allows you to either sit, stand and hang over the edge of the pool, or squat.

Water immersion can be known to shorten the time spent in labor. For most women, the delivery isn't even the hardest part, it is the labor. A lot of women report that giving birth in water is a lot less stressful, which you know is a lot better for the baby. The experience that you have is also more organic and a lot different than the one you would have if you were in a hospital room. A lot of women who opt for a water birth that can have their baby directly into their arms.

Naturally, the complications must be assessed. If you are

giving birth in water from home, the same risks are going to apply with not having medical staff on hand to assist you if any complications occur. Also, if the water is too hot, this can begin to overheat and cause fever during delivery. Once the baby is born, it is important to regulate their temperature right away and clear their lungs, nose, and mouth of fluids. You need to make sure that you are ready to do this as soon as the baby is born.

The Aftermath

One of the main worries after giving birth is how long the healing process takes. Women are very resilient. Whether you have an unmedicated vaginal birth, a C-section, or a water birth from home, you are going to need a lot of time to rest. Take bed rest, and enjoy this bonding time with your new baby. There isn't much that you need to know about what happens after you give birth because this is simply when your recovery process begins. As your body heals, you are going to be spending the rest of your time getting to know your baby and creating that irreplaceable bond.

A lot of women wonder when it is safe to begin having sex again after they give birth. While there is no concrete timeline, doctors do say that the highest chance for experiencing risks and infections come within the first 2 weeks after giving birth. As long as you feel up to it and physically ready, then you can start having sex as soon as you want to. Know that, depending on what kind of delivery you had, there will be different levels of pain that likely did not exist before. If it is too painful, try to wait at least a few more days or weeks before you try again. Keep the communication open with your partner on whether you even feel like having sex yet. Your body will have just gone through a lot of intense pain and hard work, so it is perfectly understandable if you are not in the mood right away again. If you are worried about the tightness of your pelvic floor, don't forget to still do your Kegel exercises to ensure that they remain toned.

Chapter 9: You're Having Twins

Finding out that you are pregnant can be life-altering, but finding out that you are pregnant with twins can change even more aspects of your life. It can be fairly easy to prepare for one baby but knowing that you are expecting two might send you into a panic. While there is no need to panic, you probably have a lot of questions about how you need to prepare for the delivery of two healthy babies. The great thing is you are receiving two blessings instead of one, like most women. Having twins can be the most exciting news to receive, and as long as you are prepared, your pregnancy should not be much different than any other traditional pregnancy.

The following are some facts about twin pregnancies that you have likely never heard before:

1. You Are More Likely to Have Twins in Your 30s or 40s: In a lot of cases, having twins naturally tends to happen to mothers who are already out of their 20s. According to research, after you get out of your 20s, your ovulatory cycles are going to be different. Because of this irregularity, when you do ovulate, you might be ovulating two follicles at once. This is how twin pregnancies happen!

2. You Will Need to Have More Doctor Appointments: When you are pregnant, routine doctor visits are going to become a part of your monthly routine. These

appointments happen because your doctor needs to monitor the growth and development of your baby. Naturally, if you are expecting two babies, there will need to be extra monitoring. Two babies are going to be sharing the space that is normally only used by one baby. You can expect to have more ultrasounds if you are expecting twins.

3. Morning Sickness Tends to Be Worse: Every expectant mother struggles with morning sickness, but those expecting twins will likely see more of this. It is the sudden increase of hormones that typically makes you feel nauseated, so you are going to be getting a double dose of hormones when there are twins involved. The good news is that even despite carrying two babies, the morning sickness tends to fade away between weeks 12-14, just like any other pregnancy.

4. You Won't Feel the Kicking Earlier: It is a common misconception that you will feel your babies moving around sooner than you would if you were having a single baby. Developmentally, your babies are going to be growing at the same rate as any other baby in the womb, so you shouldn't be able to feel any additional movement or kicking any earlier. Fetal movement can tend to feel like gas, so a lot of women might not even realize that the baby/babies are kicking right away.

5. Weight Gain Is Increased: This one seems fairly

obvious, but if you are carrying two babies, you are going to probably gain more weight. If you are of average weight for your height and you get pregnant with twins, you can expect to gain around 37-54lbs. A healthy amount of weight gain for a mother carrying twins is no less than 15lbs and no more than 40lbs. Your doctor is going to be monitoring this closely.

6. You Are More Likely to Develop Gestational Diabetes: If you were to develop gestational diabetes when pregnant with twins, one of the main risks is that you will have larger babies and then you will have to deliver by C-section. Gestational diabetes is common during pregnancy at times, but if you develop it while you are pregnant with twins, you will have a higher risk of developing type 2 diabetes later on in life.

7. Labor and Delivery Usually Come Early: Statistically, mothers who are carrying twins tend to go into labor at around the 36-37 week mark. Because the babies are probably going to be born early, they have more of a risk of developing respiratory issues. The babies might also be born underweight.

What You Need to Know

Knowledge is everything when it comes to pregnancy, and this is especially true when you find out that you are expecting more than one baby. As soon as you get the wonderful news, you can begin planning for the future. Not only do you need to think about your birth plan, but you will also need to consider if your current home is big enough and if you and your partner are financially stable to support these babies. It is never too early to get prepared for your twins. While your body might not feel or look extremely different with twins inside, you have less than a year to prepare to take care of two little bundles of joy.

Make sure that you are keeping your body as strong as possible. Every pregnant woman should be taking prenatal vitamins, but you truly need to make sure that you are getting enough nutrients because two babies are going to be relying on you for nutrition. The exhaustion can feel overwhelming at times, and you are probably going to need to get off your feet a lot to give yourself some much-needed breaks. Keep in mind that you are going to be eating a lot more than you are used to eating. With two babies needing nourishment, you might feel like your stomach is now a bottomless pit.

Folic acid is especially important for twins because they ward off birth defects. The recommended amount is 1mg per day for twin pregnancies, as opposed to 0.4mg for single-baby pregnancies. One of the main birth defects that are seen in twin pregnancies is spina bifida. This is a defect that occurs when the spine is not able to develop correctly, causing complications later on in life. The folic acid is going to keep the babies strong and healthy, ensuring that they can each fully develop.

Spotting is something that can worry any pregnant woman, and that is understandable. When you become pregnant, your period stops as your baby grows inside of your womb. It can be normal to see some spots in a traditional pregnancy, but you might see even more of this if you are having twins. Of course, a mother's first thought when she sees spotting is that she is having a miscarriage. Unfortunately, this can be the case, and it is more common for mothers expecting twins or triplets. If you do notice spotting, you don't need to panic, though.

Light spotting instead of cramps is your body's way of transitioning out of having periods and into being pregnant. If you begin to cramp regularly, pass large blood clots, and remain actively bleeding, then this is going to be more of a cause for concern. If you are ever unsure about the way your body is functioning during your pregnancy, you can always consult your doctor. It never hurts to ask, and you should definitely feel at ease during your pregnancy because you need to understand what is going on with your body.

It is not impossible to vaginally deliver twins, even triplets, but know that you are likely going to need a C-section when it comes time to deliver your babies. As explained, you are likely going to deliver your babies earlier than a mother who is having a traditional pregnancy. For this reason, your birth plan must be made sooner and your hospital bag should be packed earlier. Everything that you would do for a traditional pregnancy, you need to do just a little bit sooner. Remember, you are going to need to set up two cribs and potentially even two nurseries depending on if you'd like to keep the babies together or in their own rooms. Make sure that you give yourself and your partner enough time to do all of this because the weeks can go by very quickly.

Announcing to your loved ones that you are expecting two bundles of joy can be very fun. Everyone is going to be incredibly excited, and you will probably find that a lot of your friends and family members are going to probably step up to ask if you need any help. Take this help when you can! You will be thankful that you did. Before babies are born, you might not think that you need a lot of help. Things can progress very quickly when you have two crying babies in each arm who need to be fed, though. Be grateful for any help that is offered to you, and know that just because you are capable of doing it only with your partner does not mean that you should have to.

It can seem like your body is going through a lot more than a typical expecting mother's body, but just remember, the duration is not going to be any longer. At most, you will still only need to get through nine months (or less) of pregnancy. Your body is strong and resilient, and it will still know what to do, no matter how many babies you are having at once. A lot of mothers wonder if there are any early signs that can indicate that twins are developing. While there aren't any concrete signs that will surely confirm that you are, here are some symptoms that you can look out for:

- Family History: If someone else in your family has given birth to twins, this automatically increases your likelihood. While chance still is the biggest factor when it comes to how many babies you will have, the twin gene is one that can be passed down from generation to generation.

- Fertility Treatments: If you are having trouble conceiving, you might seek treatments that will increase your chances of becoming pregnant. These hormonal treatments can often work so well that they can potentially give you twins. A lot of women who go through IVF (in vitro fertilization) have been known to become pregnant with twins.

- Higher BMI: Your BMI stands for body mass index. There are plenty of charts that can allow you to track your BMI, or your doctor can let you know what yours is. If you have a higher BMI, this can be a factor in becoming pregnant with twins. Those who have a BMI of 25+ typically have an increased possibility.

Multiple Childbirth

When the time comes to give birth, you might be wondering how it is even possible to deliver more than one baby at a time. To put yourself at ease, know that millions, even billions, of women have gone through this before and have ended up with healthy babies. There is no doubt that your delivery is going to be eventful, but this is normally the most exciting part of the process of birthing twins. There are three main classifications that you need to know about that will determine how you will give birth to the babies:

- Monochorionic monoamniotic (Mo-Mo): This is when your babies are sharing the placenta and amniotic sac.
- Monochorionic diamniotic (Mo-Di): This is when they are sharing a placenta, but they each have their own amniotic sac.
- Dichorionic diamniotic (Di-Di): This is when each of your babies has their own placenta and amniotic sac.

Early into your pregnancy, your doctor will be able to tell you which of the above situations applies. With Mo-Mo twins, concerns normally arise during the delivery time because there is the possibility that the babies could get tangled up in one another's umbilical cords. While this does not always happen, it is standard that Mo-Mo babies are delivered by C-section to prevent this complication altogether. Because this is the safest way to deliver these twins, your doctor is likely going to explain this to you after the first couple of ultrasounds.

Regardless of your babies' classification, your delivery room is still going to be prepared to help you deliver either vaginally or by C-section. Much like traditional labor, a lot can happen in those few hours. In general, if you have babies that are pointed down in the correct position, a vaginal delivery is probably going to be possible. It depends on your own comfort level and your doctor's recommendation whether or not you try to deliver vaginally or just schedule a C-section. Sometimes, one baby can be in the perfect position for a vaginal delivery, yet the second baby could be facing the wrong way. This is to be expected of twins since they are two different babies. There is a lot of moving around that can happen during the last few months of your pregnancy.

There are some instances where the mother can deliver one baby vaginally, yet needs to have a C-section for the second baby. This is not uncommon, and if it is in your babies' best interest, then your doctor is going to let you know if this should be the birth plan for you. Every step of the way, your doctor is going to be keeping you updated and provide you with recommendations on what they believe is the most successful decision to make during delivery. This is why it is important to always keep an open mind about your birth plan; it can change in an instant.

Keep in mind that both babies aren't always going to be ready to come out at the same time. When you go into labor, this might only be triggered by one of the babies. Your water could break, just as it would in a traditional pregnancy, and you might give birth to your first child. Then, the waiting begins. Normally, one baby is always going to be ready sooner than the other. This is why mothers who are expecting twins can have a different type of labor; it can almost feel like double labor. If your second baby takes minutes, or even hours, to finally be ready to come out, you are going to have to endure even more anticipation and waiting.

You will actually be giving birth in an operating room just in case either of the babies needs additional assistance during delivery. You can expect to be accompanied by your partner, any loved ones you invite into the room, your doctor, one nurse for each baby, and neonatal intensive care doctors standing by. While this might seem overwhelming, this is necessary because of how different delivering twins as compared to delivering a single baby. Know that every single person present is there to support you and help you. They want what is best for you, and no one is going to be judging you or pressuring you to deliver your babies in a certain way. The only time recommendations are going to be made is when they will clearly benefit your babies.

Homebirth is not recommended for twins because of all the complexities that can happen during your delivery. While a lot of women dream of having a home birth, this just isn't exactly going to be a reality when you are having more than one baby at a time. Waterbirth in a hospital is still an option, though. If you do want to experience the comfort of having a water birth, discuss this with your doctor early on. They can have everything set up for you in the room, but know that you might have to be moved back onto a hospital bed if you do need to undergo a C-section or any other procedure during the delivery. The hospital is always going to try to accommodate your requests and desires because they know this can be a very special, yet stressful, time for the expecting mother.

Remember that your partner is also going to be handling a rollercoaster ride of emotions. Though they will not be giving birth, they are going to be supporting you in every way they can. Whether it be distracting you or holding your hand during any painful moments, your partner will also be under a lot of excitement and anxiety at the same time. It can almost feel like they are helpless when they are there with you as you work through your labor. Do your best to show your appreciation for them, even if it means a simple hand squeeze from time to time to reassure them that they are a part of this process too.

Chapter 10: Dad's Role

It is talked about less often, but the dad's role throughout pregnancy and delivery is an extremely important one. Your partner is in this with you, and this is their child too. Just because they did not get to feel any of the morning sickness or baby kicks does not mean that they aren't just as invested as you are in the whole process. This chapter will focus on what the dad's role is and how to work through certain feelings that arise or questions that come up. There is a myth that tends to circulate that a dad does not have to do much at all when a mother is pregnant, but that is not even close to the truth. Not only is the dad going to be the main support system, but he is also going to be learning and discovering just as the mother will.

The Importance

Feelings of cluelessness are normal for first-time dads. This is a brand new experience, and it should not be expected of every dad to know exactly what to do and when to do it. Just as the mother is going to be dealing with different changes, the father will also have to do the same thing. The main way to be a helpful father to an expecting mother is to just be there for her. Accompanying her to all of her doctor appointments is the first step. This will provide her with a sense of support, and you will also get to experience all of the same news and information that she will experience.

Try to do some research on your own time. The more you can learn about pregnancy and delivery is going to help your partner. Just as her own education on her pregnancy is valuable, your education is deemed just as valuable. Taking initiative is what makes you a great father from the very beginning. When it comes to picking out names, participate in the process! This is your chance to make a decision with your significant other. Think about the names that you like and make suggestions when the mother decides that she would like to talk about what you would like to name your new baby.

Doing housework is a great way to be helpful to an expecting mother. As her pregnancy progresses, she isn't going to be able to do all of the chores that she usually does. All of the bending down and walking around that can be avoided will help to put her body at ease. Communicate with her every chance you get. If she isn't feeling well, ask her directly what you can do for her that would help. A significant other that is willing to ask is a lot better than one who simply stands on the sidelines and waits for instructions.

What to Expect

In the beginning, you aren't going to notice that many changes. The expectant mother might feel sick more often than usual, but you can help by ensuring that she stays hydrated and well-nourished. Remind her to take her prenatal vitamins, and cook nutritious meals for her when she is hungry. In the first trimester, you shouldn't have to change much about your typical routine as a couple. The symptoms that she will be dealing with should be manageable, and if they aren't, you can take her to the doctor to see if there are any solutions that will make them easier to handle.

As the pregnancy progresses, the expecting mother is going to reach a point where she might stop working and stop driving. This is where you are going to have to pick up the slack. You will be the one driving her to her appointments, running errands, and going anywhere else that you need to go. Whether it is late-night runs to the supermarket for food or trips to the pharmacy to pick up medication, you can expect to be doing it all. This is the point where it will usually become more tiring for you. Again, if you are prepared for all of this, there is no reason for you to become stressed out at the thought of it.

When the birth plan is being created, you should have a say in this, too. While the expecting mother is going to have her own preferences, she will likely be asking you what you think about her choices. Be honest with her, and offer any helpful advice that you feel will make the labor and delivery easier. If a home birth or water birth is scheduled, do your best to make sure that everything is going to be in place when the time comes. Being a great father begins with being a great planner; think

133

about every detail.

How to Help

Do not tell her what to do. No matter what you are communicating about, an expecting mother does not particularly need to be told what to do regarding her own body and how she is feeling. While you might have great ideas, you can bring these up to her, but don't be offended if she decides that something else is going to be better for her. Remember, you can't feel exactly what she is feeling. Being there for support and to bounce ideas off of is extremely helpful, but being bossy or controlling is not. You need to let her take the lead when it comes to her pregnancy.

Be there to listen to her. There will be times when she simply wants to vent or complain about her symptoms. Let her do this. While there might be nothing she can do but wait them out, at least she can have you there as a support system who will always lend a listening ear. She might ask you for advice if she is unsure of things and this will bring you even closer together as a couple. Each decision that the two of you make together is going to impact your baby. While you might not know exactly what you are doing if it is your first time, let those instincts kick in.

Take her shopping for baby items. Once the first trimester is over and people have been told that you are expecting a little bundle of joy, a lot of the fun can begin. Most couples create a baby registry at a store of their choosing. Aside from these items that will be given as gifts, there are still plenty of things that the parents will have to purchase as they prepare for the arrival of their child. Going shopping for these things really solidifies the idea that your baby is going to be there soon. Do things for the baby's nursery, as well. Being able to decorate and design the nursery together is a great bonding experience.

Identifying Feelings

As a soon-to-be-father, you are going to have so many emotions running through your mind and heart. While the mother usually gets to express herself more frequently, know that all of your emotions are also valid. You might be worried about how you are going to care for the baby because you are unfamiliar with what to do, but you also might be incredibly excited to mold a young mind with your own morals, values, and traditions. No matter what the case is, express yourself! The expecting mother will appreciate that she isn't alone with any of her feelings. Fathers can often take a back seat to the point where it might seem like they don't have any strong emotions, but that isn't always true.

You are about to take on several new responsibilities, all in a short matter of time. Just as the mother might have some things to change about her lifestyle when she finds out she is pregnant, so will the father. For example, if you enjoy going out on the weekends with your friends, you might need to spend more time at home as the expecting mother experiences more intense symptoms. While you cannot tell what it is like to physically feel these things, you can definitely support her as she goes through them. If any feelings come up that are overwhelming (either positive or negative), talk to her about them. She will appreciate your openness. You don't need to pretend that you know exactly what is going to happen because let's face it, you both probably don't. Pregnancy is a learning experience that you will work through together.

Sex during Pregnancy

The only reason to avoid sex during pregnancy is if either of you is not in the mood to have it. There is nothing that you will do to hurt the baby while you are having sex; that is just a myth. Feel free to be intimate with one another, and know that your baby is still going to be growing and developing just fine. If you do want to take some extra precautions, know that your partner's breasts are likely going to be more tender than usual. Any grabbing or squeezing might feel more intense than usual, so keep that in mind. Of course, if she expresses that there is any pain, you should stop immediately. Otherwise, feel free to have as much sex as you both want to, intercourse included.

A lot of couples find that the pregnancy hormones actually do a lot for the woman's arousal. She might feel extra willing and able to have sex in the beginning. As her belly begins to grow, you might have to find some new positions that allow you both to be comfortable because anything that involves her bending forward or being on her stomach for too long will understandably be uncomfortable. Much like the sleeping position, if she can lie down on her left side while you position yourself behind her, much like spooning, this tends to be a very comfortable and pleasurable position for couples who are expecting.

Consider that she might be more emotional than usual. Do your best to incorporate a lot of foreplay before you begin having sex. If you are too rough, this can be off-putting to a woman who is currently producing high amounts of hormones that make her feel more tender and loving than usual. Allow her to be the center of attention, and ask her what feels good. Communication does not have to be a mood-killer; it will actually help you become better lovers.

Overcoming Intimacy Issues

Even though she is in the mood, you might have trouble getting into the mood yourself. This is okay, and this is normal. Pregnancy changes a lot. It forces you to think a lot more responsibly and practically than you would have before. There is also the issue of you feeling that you are going to hurt the expecting mother if you advance in any type of intimate way. Rest assured that she will be able to tell you if something hurts or if it is uncomfortable. A lot of pregnant women regularly have and enjoy sex throughout their pregnancy with no problems, physically or emotionally.

Understandably, there might still be a few things that you are worried that you will have to work through. Talk to her about your feelings, just as mentioned earlier. Working together, you can overcome any worries that you might have in order to get back to the core of your intimacy. Starting with simple touching and massage, these acts of intimacy can go a long way and allow you to start having sex again. She is going to appreciate all of the little things you do for her, even if they are not sexual. Opening doors for her and cooking her meals are little and intimate ways to show her that you care.

A Dad's Role during Delivery

Early Labor

As the woman enters early labor, your main job is to be her distraction. She is going to be feeling contractions, and these are uncomfortable. Do your best to take her mind off of them, but do not make her feel ignored. If she needs to complain, be her ear to listen. Read to her, talk about some of your favorite things, bring up funny memories, and do anything you can to get her mind focused on something else. If she stays too focused on the pain, her active labor is going to feel even worse. Try to get her up and moving. Walking around can alleviate a lot more pain than simply staying still. Walk her up and down the hallways if she feels like she can.

Active Labor

As you know from any classes you have taken or any research you have done, active labor means more active contractions. They are going to become stronger and closer together, and at this point, you will likely need to provide your hand for her to squeeze. Rub her back and reassure her that she is doing a great job. If you notice that she is starting to panic, try your best to get her back to a calm state of mind. Just as you learned in class, you are going to be her support system during this time. Try to work on breathing techniques that you have learned. Know that she is naturally going to be agitated and moody during this point. Allow her to have this moment because you don't know what she's feeling. She might be snappy, but know that she is definitely appreciating the little things you are doing for her.

Delivery

The moment has come - the baby is on its way! This part happens very quickly sometimes, and it can be hard to absorb everything that is going on. The most important thing that you can do here is to remain calm. If you are calm, then she is going to know that things are okay. The instant you lose your cool, she is going to feel panicked. If she is delivering vaginally, you can hold her hand and motivate her as she pushes. Encourage her to keep going and that it is almost over. In a C-section, she isn't going to be able to feel and see as much, so you can be her eyes. If she wants to know what is going on, you can describe it to her.

A Dad's Role after Delivery

There are normally two impulses that you will feel after your baby is born - you will want to cry and you will want to take photos. Both are completely valid reactions, as a miracle has just occurred. Be mindful that the mother has gone through so much to get to this point, and while she is definitely going to appreciate having pictures of the moment, she might not want a camera in her face for too long. Take a few shots, and then put the camera down so you can meet your baby together. If your baby is considered at-risk, then the baby will likely be taken to the nursery shortly after delivery so the mother can rest and the baby can be monitored. You can alternate between visiting with your child and keeping the mother company. If the baby is not at risk, the mother will be handed her child directly after giving birth.

In between all of this, you can make phone calls to inform your loved ones that the baby has finally arrived. It is going to be a surreal and joyous moment that you will never forget. When you go back to visit your partner, let her know how well the baby is doing, and also be sure to mention how amazing she was at delivering your little bundle of joy. She might still be in shock from the entire process, but keeping her calm and reassured is what will bring her back down to a calm state of being.

Some mothers who have to deviate from their birth plan might feel a little upset at this point, and if this has happened in your case, remind her that it was what needed to be done to have a healthy baby. If you tell her how great the baby is doing and that all of the right decisions were made, she will eventually get over not having the exact birth plan of her choosing. It can naturally be a very overwhelming time, and at the moment, it might feel like the doctors were making all of the decisions. Reassure her that you were there every step of the way and that you agreed with all of the decisions that were made. It will help her to know that you were looking out for her body and for your baby. From this moment on, the mother should feel your love. Make it a point that you are going to love her in every single moment, from childbirth to simply being together at home. Loving her always is how you are going to keep your own personal bond as strong as new parents.

Chapter 11: Postpartum

The intense part is over - you have a baby now! All of the anticipation and hours of labor have likely all melted away the instant you set your eyes on your newborn baby. This is when all of the real fun begins. You are now responsible for raising a child, and you are going to continue to learn even more about being a parent. While you are doing all of this, you are also going to be simultaneously recovering both physically and emotionally. This chapter is going to breakdown everything you need to know about your postpartum stage and what is to be expected.

The First Week

What You Are Feeling

After you have your baby, you are going to be feeling a whirlwind of emotions. Surprisingly, not all of these emotions are going to be cheerful and happy. Remember, you have just gone through nearly a year of carrying a developing baby, only to end up delivering it and then eventually caring for it. This is a lot of pressure that is put on you as a mother, and while you have a partner who is willing to support you, there are some things that your partner did not have the chance to experience along with you. These are some of the feelings that most mothers do not realize can occur after giving birth:

1. Sadness: Yes, it is normal to feel sad after you give birth. There are a few reasons why this might happen. Postpartum depression is a very real condition that a lot of mothers experience. Even when you are overjoyed that you have a brand new baby, the depression can still set in. Talk to your doctor if you believe you are experiencing this depression. Some sadness can be because you are no longer pregnant, and you have become so used to being pregnant. Even though you have your baby in your arms now, not having your baby in your belly shows just how fast their childhood can go.

2. Fear: Getting home from the hospital and being alone as a family, your first instinct might be to freak out. You've never done this before; it is natural to be scared. The thing about parenting is that you are going to learn as you go. Just because you might not have it all figured out right now does not mean that you can't learn. Sure, you might make mistakes, but every single parent does.

3. Anxiety: When you bring your baby home, it might feel impossible for you to relax. You are constantly going to be checking on your little one to see if they need anything. Don't let yourself get too jittery. Remember, you are in recovery at this point. You can only do so much, plus, you have a partner who is willing to help you. Let him help!

What You Are Wondering

You are likely trying to decipher what your baby is thinking and feeling. All your baby can do right now is cry, become fussy, and sleep, so you might be left wondering how in the world you are supposed to know what to do next. Your motherly instinct is going to kick in. A newborn baby normally only needs a few things: feeding, sleep, a clean diaper, and rocking/cuddling. If one of these doesn't seem to soothe your baby, try another. This process is definitely going to involve a lot of trial and error, whether other parents ever admit it or not.

Your first week home is your chance to form a routine. Newborn babies usually eat around every 2-3 hours, so you can time any diaper changes based on this feeding schedule. Your baby is likely going to sleep a lot, and you might be very tempted to wake them up so you can play. Avoid doing so because their body is still adjusting to being outside of the womb. Things feel different for them too, so they need to do their own form of regulation. You are going to be up and down throughout the night, but that is to be expected.

Some babies are great sleepers; others can't stay asleep for more than an hour at a time. You will find out how well your baby sleeps right away. There isn't too much you can do for your baby if they are simply fussy. This will get better as the baby grows older, but for now, you just need to keep checking on them and ensuring that everything is as comfortable as possible where the baby is sleeping. Try putting your baby down to sleep after they are fed and burped. When they are full, they are more likely to feel comfortable enough to stay asleep for a longer period of time.

The Beginning of Breastfeeding

The first few days after your baby is born, your body will generally produce enough milk for you on its own. It is milk that is rich in nutrients that your baby needs. It is normal for your breasts to feel firmer within the first 3-4 days after producing this milk. Even if your body takes a little bit longer to produce the milk, this is perfectly normal because every woman is different. If you are able, begin breastfeeding a few hours after your baby is born. When you are still in the hospital, the nurses will be there to assist you with getting your baby to latch properly.

If you intend on breastfeeding exclusively, then it is wise to avoid giving your baby a bottle or pacifier because this can cause confusion when it comes to latching. Being able to latch onto your breast is going to be a different feeling than latching onto an artificial nipple or pacifier. To get your baby to begin feeding, simply hold them in your arms and place their mouth near your breast. They will normally have the natural instinct to latch on and begin eating.

Once you get home from the hospital, you will have to keep an eye on the signs of hunger. These include when your baby moves their head from side to side when their mouth opens, if their mouth starts to pucker, or if they begin to nuzzle against your chest. The more you breastfeed, the more familiar you will become with these signs. If your baby is acting particularly fussy, you can try getting them to latch on because it could also mean that they are hungry or need the comfort of being latched to the mother. You might need to guide your nipple into your baby's mouth by supporting your breast with one hand and positioning your baby with the other. If your baby begins to suck without getting much milk, this is an indication that they are not properly latched on. Try again, and remember, this part is going to take practice from both of you.

Expert Sleep Strategies for Newborns

1. Be Aware of Light: If you are putting your baby down for a nap during the day, you will want the room to be dim but not fully dark. Any bright lighting is simply going to tell your baby that it is "go" time, and they will be more likely to want to stay awake.

2. Put Your Baby Down When They Are Drowsy: If you wait until your baby is fully asleep, setting them down in the crib might create the exact opposite effect than what you are trying to accomplish. This sudden change can wake your baby. Try to place your baby down when

they are drowsy and just about to fall asleep. Timing is everything for this strategy.

3. Give Them Time to Self-Soothe: If your baby is asleep in the crib, they are going to naturally stir and make noise from time to time. Before running into the nursery, allow your baby time to get comfortable again because a lot of the time, a baby is able to self-soothe and go back to sleep.

4. Avoid Eye Contact: It sounds funny, but if you are trying to put your baby to sleep, avoid making direct eye contact. This can be engaging in a newborn, and it might cause them to want to stay awake longer. Whether you are rocking your baby in your arms or in a rocker, try to keep your gaze neutral and not directly on the baby.

5. Feed Your Baby Late at Night: While this will sometimes happen inevitably, it is a good idea to semi-wake your baby between 10 PM and 12 AM for a feeding. This will allow them to stay full and comfortable while also promoting longer stretches of sleep so you and your partner also get the chance to rest through the night.

6. Be Relaxed on Diaper Changing Schedules: It might be tempting to change your baby each time they wake up, but sometimes, waking up does not mean that your baby is ready to stay awake. It is important to learn

your baby's wet diaper schedule in order to see if they are getting enough food. Definitely monitor this for the purpose of the baby's health, but if you do pick them up to change them every time, this could actually be disrupting their developing sleep schedule. Using moderation is the key here. Make sure that you put on a heavy-duty diaper before your baby is going to sleep for a longer period of time.

The First Six Weeks

What You Are Feeling

At this point, you might be experiencing what is known as perineum soreness. This can happen because a lot of women tear in this area if they give birth vaginally. Your perineum is the skin between your vagina and anus. Even if you did not tear, you likely still experienced pressure there during the delivery, so you might feel some pain. Afterbirth pains are also fairly common during this time. These will feel like standard belly cramps, and they happen because the uterus is shrinking back down to its original size. If you had a C-section, it is common for your incision to feel a bit sore, as well.

To ease any of the postpartum pain mentioned above, you can perform Kegel exercises to strengthen your pelvic floor muscles. You can also place an ice pack on your perineum to directly ease some of the pain. Sitting in a warm, shallow bath is also great to ease any type of vaginal or abdominal discomfort. You can add sea salt to cleanse yourself and your bathwater. If the pain does not subside on its own, you can ask your doctor for more options or medications to assist you.

Vaginal discharge is normal during this time. Even after your baby is born, your uterus is still trying to get rid of certain tissue and blood inside of your body. The discharge will look like period blood, and it might even include some blood clots. Over time, your flow will get lighter. You can wear period pads until this subsides. It can last for a few weeks or even a month after you give birth.

What You Are Wondering

If you begin sweating a lot more after giving birth, this is normal. It tends to happen especially at night, and it is caused by all of the hormones that your body has created during the pregnancy. You might also be wondering why you are still so tired after you have given birth. Even though you are not physically carrying your baby inside of you anymore, you are caring for your baby at every hour, day and night. Do your best to sleep when your baby sleeps so you can preserve as much of your energy as possible. Don't be afraid to ask for help! Let your partner soothe the baby, and let any loved ones come over and help if they offer. Their help will allow you the time to rest.

Another burning question is when you are going to lose your

baby weight. Immediately after giving birth, you should lose around 10lbs. In the next few weeks, you will also naturally begin to lose weight. To get your body toned and back to its original state before you became pregnant, staying active and eating healthy are the best ways to do this. There is no secret to dropping the pounds overnight, and you do not have to immediately get back into the gym and workout for hours a day. Simply get up and moving. Taking walks and doing low-impact exercises like yoga and Pilates can help you. Also, keep in mind that what you eat still matters because you are breastfeeding. Even if you are not in a rush to lose any weight at all, your baby is still receiving nutrients from the foods that you eat.

Physical and Emotional Changes

Your body is going to look different after you give birth; every woman experiences this. You might have stretch marks that you didn't have prior to your pregnancy. The skin around your belly might be loose. Remember that you just gave birth to a healthy baby that you spent 9 months growing inside of you. This is a lot for your body to handle, so yes, things are going to look different. This doesn't mean that they will look different forever, though. Try not to be so hard on yourself or compare your body to any other postpartum body that you've seen. Your metabolism is unique, so it is going to take some time for you to get back to your original appearance. If you can help it, try to overlook these changes and remind yourself that you have a beautiful baby now.

Emotionally, you can be going through a lot at this point. There will be times of pure exhaustion because of all the broken sleep you are getting. There will also be times of elation and joy as you watch your baby grow and learn. It can be overwhelming with just how many feelings you can go through in a day. There is also the possibility that you can develop postpartum depression, as mentioned earlier in the guide. If you ever feel that you cannot handle your emotions, or if you believe that something does not feel right, consult your doctor.

Getting Back Into Shape

As mentioned, when you feel ready to get back into your pre-pregnancy body, go for it! There is no rush to get there by a certain deadline, though. Do what feels right to you. Low-impact exercises that focus on building up core strength are the best for getting your belly flat. When you were pregnant, there were certain muscles that you had to avoid putting a strain on for the safety of the baby. Now that you have this freedom again, work your way into exercising slowly. If you overdo it in the beginning because you are eager to get back into shape, you could end up hurting yourself and setting yourself back for even more weeks.

Create a realistic workout routine for yourself that includes exercises that are appropriate for how your body currently feels and for the free time that you have. Make an arrangement with your partner for 30 minutes to an hour where he will commit to taking care of the baby so you can get this done. As long as you are willing to stick to a routine, you will be able to get back into shape fairly easily. All it takes is the commitment to taking care of yourself.

Reasons to Do This Again Someday

After all that you have been through, you might feel that you don't want to have any more kids. This is valid, and a lot of women make this decision because of what they had to go through during pregnancy and delivery. On the other hand, even despite all of the pain and hard work, many women feel that pregnancy is worth it every single time. If you want to put your body through it again, have as many children as you and your partner desire!

If you want your baby to have siblings, this can also be a reason to consider having more kids in the future. Having 2 young babies at once can be difficult, but if you wait a few years, you might feel keener on having another child in order for your firstborn to have a little brother or sister. No matter what you decide to do, know that there is no pressure to ever have another child again. The decision is a personal one, and it is solely up to you and your partner.

Conclusion

Having a baby is something that you will never forget. There is no other experience like it, and this is why so many people consider childbirth to be such a miraculous process. After growing your baby inside of you for so long, the bond that you have as soon as that child is born already exists and is as strong as can be. Raising a child is hard work, and after going through an entire pregnancy and delivery, you will likely have a newfound appreciation for all of the mothers that you have ever known.

As you go through each trimester of your pregnancy, the main thing you need to realize is that you are not going to be alone. With the support of your partner and the wisdom of your team of doctors and nurses, all of your questions and concerns are going to be handled. Each thing that changes in your body will be felt and explained if you feel that you need an explanation. When you begin to experience your first round of pregnancy symptoms, know that there is always something that you can do to alleviate them. Having pregnancy symptoms is a sign that your baby is developing as it should. While it can be rough on you, know that these symptoms are happening for a reason.

Not every pregnancy is going to look exactly alike. You might start showing right away or you might barely even show at all. Don't compare yourself to anyone else because this is your baby and your body. Know that you always have choices, from what happens during your birth plan to what you'd like your doctor to test your baby for while it is still in the womb. Ultimately, you become a mother as soon as you get the confirmation from your doctor that you are pregnant. That motherly instinct kicks in a lot faster than you think.

As promised, this book was made for the purpose of providing you with reassurance. You are a strong and capable woman, and your body knows exactly what to do in order to develop and deliver a healthy baby. With the tips on how to ease your sickness and ailments, you will be able to get through each trimester like a champ. By understanding how to work with your partner and communicate during each step, you will both feel included in the process of pregnancy and the delivery alike. When you know what to expect at each doctor's appointment and in the delivery room, you will be able to enter each situation with the confidence that you need in order to get through it. The sooner that you are able to endure all that comes with your pregnancy, the sooner you get to meet your wonderful new addition to the family.

The moment that you discover you are pregnant, this book is made to guide you through every step of the way so that you do not feel scared. Instead of wondering about the worst things that can happen to your body or the baby, you should be looking forward to the positive things instead. This guide should inform and educate you on topics that you are going to encounter as you experience your pregnancy journey. You will understand why it is a journey as you realize things about yourself and your body that you likely didn't even know was possible before. A woman's body is incredibly resilient and tough; most people do not give it enough credit. When you can recognize that in yourself, it is something to feel proud of.

No matter what decisions you make during your pregnancy, know that you are doing what is best for you. Without the influence of anyone else, you should have an idea of what you want for your baby, your body, and your family. This is what being a mother is all about. By learning how to accept these ideas that you come up with and have the confidence in yourself to make them happen, you are already being the best mother you can be. Never forget that childbirth is not something that simply happens on its own. A successful birth story is a combination of a healthy baby and a mother's strong will to do her very best.

Part 2: You and Your Baby Can Sleep Through The Night

A Step by Step Manual for Exhausted Parents on How to Train Your Baby to Sleep Every Single Night in 7 days!

Introduction

You knew that bringing home your bundle of joy meant you wouldn't sleep well for a period of time, yet this time frame seems to never end. You are stressed. Your anxiety is worse than before. You are struggling to make your baby fall asleep and this is causing you more problems than you ever imagined. Your patience is thin, you can't make rational decisions, your work performance is low, and you are not getting along with a few of your family members. No matter what you have tried, you cannot get your baby to fall asleep. Nothing is working and you don't know what to do.

Fortunately, you have already taken the first step to help your baby fall asleep successfully every night, just by choosing this book. Here, we will discuss two of the best methods to help your baby fall asleep so you can get a good night's sleep too. Furthermore, you will learn the 10 habits that you need to avoid to ensure your baby sleeps promptly.

I am Harley Carr, and I am the mother of three children. Raising three kids is such a challenging role. I've been through a lot of difficulties during their first year of life, especially concerning their sleeping patterns and feeding schedules. I have been changing diapers for the last eight years! This is my life and I was able to manage them (of course with the help of my partner). I was lucky enough to survive those sleepless nights.

However, I also know that not everyone has a partner to help them. There are many great single parents out there who are in the same boat. This book will help you too. I remember many times where my best friend, a single parent, called me in the middle of the night ready to pull her hair out. She burst into tears so many times, as she wished so much that she didn't have to do it all alone. After taking on the 10 habits, which we are about to discuss, she successfully got her child to sleep every night.

To the mother who has twins or multiples, this book will not leave you out either. Your struggles are similar to the rest of us, yet special as you hold more than one baby. This gives extra challenges, ones that another friend of mine has discussed with me. They struggled with breastfeeding to the point that they felt they needed to give up. Because she and her partner worked different shifts, they each had to juggle two babies at the same time and it became nearly impossible, especially when they lacked patience due to sleep deprivation. She did continue to breastfeed, citing a twin pillow giving her the best support when breastfeeding.

This book is for the person or step-parent who doesn't have a child of their own but cares for another person's baby. Whether you are in a relationship with the baby's parent or you are a caregiver, you will learn ways to help the baby and everyone else in the situation receive a good night's sleep. Taking care of a child as a caregiver brings extra challenges as the baby is aware that their parents are not around. This can add stress to the baby, which makes it more difficult for them to sleep. As long as everyone who will have the baby day and night is on the same page with sleep training, everyone can make this mission successful.

Here is an example of an alternative care situation in which both parties will need to be in sync with the sleep training procedure: Lisa is a newly single mom who recently left her husband after dealing with domestic abuse. Afraid that the baby's father will harm her son, she does what she can to ensure that she has their baby at all times. Her friend, Jasmine, decided to move out of the college dorms and into Lisa's new apartment to help her with the baby. Lisa, who is struggling with postpartum depression, is now facing a divorce and a loss of income. Falling into a deep depression, she is unable to sleep most nights because her baby doesn't sleep well. Jasmine does everything she can to care for the baby during the night as well, but this is causing Jasmine to fall behind on schoolwork. Soon, she starts failing her exams and doesn't get her assignments completed. Jasmine is afraid she will flunk out of school. She knows the baby isn't her responsibility, but she feels the need to help her best friend.

I am also writing to the parent who feels like they do it all, even when they have a partner. Your significant other might be out of town working, busy with long days at the office, or simply doesn't help out as much as you need them to. You might work at home and take care of your children. You do most (perhaps all) of the housework and are overstressed due to a lack of sleep.

Each one of us has a different story. But, no matter what your story is, I am talking to *you*. Together, we can help you overcome the struggle to get enough sleep. It doesn't matter who you are, what you believe, or how many people are in your family. Your family can consist of you and your baby, friends, other family members, a boyfriend, girlfriend, or fiance, *whatever*. You will receive the sleep training help needed to continue to grow your healthy family and environment.

In this book, I will share my insights and tips about how to cope and manage challenges and difficulties during your baby's first year and most importantly how to help them sleep soundly and consistently without compromising their health or physical and emotional development.

Once you've read this book, you will know what sleep training is and understand the steps you need to take so your baby sleeps through the night. You will learn when the time is right to start sleep training, what you need to expect, and how you should handle these expectations. We will discuss which sleep training method is the best for you, your baby, and your family. You will learn the secret sauce to sleep training and receive step-by-step guidelines to ensure your baby sleeps soundly every night. Furthermore, you will learn the 10 habits you need to avoid to make sleep training successful. You will not only get your baby to sleep well each night, but everyone else in the household will get quality shut-eye as well. Thus, you will think straight, your anxieties will dissipate, and you will make better decisions. Hold on, I haven't even mentioned the greatest part of this process yet—you will begin to really enjoy your role as a parent while maintaining great relationships with your partner, family, and friends.

My promise to you is that this book will fully equip you with the knowledge and skills you need to successfully sleep train your baby. You will set up the perfect feeding schedule to help your baby maintain a 24-hour routine. When your little one adapts to their new routine, they will sleep soundly throughout the night. This will have obvious positive effects for your baby, but also for you, and everyone else in the household.

At the moment, you feel like you are starting to lose your mind. You feel like your marbles have spilled and are rolling everywhere. You try to catch them, but all you do is kick them into more chaos as you chase them, just as you and your baby continue to struggle with the lack of sleep more and more despite your efforts. On top of this, you surely have other stressors in your life. You have no idea what to do and you feel like you have already done everything humanly possible. While some steps worked in the short-term, nothing is working long-term.

You might even be so desperate as to be looking at hiring a sleep consultant for 72-hours of in-house training. The biggest problem with this is that it is a stranger and they cost close to $7,500. You have a baby and other responsibilities and cannot afford to spend this type of money to help your baby sleep.

Good news—you don't need to look at a sleep consultant because *you* can take care of sleep training using the system in the contents of this book. Not only will this allow you to save money, but you will find the best solution for you personally in the following chapters. It will answer all of your questions and will give you the complete steps on how to train your baby to sleep every single night. Put simply: It will help you survive. You can escape those sleepless nights and avoid the harmful effects that sleep deprivation causes to babies and parents. These dangerous effects can:

- lead to obesity

- have a negative effect on the immune system

- disturb memory

- lower cognitive scores

- cause moodiness

- overstimulate your baby

- lead to inattention and hyperactivity

- increase separation anxiety

- delay the baby's growth

- make vaccinations less effective

- lead to long-term social and emotional problems

- possibly be linked to autism

- reduce parents' patience

- reduce parental focus

- lead to fatal consequences when a parent is too sleep-deprived

Don't wait for another night. Read on for the absolute best sleep training advice, so everyone in your household can finally get a much-deserved good night's sleep!

Chapter 1: What Is Sleep Training and What Are the Harmful Effects of Sleep Deprivation?

Sleep Training

Sleep training is a process that has become more common over the last several years. It is when you help your baby learn how to soothe themselves to sleep and stay asleep for the rest of the night.

It is important to note that babies will learn sleep training at different intervals. Some babies will fall asleep easily while other babies will struggle to soothe themselves into a deep sleep. There is also the possibility of your baby falling asleep quickly but still waking up in the middle of the night and having a hard time getting themselves back to sleep. No matter how your child reacts to sleep training, they will all need help to learn the process.

When can I start sleep training?

There is a lot of debate on what is the best age to start sleep training your baby. Some people say that you should begin as soon as they come home from the hospital. However, most experts will tell you to wait until your baby is four months old. You want your little one to develop regular nightly feedings and a sleep-wake schedule, or at least as much as possible before you begin training. Once you start noticing that your baby is on a bit of a cycle, you can start sleep training. Remember, each baby is an individual and this means they will all vary in sleep characteristics too. For instance, you and your friend start sleep training at the same time. You notice your friend's baby is quickly learning to soothe themselves to sleep, but your baby is still struggling. In this case, your baby might not be ready for sleep training. They might also need less sleep and are not as tired when you start to get them ready for bed.

You should always communicate with your baby's doctor when you are thinking about starting sleep training. Let the doctor know your plan as this is something you can update them with throughout the process. This is helpful for all parents, but especially single parents as it gives you another person to support you during this time. Emotional and psychological support can help ease any problems that arise and make you more confident in the sleep training process.

How to prepare for sleep training

To help you prepare for sleep training, you should follow these tips:

- **Choose a consistent bedtime.** One of the first steps in getting your baby ready for sleep training is to set a bedtime. Experts state that the best time for your baby is between 7:00 and 8:00. You might already have a time that you follow, but not as closely as you should. If you decide to lay your baby down for bed at 7:30 p.m. you need to stick to this time as much as possible. Keep in mind, life is unpredictable, and you will most likely have days that you can't lay your baby down directly at this time. For example, you are driving home from a family member's house after an emergency situation. In this case, your baby might fall asleep on their own as you drive, which can cause problems as you wake them up to bring them inside for bed. The key to a slight change in their routine is to remain calm and realize it happens. As long as you are consistent with their bedtime in the following nights, your baby will not be affected by one late bedtime.

- **Establish a bedtime routine.** You should start a bedtime routine before you begin sleep training. Most experts say you can start a routine at four weeks old, but don't worry if you haven't started a routine and your child is older—simply create the routine and begin. It is never too late! Your routine can be anything from giving your little one a nice warm bath to reading a short book. You might sing a song or speak to them

171

about your day in a soothing voice. No matter what you decide, you want to make sure it is calming and relaxes your baby.

- **Ensure your baby does not have a medical condition that may affect their sleep.** This is one reason it is important to talk to your baby's doctor before you start sleep training. The pediatrician can perform an exam to make sure your baby doesn't suffer from any type of medical condition that can keep them from getting a good night's sleep. If you find out that they do, follow the doctor's orders to give your baby the best success rate for sleep training.

- **Establish a daytime schedule that you can follow.** A daytime routine is just as important as a bedtime routine. Ensure that you lay your baby down for a nap at the set times, follow a feeding schedule, and keep them busy throughout the day so they are more tired when it is time for bed. The more secure your baby feels the more success you and your baby will have with sleep training.

What are my sleep training options?

There are many sleep training options, but we will focus on two of the main methods:

1. **Cry it out method.** The cry it out method is one of the most debatable approaches because some people don't understand this method. Many people feel it leaves your baby to cry in their crib until they fall asleep. This is not true. While your baby will most likely start crying when you start sleep training, you want to have a set time for the cry it out method. For instance, you might allow your baby to cry for a couple of minutes before you go back in there and comfort them, without picking them up. Once they calm down, you will leave the room again and wait to see if they fall asleep. If they are still crying after a couple of minutes, you go back into the room to comfort them as they continue to lay in their crib. For example, you might rub their back and hum softly.

2. **No tears method.** In this method, you will comfort your child immediately when they start crying. This is a gradual approach that will give you the same results as the cry it out method.

Harmful Effects of Sleep Deprivation

You know how sleep deprivation can affect you. Take a minute to think about how it can affect your baby. You might think that your little one is getting enough sleep. After all, they seem to sleep all the time, especially when they are only a few months old. However, about 30% to 40% of children are not getting the sleep they need (15 Ways Lack of Sleep Is Harmful To The Baby, 2016).

There are many reasons for sleep deprivation in babies and it can be hard to know if they are overtired because they can't directly tell you. But don't worry, they will let you know in other ways. Here are some symptoms of sleep deprivation your baby might exhibit:

- You have trouble feeling your baby.

- They rub their eyes often.

- Their eyelids flutter a lot.

- They yawn often.

- They seem easily irritable.

- They are not interested in their surroundings or other people.

- You notice your baby is scared of bedtime. This is a symptom most commonly seen in older babies.

- They don't sleep often during the day or you notice a decrease in the amount of time they sleep that does not correspond to their age.

- You notice your baby pauses breathing while they are sleeping.

You need to be aware that you will see one of two of these signs now and then. For example, if your baby had a difficult night falling asleep or didn't sleep well this causes them to yawn, rub their eyes, and they won't want to eat like they normally do. Because these symptoms are not every day, there is no need to worry. Your child will get a better night's sleep the next night. If you start to notice these symptoms every day for a couple of weeks, then you will want to visit your baby's pediatrician.

Now that you understand the symptoms of sleep deprivation in babies, now we'll explore how else it can affect your baby.

Can cause obesity

Babies who don't get the necessary sleep are more likely to become overweight by three years old. Sleeping affects many parts of the body and mind, including your baby's metabolism. It becomes slower with a lack of sleep, which makes your baby gradually increase weight. The extra weight gain happens because of an imbalance of energy which affects several hormones, such as leptin, insulin, growth, and ghrelin.

Johns Hopkins University completed a study that showed that an extra hour of sleep a baby receives during night decreases their chance of obesity by 9%, whereas a baby who sleeps less than their needed time increase their chances of obesity by 92% (15 Ways Lack of Sleep Is Harmful To The Baby, 2016).

Negatively affects their immune system

Children who do not receive the sleep they need are more likely to become ill because their immune system suffers. It is easier for a baby to catch the flu or cold when they do not get the sleep they need. The UCLA Cousins Center conducted a study that showed even a small amount of sleep loss can negatively affect the immune system. It causes tissue damage and triggers inflammation (Elsevier, 2008).

One of the best ways to fight off bacteria growing in a baby's body happens while your baby is sleeping. Disease fighting proteins are released from the immune system, but they can only be released when sleeping. Therefore, the longer your baby is awake, the fewer proteins their immune system will produce. With a lack of proteins, it is also harder for your baby to fight off any illness that enters their system, which means they are sick for a longer duration.

This can happen whether your baby loses an hour of sleep a week or an hour every night. But, the longer your baby goes without the necessary amount of sleep, the more serious this effect becomes. Therefore, if your baby is showing signs of sleepiness, especially on a regular basis, you need to take the time to increase their amount of sleep every night.

Disturbs memory

You know how much you struggle mentally when you don't get a good night's sleep. Your baby will also struggle in this way when they don't get the sleep they need. A lack of sleep impairs functioning within the brain, causing difficulty in learning and impairs memory. Your baby is learning every day. They might not remember what they see as a baby when they grow older, but they are still learning and taking in their scenery, nonetheless. They are learning who to trust and about their surroundings.

When your baby suffers from a lack of sleep, they cannot comprehend their environment strongly. They will struggle to store memories as they do not get enough Random Eye Movement (REM) sleep, which consists of 50 to 80% of their sleep (15 Ways Lack of Sleep Is Harmful To The Baby, 2016). Professors at the University of Arizona conducted a study that focused on memory and sleep of babies at 15 months old. For 15 minutes, the babies listened to a fake language recording. Four hours later, the professors tested all babies and found that the ones who napped prior to testing remembered the recording better. Furthermore, they became more flexible in learning. The babies who did not nap before testing did not remember the recording at all.

Lowers cognitive scores

With the disturbance of memory, it is not surprising that a lack of sleep also lowers your cognitive scores. A child's brain is constantly developing, and this means less sleep can permanently affect your baby's mind. Researchers at the University of Colorado concluded through a study that the brain forms new cell connections when a child is sleeping. In fact, the left and right brain forms close to 20% of its connections during sleep (15 Ways Lack of Sleep Is Harmful To The Baby, 2016).

One of the best ways to ensure that your baby will get enough sleep is to give them an early bedtime. Think of the amount of time it takes your child to fall asleep and when they should fall asleep to make certain they get the amount of time they need. For example, a five-month-old baby should sleep 12 to 15 hours in a 24-hour period. If your baby naps two hours a day, this means they need at least 10 hours of sleep at night. You put your baby to bed at 7:30 p.m., but they never fall asleep until about 8:30 p.m. You need to get your baby up at 5:30 a.m. to get them ready for daycare so you can go to work. This means, at most, your baby gets eight or nine hours of sleep, falling below the recommended 10. Because your baby takes about an hour to fall asleep, you want to put them to bed at 6:30 p.m. They will fall asleep by 7:30 p.m. and get at least 12 hours of sleep every day.

Makes your baby moody

There is something that you can never truly control with your baby—their moodiness. It is something that everyone struggles with, but most adults can control their moods. This is something that your baby cannot control because they simply do not have the ability yet. Therefore, you need to do everything you can to help your baby's moodiness and, thankfully, one of the biggest steps you can take is sleep training.

When your baby does not get the sleep they need, they get fussy and frustrated quickly. While most babies will cry easily, they tend to bounce back quickly. If you notice your baby cries for several minutes or you struggle to get them to calm down, your baby might be sleep-deprived.

Overstimulation

Like you, when your baby does not get enough sleep, they become overtired. When this happens, they become overstimulated and this makes it harder for them to fall asleep. Overstimulation causes more stress on your baby, which causes them to become moody and more prone to fits. Your baby can't bring themselves out of this situation, they need help and the best way to do this is by making sure they get the sleep they need for their age.

Hyperactivity and inattention

You know you lack focus when you do not get enough sleep and your baby is the same way. However, the difference between you and your baby is you lack energy and they gain energy. Sleep-deprived babies tend to become hyperactive. It is important to be cautious of your baby's sleep schedule before you or a doctor starts to wonder if your hyperactive baby is developing ADHD or ADD. Hyperactivity because a baby is overtired and symptoms of ADHD are often confused. The best factor to look at when you are trying to distinguish between the two is that children are usually older when doctors diagnose them with ADHD. You should also keep an eye out for other symptoms of tiredness such as rubbing their eyes and moodiness.

Increases separation anxiety

Once your baby understands object permanence, they will develop separation anxiety. Separation anxiety is when they throw a fit, cry, or struggle when they realize you are no longer in their sight. Separation anxiety usually starts around nine to 10 months of age but can develop as early as six months old. Your baby can develop separation anxiety after sleep training, but it is more common for babies who are sleep deprived. Studies prove that babies who get the sleep they need have an easier time self-soothing when they are alone (15 Ways Lack of Sleep Is Harmful To The Baby, 2016).

Slow growth

Even though you do not always see it, your baby is constantly growing mentally, emotionally, and physically. Every day is a learning experience for them, and these situations help them grow in various ways. Babies who do not get the amount of sleep they need will develop at a slower rate than babies who do get the sleep they need. All types of growth are disturbed from their height to their developmental milestones. When a baby sleeps, about 8% of the somatotropin growth hormone is released. When a baby does not get the amount of sleep they need, this percentage drops.

Vaccinations are less effective

According to a study by the University of Pittsburgh School of Medicine, vaccines are not as effective for sleep-deprived babies. This study noted that the vaccine produced 12% fewer antibodies in babies who were sleep-deprived (15 Ways Lack of Sleep Is Harmful To The Baby, 2016).

Long-term emotional and social problems

When a child is sleep-deprived, they will avoid social activities because they feel it requires too much effort to interact with other people. They will also struggle with expressing themselves, whether it is verbally or nonverbally. Lack of sleep creates more negative emotions and makes children less likely to remember positive experiences. Your baby might feel more stressed and then have trouble learning new skills, making them fall behind in comparison with their peers. If your baby doesn't get the sleep they need for a long period of time, anxiety and depression can develop.

Might be linked to autism

Over the last several years, researchers have looked into what causes autism as it is on the rise in children. While scientists continue to find out the causes of autism, as many are relatively unknown, it is noted in their studies that sleep-deprived children have a higher risk of developing autism. A study conducted by psychologist Terry Katz and neurologist Beth Malow concluded that children who had autism, but no other health problems, could manage some of their symptoms when they received more sleep. Not only did their repetitive behavior decrease, but so did their anxiety.

Lack of patience for parents

There will always be moments where you feel frustrated as a parent. However, parents tend to have more frustrating moments when their baby is sleep-deprived. Because your child is exhibiting moodiness, struggling to focus, hyperactive, and overstimulated you become easily frustrated after they show these types of behaviors regularly or for a long period of time. Your patience wears thin over time as this is a human trait. Ensuring that your baby gets the sleep they need can help decrease the frustrating behaviors and give yourself more patience.

Parents lack focus

When your baby does not get the sleep they need it makes you sleep deprived as well. This will affect your focus and ability to monitor the many needs of your baby. For example, you might not realize that the formula is too hot or that the temperature of your baby's room is too cold. It is easy to lose focus on specific tasks and duties when you are tired.

Fatal consequences of parental sleepiness

It seems not a day goes by where you do not hear about a road accident. However, what you do not hear is about these accidents is that 1,000 fatal road accidents happen annually due to a lack of sleep. Because you lose patience quickly, you are tired, emotionally and mentally drained, and you lose focus you are more likely to end up in an accident.

Drowsy driving is just as bad as drunk driving. If you are feeling tired, take time to take a 10 to 15-minute nap before you get on the road. If you are driving and feel that it is getting hard to keep your eyes open, pull over in a parking lot or safely on the side of the road and rest your eyes. Call a friend or family member if you need someone else to drive you home safely.

Chapter 2: Family Structure (Teamwork Works!)

Your family can consist of many people, friends, blood relatives, neighbors and maybe even coworkers. However, no matter who your family consists of, it is important to realize the importance of them and the teamwork they can offer.

No matter what your role is in the family, you need to remember the word "teamwork" because it really does work. To ensure your baby gets the most out of sleep training, every member needs to work together. Even if you have a babysitter for the night, you need to make sure they understand your baby's routine. Walkthrough the routine with them and leave a note that shows the babysitter the steps of the routine. Some parents like to place pictures of their child's bedtime routine on the child's wall. When the child is older, they can look at the picture and understand what is next in the routine.

For this chapter, we will focus on three different structures within your family: dad, grandparents, and a partner. Each person will play a significant role in your baby's life and help ensure that sleep training works for you, your baby, and your family.

Role of Dads

American society often places the role of the dad in the family on the sidelines. We still live in a world where the mother is thought of as the nurturer and the main parent for the children. Fortunately, this view is starting to change dads. In fact, there are a number of dads who want to do everything they can to help their baby adjust during the sleep training period.

If you have a family with a dad, they must become just as important in the sleep training process as you. Forget about what society has told you when it comes to dads in the parenting relationship. They can do nearly everything you can do. They can also be your sense of support during the difficult moments, such as the nights where your baby is teething and sleeping their normal number of hours is becoming more and more difficult. But, with the support of your baby's dad, you can make it through these nights.

The dad does not need to live in the same house as the mom to take part in sleep training. If there are two different homes, communicate with each other and come to an agreement on what is the best sleep training routine for your baby. Be respectful of each other and follow through with the plan. Remember, slacking in one home because one of you does not agree with every step of sleep training will harm the child more than anyone else. It is always best to keep the baby in a routine.

Here are a few tips to include in the sleep training when it comes to the dad's role:

- **The baby's dad can help put them back to sleep at any age.** Some people believe that when breastfeeding, the mom always needs to get up and put the baby back to sleep, but this is not necessarily true. A mother can always prepare the milk for the nighttime and the dad can bottle feed. Another way dads can help is to get up during the feeding and then burp the child when the baby is done with feeding. This will allow the mother to go to bed a get a bit more sleep. Furthermore, when your baby is starting to wean from breastfeeding, they will continue to wake up at certain times during the night out of habit. Dads can easily take a turn to soothe their baby back to sleep.

- **Dads are great at being a shoulder to cry on.** Sleep training, even when you do your best to remain calm, is hard. You will feel stressed at times and you might even have moments where you think, "I can't do this anymore." These are some of the best moments to talk to the baby's father. They will understand where you are coming from and offer you support. There is nothing wrong with venting about the process as this can help you remain consistent and keep everyone focused on the goal.

- **Include dads into the bedtime routine.** You can always take turns when it comes to the bedtime routine. For example, you might give the baby a bath and the dad might read to them. Then, you both put your baby to bed by tucking them in and telling them goodnight. You can both take part in the bedtime routine every step of the way as well. Don't think that the steps need to be split or one should do most of the steps and then both of the parents tuck the baby in.

- **Take time to feed the baby with a bottle.** Not all babies are breastfed and if your baby takes the bottle, then the dad can take charge of some of the nightly feedings. You might decide between you to take turns or focus on what is best when it comes to your work schedules.

Role of Grandparents

Grandparents are great to lean on when it comes to sleep training. While they might have their own ideas on how to sleep train a baby, grandparents are great people to look to when you need some emotional or psychological support. They have been in your shoes and understand how stressful it is to sleep train a child. Even if they didn't sleep train, they understand the difficulties in getting a baby to sleep through the night and will understand when you need a shoulder to cry on.

It is important to remember when considering grandparents as support is that you might need to speak up and ask if they will help you. Some grandparents will jump at the chance to help and will constantly ask you if you need anything, while other grandparents will give you space and wait for you to come to them. By now, you understand the grandparents better than anyone else. But no matter what your relationship is like with them, you always need to take time to explain the process to them.

Understand that grandparents grew up in a different time and if they criticize your methods, they are not trying to hurt you. They might feel their advice will help you. Listen to what they have to say and do your best to explain your process. Try to get them to understand the importance of consistency and be patient. Your baby's grandparents have the best interest at heart for your baby and they will do what they need to.

No matter what your relationship is with the grandparents, you need to focus on the special relationship between your baby and their grandparents. Here are a few factors about their special relationship:

- **Love is unconditional.** There is nothing that your child could do that will make the grandparents stop loving them. This is the same love that you feel for your child.

- **It is usually more carefree.** Grandparents have already raised their children and now they want to focus on the fun part and be a grandparent. This can help you greatly, especially if they will take time to rock your baby before bed or get up in the middle of the night to soothe your baby back to sleep. Most grandparents have more patience for their grandchildren than you have for your child. This isn't bad, it is typical when it comes to this relationship dynamic.

- **They might have more time.** Grandparents might be retired and do not have the same day-to-day tasks and responsibilities that you do. This allows them to stay with the baby and make sure that they are following their schedule while you are working or running errands.

Share Sleep Training with a Partner

The first step to sleep training with your partner is to get on the same page. Whether you are roommates, married, dating, or co-parenting, you and your partner need to have strong communication skills in order to effectively sleep train. Sit down and talk about the sleep training schedule, the nighttime routine, and the best time to lay your baby down to sleep. You need to have a bedtime that works for both of you, especially when tag-teaming the sleep training process. You both need to agree on which sleep training method you'll be applying to. If your partner is not sure they can listen to your baby cry for some time, for example, you'll probably opt for the no tears method.

Decide if you will split the sleep training responsibilities evenly with your partner or if you will hold most of the responsibilities. Every situation is different, and you need to find what works best for you and your family.

Go through the process together (without your baby) before you start sleep training to make sure that you both understand the process completely. Walk and talk it out from start to finish. For instance, if the bedtime routine starts with a warm bath, walk into the bathroom and discuss the length of the bath. Then move on to the next step. Will you have pajamas ready for your baby to put on in the bathroom or will you bring them into their bedroom? Continue this practice run through all the steps in your sleep training process.

Finally, choose a convenient date to start the sleep training process. You should start your training strong, so it is imperative that the first week works for both of your schedules.

Chapter 3: Multiple Births (Twins)

Every parent of twins or multiples will tell you that taking care of more than one baby is a monumentally bigger challenge. There is a lot of truth to this, especially if you are a single-parent household. While two parents can switch time with the twins and do their best to take care of feeding, diaper changes, and attention together, it is harder when you are the only parent taking care of two babies. There are also other factors involved if you are a parent to triplets or more babies. You can get a sense of how difficult trying to manage more than one baby can be when you only have one child to care for.

Taking Care of Two Babies

Personally, I can only imagine what it is like to take care of two babies. My experience comes from caring for my own children and watching my friend care for her twins. Of course, I have also checked out a couple of reality shows on raising multiples, but this doesn't compare to a parent or parents who take care of their twins every day.

One of the first questions that might come to your mind when caring for twins is, "How can I make this easier?" Chances are, you have already tried everything you can think of and some steps might have helped, but there are still several struggles you need to face. You are stressed and looking for help to alleviate your challenges.

First, it is important to remember that you are not alone in this category. Every new parent, even when they have a partner, can use more support. In fact, there is never enough support for parents. With this in mind, if you do have a partner, you need to remember that they don't have enough support to give you. Even if they help you with your babies with every feeding, your partner might also feel like they still haven't given enough help. Therefore, blaming each other will not help the situation. You need to support each other and recognize how much you are both doing as much and as often as you can.

If you start to feel your stress building, plan ahead so you can take a break or get some extra help for a couple of days. This might mean you contact your parents, in-laws, siblings, friends, or ask your insurance company if they will pay for a home nurse or night nurse to come and visit.

Breastfeeding may become another struggle when it comes to parenting multiples. You need to find a method that works for you. Some parents will get a twin nursing pillow to help them feed their twins at the same time. Of course, this method is not always possible. Sometimes, you need to feed your babies at different times, and this can cause problems when it comes to napping and bedtime. Take a few deep breaths and remember, these struggles are temporary.

Another tip when it comes to taking care of multiples is to take as much maternity leave as possible. You will need this to help get into your groove and take care of your babies. Some parents combine their vacation with maternity leave. Other parents will make sure that if their baby is sick that their Human Resources department knows this as then they might get a few extra days by using their sick time instead of maternity or vacation.

Finally, get a good foundation of support—not just from your friends and family. Find other parents with multiples in your area or online who you can talk to. They understand what you are going through and will have ideas that you can try with your family. Psychologically, when we know that other people understand our situation, we can handle every day a little easier because we know that we are not alone. Let me repeat, so you always remember this—you are not alone.

How to Sleep Train Twins

Most of the resources you receive about sleep training focus on caring for one baby, but sleep training multiples is just as important.

One of the first steps you need to accomplish is whether your twins will sleep together or apart. You might wonder if it is common for your babies to disturb each other when they are sleeping or if they will sleep better when they are co-sleeping, which is sleeping in the same bed. A few studies show that a little over half of the parents allow their babies to co-sleep, at least for the first couple of months. Many other parents will place the cribs next to each other so their twins can still comfort each other but have their own space.

The research of co-bedding twins comes up with a lot of debate, even from the experts. Some people believe it is healthy for your multiples, especially in the first few months. Twins are used to being next to each other, as they were in the womb. Other experts state that because there are no real benefits shown with co-sleeping and that it is best to ensure your twins each have their own crib. The bottom line is you need to do what you feel is right for you, your twins, and your family. If you do decide to co-bed, there are several ways that you can do this. Some people like to lay their babies side by side while other people will lay them head to head or feet to feet. No matter what you decide, the best step to take is to make sure they have enough room for themselves. They will be aware of their twins and won't harm or hit their sibling.

To help ease your worries about sleep training twins, here are some tips to follow:

- You don't need to place any type of barrier between your babies when they are co-sleeping. Barriers can hurt babies more than help them.

- The risk of SIDS for twins declines if they room-share or sleep in the same room with you for the first six months.

- Always lay babies on their backs when they are going to sleep. This will reduce the risk of SIDS.

Sleep patterns in twins are a bit different because they follow their gestational pattern over age, especially if they are born prematurely. Other than this, the way they sleep and how you will sleep train twins is similar to a single baby. For instance, you will develop a plan and find out what method will work best for you and your family. The biggest difference is that you have two (or more) babies instead of one. Most parents of multiples state that one of the best steps you can follow when you are sleep training is to do your best to feed and put your babies down to sleep at the same time. This might not be possible, especially if you are a single parent and struggle with feeding your twins at the same time. Do your best and your babies will fall into a routine, especially if you remain consistent.

Routines are just as important as multiples as they are with twins. Studies show that parents with multiples are more likely to follow a routine and receive help from other people. However, the amount of sleep deprivation that mothers have is the same whether they have one baby or more than one.

What to Expect and When

In reality, it is hard to know exactly what to expect and when each baby is different. They tend to follow their own schedule when it comes to growth and this can affect sleep training. The main goal for most parents with twins is to get your babies on the same schedule, especially when it comes to sleeping. Fortunately, sleep training will help.

Twins who are born prematurely will need more sleep during the first few weeks. It is also important to note that if your twins are born early, you might need to push back sleep training for a few weeks or so. For example, most parents will start sleep training once they receive approval from their child's pediatrician, which is usually between four to six months. But, if your twins were born a couple of months early, they won't be ready at the average time. You need to focus on their gestational age over actual age, so you might not start sleep training until between six to eight months.

To get your babies established in a routine, here are a few tips for you to follow:

- **Double-duty feedings.** It isn't easy, but you want to do what you can to make sure your babies eat at the same time as this will give them a stronger chance of falling asleep around the same time.

- **Have your babies nap at the same time.** Whether you decide to co-bed your twins or give them their own crib, you want to lay them down at the same time. One might be a bit drowsier than the other, but the other twin will quickly catch up.

- **Establish a good bedtime routine.** You might start with a bath as this will get your babies to understand that the sound of their bath means it is soon bedtime. After bath time, you want to ensure that you are playing soothing music or read them a story quietly. Doing something that is relaxing will help your babies fall asleep and stay asleep.

- **If one baby wakes up to eat, wake the other baby.** Of course, it will be hard to wake up your peacefully sleeping baby but doing so will keep your babies on the same schedule. Plus, once you get the twin who is up and eating to sleep, the other twin will wake up and they will continue to take turns throughout the night. This will mean, whether you are a single parent or have the help of a partner, you will get little to no sleep. Furthermore, the twins can keep waking each other up, which means you will have two tired and crabby babies the next day.

- **Establish small goals.** Chances are you have a lot of goals when it comes to keeping your twins on the same schedule. While this is great, the trick is to make sure that you establish small goals. Remember, your babies are usually a bit behind a single baby, especially if they are born prematurely. Keeping your goals small will help your babies thrive and keep you from becoming stressed because you are not where you want to be. Always get excited over the smallest achievements, such as feeding twice a night instead of three times.

- **If one twin sleeps through the night, it is okay to separate.** You will want to notice how your twins adjust if you decide to separate them into different rooms, but many parents do this as one twin might start sleeping through the night before the other twin. When this happens, it is a good idea to look at moving your little sleeper into a different room, even if it is the living room, because this will allow them to continue sleeping through the night. You can always move them back into their bedroom when the other twin is sleeping just as well.

The best routine and feeding schedule for twins

Even the most energetic mom can become overwhelmed by constantly waking up to feed her twins at different times. Plus, daily life with babies, even one, is chaotic and this only increases when you have twins. Placing your babies on a schedule will help them as they will sleep, eat, and play together. It will also help your emotional, mental, and physical health, which is extremely important. If you don't take care of yourself, it is harder to take care of your little ones.

While you want to keep your twins on the same schedule, you also need to be flexible. Don't keep your nodding your baby up if they are starting to fall asleep while the other twin continues to coo and interact with you. If one becomes hungry, don't force them to wait to eat until the other becomes hungry. Go ahead and give your little one a snack. Remaining flexible will allow you to attend to the needs of your babies individually, which is extremely important. You might have one twin that is more sensitive and needs more sleep and cuddles and one twin who shows more independence and doesn't need to sleep as much.

Through your flexibility and doing what you can to follow a schedule you set, your babies will start to follow the schedule over time. It might take several months and a lot longer than one baby, but this is how it works with twins. Following the cues of your twins will help them thrive.

Bath time

Splashing in the bath is double the fun when you have multiples. While some parents feel they can only bathe one baby at a time, as bathing just one baby is an intimidating task, to begin with, it is still best to bathe your twins together when they reach a certain age. Because newborns are more fragile, it is best to bathe them separately. Once you feel your babies are ready to take a bath at the same time, here are some tips to help you and your babies adjust:

- **Forget the bath seats.** Bath seats can tip when your baby is in the tub. They tend to give parents a false sense of security. While it might feel nice to have the extra help from the seats, nothing is better than your constant supervision. Plus, they make the bath less fun as they restrict your babies.

- **Start bathing them together when they can sit up without assistance.** Your babies will tell you when they are ready to take a bath together and this is when they can sit up without your assistance. When you start bathing them, you will want to have a slip-proof mat, always be within grabbing reach, and only have about two to three inches of water.

- **Your twins might go through phases where you need to split them.** Some babies enjoy getting their hair washed while other babies dislike this part. If one of your babies cries because they are getting their hair washed and this upsets the other twin, you might want to look at splitting them up for bath time. Continuing this process while they are together can cause them to dread bath time, which should always be a fun, relaxing activity.

- **Prepare for post-bath.** Chances are you will only take one twin out at a time, so you want to ensure you are prepared with a towel, pajamas, and a bouncy seat ready for the first twin to come up. Don't place the babies too far away from you. Remember, you always want to be in close contact so you can grab them in case they fall.

Problem-Solving (How to Deal with Your Crying Twin)

The way babies communicate is with their cries. As a parent, you start to learn what your baby's cries mean. You will learn they have a cry when they are hungry, a different cry when they are overtired, when they are scared, etc. While it is never fun to hear your baby cry, especially when they are having trouble calming down, it is normal. However, this doesn't mean it isn't stressful, especially for new parents and parents with more than one baby.

One factor you should be aware of is that there are no studies to prove multiples cry more than a single baby. It might seem this way at times, especially if your twins take turns crying, but it doesn't mean that you need to hear them cry more. What determines how often your baby cries depends on their personality. Sensitive babies will cry more because they are more sensitive to sound, touch, light, etc. When your baby is more laid back, they will cry less. Each baby will have their own special personality, and this means one twin might cry more than the other.

So what can you do when your baby is crying and you can't seem to calm them down? First, you want to remain as calm as possible. While this is not easy, it is the first step to calming a baby. Both of your babies can sense how you feel and if you feel stressed, they will begin to feel uneasy and both can become inconsolable, which will not help the situation. Here are a few more tips to help you soothe your crying babies:

- **Set your babies together.** If you don't co-bed or your twins are not side-by-side, place them together. One of the magical characteristics of twins is that they have a natural ability to soothe each other.

- **Let them cry, but check on them.** It is hard to hear your baby cry, but sometimes what they need is a good cry. When you have tried everything and starting to feel overwhelmed, take a bit of a break. Set your baby down and allow them to cry. This won't harm them. They might even fall asleep. If your baby is still crying in a few minutes or after you feel better, go back in and try to calm your baby again.

- **Use soothing methods.** There are many soothing methods that you can try on your baby. For example, you can rub their back while they are in their crib, rub their little cheek, rock them, gently sing to them, or entertain them. Another struggle when it comes to soothing methods for twins is that your babies might have different methods they need at that moment.

- **Prioritize needs.** It can happen with twins often—they start crying at the same time and you are alone. The first step is not to panic. Attend to your babies calmly and see why one is crying and note what you can prioritize first. For example, if one baby is sick and the other baby is upset because their twin is sick, you will soothe your sick little one first. If one baby is crying louder than your other baby, you might tend to that one first. If you walk in the room and immediately notice one baby is crying because their pacifier fell out of their mouth, help them and then attend to your other little one.

Helping yourself cope with crying twins

You always need to remember that your mental, emotional, and physical health is important. As a mother, I know how easily this is forgotten, especially when you have upset babies.

I had to slowly learn that to truly care and help my children, I needed to focus on myself first. This is a hard realization to come to as a mother because we feel selfish. But, taking care of our own health is not selfish, it is powerful as it allows us to care for our babies better.

If you need help when it comes to your babies because you feel overwhelmed by their cries—reach out for help. Here are some other tips to consider to help you deal with the crying.

- **Let go of the guilt.** As mothers, we have loads of guilt that we carry around with us on a daily basis. We feel that we don't do enough for our babies or that we aren't enough for them. We want to give them the best, but we feel like we can't. I have been there, and I know you have too. The best step to take it to work on dropping the guilt and here is why—*you are enough for your babies*. Say it out loud if you need to, "I am enough for my babies." When you feel overwhelmed, take a deep breath and keep in mind that this situation will pass, and you are doing a great job.

- **Have some "me time" every day.** It is hard to find an alone time when you have one baby, much less two or more, but it is necessary. Instead of running around trying to get all the housework done, take some time when they are sleeping for yourself. Get up a few minutes earlier and get your morning routine completed before your babies wake up.

- **It is okay to cry.** Sometimes we just need a good cry, just like our babies do. If you feel the need to cry to let out some stress or built-up emotions, go ahead and cry. Take a nice long and relaxing bath when your babies are sleeping and cry it out. You can even take time to cry yourself when your babies are crying as it might help all of you to cry it out together.

- **Remember your support system.** Talk to other moms of multiples, friends, or family members. Let them know how you are feeling. Don't keep your emotions inside as this will only cause you, and your babies, more stress.

Monitoring Your Baby's Growth

Every baby grows at a different pace, but it is important to ensure that you take your time to monitor your baby's growth so you can catch anything that does not seem right immediately. Your pediatrician will do this, but you must do it as well.

Your baby's genetics, environment, health, and activity level will play an important role in their development. It is important to note that if your baby is a little under or over the average weight or height that it is something you want to monitor, but remember it is not always bad. Your baby's doctor will help you find a solution to why they are gaining weight at a faster rate than most babies their age.

When you monitor your baby's growth, you will pay attention to these factors:

- **Weight.** To get the best weight of your baby, you will want to use a baby scale. You will normally take off their clothing to weigh them. Baby scales are used up to one year of age.

- **Length.** You will measure the length of your baby with a tape measure. You want to lay them on a table and measure them from their head to their feet.

- **Head circumference.** You can measure the head circumference to help you understand where your baby sits with their brain development. For example, if the circumference is smaller than most babies, it might signal developmental delays. If your baby has a larger than average head, they could have a medical condition known as hydrocephalus, which means they have fluid on their brain.

When you first look at a growth chart, you might think it is more confusing than it is helpful. It can be hard to understand at first, but once you have the numbers, you can use the following steps to read where your baby sits on the growth chart:

1. Decide if you are looking at your child's height or weight and note where your child fits on the side of the graph.

2. Look for your baby's age at the top of the graph.

3. Follow the lines until they meet in the graph. They will fall somewhere along the curves.

4. Once you find where the lines intersect, follow the curves so you can see the percentile where your baby sits. This percentage will show where your baby is compared to other babies their age. For example, if your baby weighs at 9%, they are heavier than 9% of all over babies. This might indicate that they are a bit underweight and you should make sure to contact your child's primary care doctor to see what you can change to help your baby gain weight. The doctor can also make sure that your baby doesn't have a medical condition that is keeping them from gaining weight.

The key to following growth charts is to remember that it is not the specific percentage that you should be worried about. While it is helpful for doctors, they will pay more attention to the patterns your baby shows within the growth chart. For example, if they were at 7% six months ago when it came to weight and they are now at 9%, they are gaining weight.

However, if the doctor sees this percentage number decreasing, they might become a little more concerned. Above all, you always want to remember that babies grow at different paces. Your baby might not have hit their growth spurt yet, while most children their age have reached the growth spurt.

Tweaking Your Toddler's Twin Routine

As your twins grow older, making sure they are on the same schedule will become a little easier. In fact, by the time they are two years old, your twins will give you a break by helping you sync up their schedules, which is nice providing they continue to keep you more than busy throughout the day.

To give you a better understanding of how eating, bathing, and sleeping work with your twin toddlers, here are some of the highs and lows to look forward to.

Eating

Your twins are about two years old and can now feed themselves for the most part. While it will get messy now and then, especially when they decide to place the noodles in their hair instead of their mouth, it eases your stress during mealtime. When it comes to drinking, you can start getting them to use cups without a lid. Some people like to allow their children to practice drinking out of "big boy" or "big girl" cups before they put any liquids in the cups. You can turn this into a little game by allowing them to have "tea time."

The biggest challenge when it comes to eating is that your twins are not the same person. What one twin likes, the other one might not. This means you might need to give them two different snacks and sometimes make two different vegetables. You do not want to force your toddler to eat the food in front of them as this will make them dread mealtime. Instead, you want to follow their lead. If they are not hungry, save the food for when they get hungry. Sometimes making food that both your toddlers will eat is a big enough challenge and you do not need to add to this challenge by having them start crying because they need to come and eat their food.

Part of their eating routine at this age is that they are trying new foods. Continue to offer your children new foods and if they do not like one type of food, wait a few weeks before you offer it again. It will be like a new food to your child because they will not remember trying it before and they might like it this time.

Bath time

If you thought babies splashed a lot in the bathtub, just wait until you place your toddlers in the tub. Sure, they can now listen to your commands of "no splashing" better than before, you can still allow them to have fun splashing and playing with toys. They are even old enough to help you wipe up all the water that they got on the floor. The best news when it comes to bath time is your twins will have the best time in the tub with each other as they play.

The challenge is that they might have too much fun, which can cause a mess in the tub. Even if you find yourself leaving the room for five seconds, you can come back to a pool on your floor. They have also learned how to team up to get into a little trouble here and there, so you need to watch out. One might be behind the curtain because they decided it is a good idea to splash you as you walk into the room. Do your best to remain calm in moments like this. Remember, they can always help you clean it up, which will help them to understand the consequences and taking responsibility.

If you find that bath time is becoming too challenging with both your twins at the same time, then you will want to look at splitting them up with back to back bath times. Of course, this might not be possible if you are a single parent. However, if you trust your toddler being in their room with the television on or playing quietly while you give the other a bath, then you can do this.

Sleeping

I will never forget getting a text from my friend at 10:30 p.m saying, "They are still talking to each other. I really wish they would fall asleep!" I smiled and found it cute, but I also understood her frustration. Your twins will love talking to each other during their bedtime. In fact, one twin might talk more and often talk to the other twin to sleep. So, while the best news is that your twins are synced with their bedtime routine, they can talk, they can get up and play, and one twin can easily keep the other twin up—and this can make for a crabby twin the next day.

The best way to handle your twins at bedtime and naptime is to let them do their little talking until they fall asleep. Usually, once one twin falls asleep the other twin will start to get bored and nod off. They might talk to themselves for a bit, but consider this their time. It is important that your twins have alone time as well. If one twin wakes up before the other twin, let that twin stay in their crib or room. This will help keep their schedules synced.

Chapter 4: Know the Reason behind the Cry

You know that your baby has different cries to tell you what they need, but you might not completely understand all of their cries perfectly. In general, there are seven main types of cries, which are discussed below.

Seven Types of Cries

1. Hungry

The earliest stages of hunger will not involve crying. Your baby will start communicating that they are hungry by showing you cues of hunger, such as sucking on their fingers, reaching for your breast, or opening their mouth and acting like they are sucking. You will notice their tongue moving to the roof of their mouth. If you do not respond to these early signs, your baby will start to become squirmy and eventually cry. Some people refer to hunger crying as a rhythmic "neh" cry that sounds low-pitched and repetitive.

The only step you can take to soothe your baby from their hunger is the obvious one: feed them. You should feed them as soon as you notice the early stages of hunger. If you delay their feeding and your baby becomes upset it can cause them to later throw up their food.

2. Tired or uncomfortable

Even before crying, your baby will show early signs of tiredness. They may rub their eyes or face, avoid eye contact, or yawn. The earlier you catch their signs of fatigue, the easier it will be to put your baby down to sleep later. When your baby starts crying because they are tired, their cry will build with intensity. Some people refer to the cry as an "owh" sound, while other people describe the cry as nasally or whiny cry. When your baby is uncomfortable or too hot or too cold, they will have the same type of cry. But in the case of discomfort, they will give you slightly different cues. Instead of rubbing their eyes, your baby will squirm or arch themselves.

When your baby is tired, your best option is to place them down for a nap. If they are uncomfortable, start by changing their diaper and looking for signs of diaper rash. Next, think about whether your baby is chilly or too warm and if any clothing adjustments need to be made.

3. Had enough

Your baby will let you know when they have had enough. Along with a cry that sounds more like a whine, your baby will try to move away from the stimuli that are making them mad or stressed. The best option is to remove your baby from the overwhelming environment and comfort them.

216

4. Bored

When your baby is bored, they will try to interact with you by looking your way, smiling, cooing, or playing in their own way. For example, they might kick their legs or fiddle with their feet or hands. Their playful manner will then turn into fussing if they feel you are not giving them the attention they are craving. You will notice their fussing turning into sounds of whining or disgruntled cries. At this point, your baby is frustrated and they want to know why you aren't playing with them.

The best step to take to keep your baby from giving you their boredom cry is to take notice of their cues of boredom. Once they start interacting with you, play with them. You don't always need to go and pick them up when they are bored. You can talk to them, smile back, and make sure they have an age-appropriate toy near them to play with.

6. Colic

A baby who cries for more than three hours is defined as colic. They are inconsolable as they cry, which sounds more like a high-pitched cry or scream. Some parents feel their baby is in pain, but colic is not painful for your baby. Most babies have colic close to their bedtime. A baby as young as six weeks old to three months can have colic episodes.

It isn't easy to comfort a colicky baby, but there are many ways you can try to soothe them, such as swaddling, swinging, playing white noise, walking with them, or giving them a back rub.

7. Sick

A baby who is sick will not give a loud cry unless they are in pain. Their sick cry will sound more like a low-pitched or whimper. They will show other signs of sickness, such as pulling at their ears, having a temperature, vomiting, or diarrhea. The best step to take is to make them feel comfortable. If your baby has diarrhea, vomiting, or a high temperature you need to contact your doctor. Your baby can quickly become dehydrated when they show these symptoms and this will only make them feel worse.

Other Reasons

Flatulence or gassy baby

You can tell if your baby is having tummy trouble if they are arching their back or bringing their legs toward their torso. Their crying will start small, similar to a whimper, but it will become more intense over time. The best step is to help them get their gas moving by gently pushing their knees up toward their stomach, laying them on their right side and rubbing their left side, or giving them a back rub.

Reflux

If you notice your baby gagging or coughing when they are eating, they might have reflux. They will often spit up or vomit after they are done eating. Reflux can also cause problems when it comes to burping, which doesn't help their tummy trouble.

One of the best steps is to place your baby in an upright position, as this will help their food stay down. In fact, a baby with reflux will tend to cry when you put them in the regular feeding position because it is uncomfortable for them.

It's important to stick to your baby's feeding schedule if they have trouble with reflux because feeding them more than necessary can make their reflux worse.

Allergies

Food allergies are the most common types of allergies for a baby and can show up as hives, gastrointestinal issues, or a rash. Your baby's allergy cry will be similar to their gassy cry. They can show the same symptoms like flatulence, as this is a sign of food allergies, making it hard to distinguish between gas and allergies. If your baby recently tried a new type of food, such as milk, fish, or wheat, you need to discuss this with your doctor at your baby's next checkup.

Other types of allergies that can affect your baby are seasonal and medical allergies. For seasonal allergies, your baby will have watery eyes, a runny nose, and a cough. It might seem like they have a cold at first, but you will notice the symptoms continuing or only showing up with certain environmental factors, such as rain.

The only way to truly know if your baby has allergies is through an allergy test, which their doctor can perform. The best step you can take is to keep a journal of your baby's allergies. Be sure to write down their symptoms, what they ate, and any environmental factors that could contribute to the allergy.

When You Can't Find a Reason for the Crying

Sometimes babies do not have a reason for their crying session. In fact, sometimes babies who cry for a few minutes to an hour have no reason at all. This type of crying moment tends to happen in the evening, which makes many people feel it is because their baby is tired or overstimulated. This can also be one of the most stressful times of the day as everyone is trying to get their evening routine done so they can go to bed as everyone is tired. In these moments, the best step you can take is to allow your baby to have their crying moment and try to comfort them if they can't calm down.

Learn to Understand Your Baby's Cry

Don't worry if you feel overwhelmed thinking that you will never learn your baby's specific cries because *you will*. You will quickly catch on to your baby's form of communication and be able to help them quickly. Once you understand your baby's cries, you will find that they cry less often and seem to coo a bit more. Before you know it, they will be learning how to talk! So, even if you feel stressed about your baby's cries now, know that they will be a thing of the past one day. Do your best to enjoy your moments by noting the different cries and learning how to effectively communicate with your baby. Doing this will only make your bond grow stronger.

Another key is to stick to the routine. Your baby needs a routine and they can become frustrated or uncomfortable when their routine is not in place. You might not think they know, but they do. Sticking to a routine can also help you identify the cries. For example, if it is close to bedtime and your baby starts crying, they might be saying they are tired now and are ready for bed.

Surviving the Crying Spells

Every baby has crying spells. No matter what you try to calm your baby's cries, sometimes it is just not what they need because they are simply inconsolable. These moments are upsetting and cause a lot of anxiety for the parent(s). While the crying won't harm your baby, it can leave you feeling like you are not enough. Studies have proven that these moments can create emotional, mental, and physical effects on parents.

The best step you can do is to take care of yourself as well. This is not always easy to do, and I know it is easier said than done, but it is necessary to do what you can to ease your anxiety and pain. Here are a few tips to help you through the process.

- **Stay healthy.** Make sure that you get all the sleep you can, take care of yourself by eating right and exercising. Ensure you allow yourself some "me time" and you will find yourself able to care for your baby more easily, even though their crying spells.

- **Breathe.** Take a few deep breaths and remember that the crying spell will not last forever.

- **Understand your own limits.** Everyone has limits. This does not make you a bad parent just because you need to ask for help or are afraid you will lose control if your baby does not stop crying. Every parent goes through this. All you need to do is place your child down and let them cry for a few minutes so you can calm yourself down. Never hesitate to reach out for help or moral support if you need it.

- **Take a break.** Do not be afraid to tell a friend, your partner, or a family member that you need to take a bit of a break. Ask them to come over and help care for the baby. Even if it is just so you can take a nap or go for a walk, it will help you and your baby in the end.

Chapter 5: A Parent's Biggest Fear

For some parents, sleep training makes them feel guilty, especially if they are using a cry it out method. They also fear that their baby will remember them not going in their room right away to check on them or help them back to sleep. While guilt and fear are understandable, they are not realistic. Part of this is the belief that the cry it out method means you do not go in to check on your baby. This is not the cry it out method at all. You set a certain amount of time where you allow your baby to fuss or cry to see if they will soothe themselves back to sleep. If they do not do this by the timeframe you gave yourself, such as two minutes, then you go in and soothe them to sleep.

The biggest fear parents have is that they will harm their baby, one way or another, by using any sleep training method. A *Pediatrics* study aims to end this fear by stating that you will not harm your baby by using any of the sleep methods, whether you focus on a no tears method or a cry it out method. You will help your child get the sleep they need and live a happy and healthy life by getting them to follow a sleeping schedule.

In this study, 43 babies between the ages of six to 16 months were placed in one of three groups. The first group used the graduated extension method which tells parents to periodically check on their baby. The second group used bedtime fading, which focuses on gradually delaying the baby's bedtime as a way to introduce sleepiness. The third group is known as the control group and only received information about the best sleep practices they could incorporate (Ruiz, 2016).

The study concluded that the first group, which used a cry it out method, did not affect their babies negatively in any way. The bonds between the parents and babies remained strong, which is something that many people felt would not be proven by this study. At the time of this study, most people felt that any type of cry it out method caused the babies to resent their parents because they did not receive what they needed. The researchers further tested the stress hormone of the baby measuring their cortisone levels. They found no difference in the stress level because of the sleep training method used (Ruiz, 2016).

This is not the only study completed to show that babies have no long-term effects when it comes to the cry it out method. There are several studies that give us the same result, telling parents that there is no reason to fear the cry it out method. You do not need to worry about damaging the bond you have with your little one to make sure they get a good night's sleep.

The studies are also here to tell you to let go of the guilt. I know this is easier said than done, but there is no reason to feel guilty about letting your baby cry for a couple of minutes before you go in to help soothe them. You are raising an independent child, and this is something you need to be proud of. Your baby will continue to grow up to know that you love them and are there for them when they need you. At the same time, they will learn how to self-soothe themselves to sleep, get a good night's rest, and allow everyone else in the household to do the same. This will keep you happy, which will also keep your baby happy and thriving.

What Science Cannot Tell Us About the Cry It Out Method

Even though there are a number of studies to support, and some that do not, the cry it out method, there are several factors that science cannot tell us. To help you understand the cry it out method a little better, we will go through myths and then state the facts about the method. From there, we can come up with our own conclusion and you can have a better idea when it comes to deciding which sleep training method you will use.

Myth: The only sleep training method you can use is the cry it out method.

Fact: There are many different sleep training methods that parents and experts feel are great methods. Some of these methods are a cry it out method while others are not. Furthermore, people continue to create their own sleep training methods that work for their babies and share them with the rest of the world.

Myth: You need to find the correct amount of time to let your baby cry while you are sleep training. You do not want to go over or under this amount of time.

Fact: You need to follow your instincts and there is no set "right" time when it comes to letting your baby cry during sleep training. Some people will wait a minute while other parents will wait three minutes. The ones who wait longer are just as good of parents as the parents who wait a minute. The amount of time you allow your child to cry does not indicate if you are a good parent or not. There is no right or wrong formula when it comes to sleep training and crying. You need to do what is best for you and what feels right for your baby.

Myth: Sleep training will hurt my baby in the long run.

Fact: As you can see from the study above, sleep training will not harm your baby. Your baby will get the sleep they need and begin to thrive even more with sleep training.

Myth: The only way to truly know that you are sleep training is when you hear a lot of crying.

Fact: While you can use this as a way to know that sleep training is working, there are several approaches that many people feel are gentler. You always want to remember to use what is best for you and what you feel is best for your baby. This means that you do not let other people tell you how sleep training between you and your baby should go. You can get advice, but you always need to follow your instincts and your heart. You need to be comfortable with sleep training, so your baby has a calm environment. You will know it is working when they start to sleep on their schedule and sleep for longer periods of time.

Myth: Once my baby is sleep trained, they will not wake up during the night and I can get a full night's sleep.

Fact: It is natural for babies to wake up a few times during the night, even if they are sleep trained. This is very common within their first year of life. The key to sleep training is you help your baby learn to self-soothe themselves back to sleep. Yes, they will wake up fewer times, which means you will wake up less, but they will still wake up from time to time.

Conclusion

Looking at the myths and facts when it comes to sleep training your baby, it is important to note that it is helpful for the whole family. Not only will your baby get enough sleep, but you will too. Furthermore, sleep training can help your baby thrive, which will support them on their road to healthy development.

Chapter 6: Why Most Training Fails

The Top 10 Reasons Sleep Training Fails

Sleep training does not fail simply because you didn't or couldn't accomplish the task. It fails because of the common mistakes that most parents make. Here are some of the most common mistakes to be aware of and work to avoid in the sleep training process.

1. Starting sleep training at the wrong time

The best time to start sleep training is when your baby understands the difference between day and night and are on their own sleep cycle. The first sign your baby is on their sleep cycle if they sleep and stay awake for a predictable period of time. For example, you might notice your baby sleeping for 90 minutes and then waking up for about 30 minutes. After noticing this schedule for a few days, you can start looking at a sleep training plan.

If you are trying to sleep train a toddler, you should stay away from starting the sleep training at the same time as other milestone moments, such as potty training. These moments naturally interfere with your child's sleep schedule and will cause the sleep training process to fail.

2. Not changing the bedtime

To ensure that sleep training is successful, you need to start at a certain time and stick to it. If you have a bedtime that is too early, your child will not be tired enough to sleep. Many people state it is best to have a bedtime that is a little later as you want to lay them down when they are about to fall asleep, yet still awake. Furthermore, it is best to keep the bedtime routine under 30 minutes and to stick with the routine. This means, especially as your child gets older, it is only one book and not two one night and then one the next night. You also want to read for the same amount of time every night.

3. Missing the medical causes of sleep difficulties

Earlier, I mentioned the importance of seeing your baby's primary care doctor before you start sleep training. Following this step will help you learn if your baby is ready for sleep training and make sure that they do not have a medical issue to keep them from successful sleep training. Sleep issues do not mean you can't sleep train your baby. It simply means that you will work with the doctor to manage these issues before you begin the sleep training process.

4. Being inconsistent

You have a busy life. You are tired after work or when it gets to be bedtime. You lose energy, which makes you question whether you have to go through the sleep training process or if you can skip it for that night. Many times, people will skip part of the process or won't follow through with their timing because they are exhausted. While this is understandable, and nothing to feel guilty about, it can cause your sleep training to fail.

Do your best to push through when you are tired. Stick to your sleep training plan as the most important part of this process is that your baby has a consistent schedule to learn. If you find yourself needing help for a couple of nights, reach out and ask a friend or family member to help you. Allow yourself to go to bed early and get up with your baby. This can help you stay consistent.

5. Challenges in the bedroom

There are several challenges that can show themselves when it comes to sleep training and some of them you might not think about. For example, if you live on a noisy street, you might not notice how the noise keeps your baby up or wakes them up as they are about to fall asleep.

Another common challenge is a sibling in the same room as your baby. If this is the case, the best method is to move the other child into your bedroom, a spare bedroom, or even the couch during sleep training.

Other challenges include light, even street lights. Lights that shine directly on your child can keep them awake. If you can read in your child's room, especially in the spot where they are sleeping, the light is too bright for them. Get blinds to block out any outside light or find a light for them that has a dimmer switch.

6. *Not being ready*

Sometimes parents start sleep training their baby too early. Sleep training is not a task that you can wake up one morning and decide you will start this process that night. You need to prepare yourself and your baby for the sleep training journey. This means that you will want to set a start date. You want to have your plan, method, and everything in place by the time your start date comes. This includes a doctor's visit and making sure any helpers understand and support the plan.

7. *Moving your child into their bedroom at the same time*

You want to make sure your baby is comfortable sleeping in their own room before you start sleep training. If you start the process at the same time you move them into their own bedroom, your child will feel too much stress as this is too much change all at once. You need to work with them and introduce change slowly into their life. You don't need to move your child into their room months before you start sleep training. It usually only takes a few nights to a week for your child to become comfortable with their new sleeping environment.

8. Feeding your child all night long

Instead of feeding your child several times during the night when you start the sleep training process, many experts state you should feed them right before bed. When you first start, even if it is at six months of age, you will still need to wake up at least once during the night to feed your baby. This is fine. You can still sleep train your child as you feed them once or twice during the night. However, waking them up multiple times or having them wake up several times to eat is not something that will help sleep training.

9. The "extinction burst"

The "extinction burst" means your baby's crying or certain behavior will get worse before it gets better. For example, you place your baby into their crib and follow the "cry it out" method. You feel pleased because the first night went better than you thought. However, the second night was the opposite. Your baby cried for over an hour. While you checked on them every 10 minutes and tried to soothe them, they would start screaming once you left the room. After the second night of this, you felt like a failure with sleep training because it seemed to get worse and not better.

The fact is, you need to hold on. It can take up to a week for sleep training to work with your baby. If it is longer than a week and you do not see any signs of improvement, you should contact your baby's pediatrician and make sure there are no underlying medical issues.

10. Switching to a bed prematurely

Most experts state you should not switch your baby to a toddler bed until they are about two years old. There are a few exceptions, such as climbing out of the crib. One mistake you can make when it comes to sleep training is switching your baby to a toddler bed and then starting the sleep training process. Your baby always needs to be comfortable in their sleeping environment before you start the sleep training process.

Misguided Approaches to Sleep Training (How to Troubleshoot Sleep Training)

The number one reason

The number one reason why sleep training fails is that people expect their babies to learn quickly. One reason for this is because there are many people who say their child learned within a few days and many experts who state babies should adjust to their schedules within a week.

The reality is, your baby is on their own time frame and they might take longer than a week to adjust. You want to make sure that your expectations of sleep training are realistic. If you have unrealistic expectations, you will create extra stress when it comes to sleep training. This will make sleep training harder for both you and your baby as the atmosphere will not be calming. To help your baby sleep, you want to create a calm and warm environment.

The key to sleep training is to remember that you are your baby's teacher. You are helping them learn a new skill—that they can soothe themselves to sleep. Many parents will give up on a task after the first night or two if they do not feel that it is working. You should always try the same schedule at least three nights in a row. If you find on the fourth night that the process is not becoming easier, consider looking at your sleep training plan and see where you can adjust. Is there something that causes your baby to become anxious? Did you start too early? Are you using a method that works for you and your baby? Do you put them to bed too late or too early? There are many factors to consider, but you are bound to find one that causes you to go, "ah, this might be the problem" and adjust your sleep training plan.

What is missing?

The biggest factor that is missing when it comes to sleep training is consistency. It is hard to remain consistent every day as your life is not always meant to follow a consistent path. However, you always need to do what you can when it comes to your baby. This means you might need to tell your friends that you cannot stay out beyond 6:30, but you need to get home to start putting your baby to bed. It means that you will need to push through your baby's bedtime routine when you are exhausted and feel that you can hardly function yourself.

If you naturally struggle with consistency, try to find an accountability buddy. This is someone, such as your friend, partner, or family member that can help you keep on schedule. They do not need to live with you, they can simply call you and make sure that you are starting the bedtime routine and staying on track. If you are struggling, they might come and help you that night or talk you through any challenges that you are experiencing.

Chapter 7: What Sleep Method is Right for My Baby? (Choose a Sleep Method That Works for Your Family)

Oh, the big question when it comes to sleep training, "Which sleep method is right for my baby and my family?" This question is always harder for people who have other young children in the home or single parents who know they will need to go through the whole process by themselves. For parent(s) with other children, they need to find something that will work for them too and this can cause other problems, especially if their baby sleeps in the same room with another sibling. A single parent will wonder what method they will emotionally and psychologically be able to handle consistently.

How Do I Pick the Right Method for Me and for My Baby?

The bottom line is, you need to focus on you and not just your baby and your family members. All sleep training methods allow you to modify your baby's behavior, so they learn to self-soothe themselves to sleep. If you will be the primary person to follow through on the sleep training process, you need to ensure that you can emotionally, mentally, and physically handle the sleep training method or you will struggle to remain consistent. You might stop trying to train your baby to self-soothe themselves to sleep after a couple of nights because you feel it is too hard. For example, if you know you cannot tolerate hearing your baby cry themselves to sleep, even when you go in their bedroom and help soothe them, the "cry it out" method might not be a suitable choice for you.

You need to choose a method that you are comfortable with because your baby will feel what you feel. If you feel uncomfortable about the method, they will more likely feel uncomfortable. This will cause them to struggle when it comes to learning the sleep training method and you will quickly deem it as a failure.

There are a lot of factors you will look at when you choose a method. Some methods you will read about and automatically know they are not the right fit for you and your baby. Other methods you will research deeply, and you might make a pros and cons list that helps you decide which method is the best. Your personality, age, baby's patterns, and personal beliefs will all come into your decision-making process.

The best advice that you can receive when it comes to picking a method is to follow your intuition. If a method doesn't feel right to you, don't use that method. There are a lot of great methods available to you and one will feel like the perfect fit for your family.

If you have a partner or are co-parenting, you do not want to leave them out of the decision-making process. Even if you are the primary parent and will do most of the sleep training, the system will only work if both parents are on board. If your partner does not agree with the method, they might not care to follow through and remain consistent, which will affect the baby more than anyone else.

Sleep Training Methods

Cry It Out Method

Contrary to popular belief, the cry it out method does not state that you need to let your baby cry in their crib until they fall asleep. The method states that you will set a period of time that you let your baby cry before you go in to comfort them. There are many different versions of this method and you will tweak it to create a strategy that works best for you, your baby, and anyone else involved.

Richard Ferber, a pediatrician, is credited with developing the main idea behind the cry it out method. While he never coined the phrase "cry it out" he supported parents allowing their babies a period to cry it out during sleep training because he felt you cannot avoid this part of sleep training.

The main theory behind the cry it out method is that if you continue to soothe your baby to sleep by rocking them or rubbing their back, you cannot teach them to fall asleep on their own. They will constantly want you to soothe them to sleep. It is important to note that crying is not the goal when it comes to this method. It is simply a part of the method. The goal is the same as any other sleep training strategy—to teach your baby to put themselves to sleep when they are supposed to and sleep throughout the night.

Jodi Mindell follows much of Ferber's "cry it out" method but is considered to be gentler. She focuses on giving her patients a variety of tips to follow to help their baby learn to self-soothe instead of parents focusing strictly on sleep training. She uses experiences from her job of treating sleep problems to help parents find the best technique within the cry it out method that works for them.

Michel Cohen is a pediatrician who supports the cry it out method. Cohen believes that you can start sleep training babies as young as eight weeks old by letting them cry for a period of time.

If you want to try one of the cry it out methods, you should follow these basic steps. Remember, you also need to pay attention to your baby's cues and how well you can handle the method. Follow your instincts for the best outcome.

1. Talk to your baby's pediatrician about when you should start sleep training your baby. They should be between

the age of four to six months, but it also depends on other factors, such as if they were premature.

2. Set a start date and make sure you have a plan. Know how long you will let your baby cry it out. For example, you might start with two minutes and slowly increase the length of time.

3. While your baby is drowsy but still awake, place them in their crib.

4. Tell your baby goodnight and leave the room. If your baby starts to cry, wait until your set time is up to walk back into the room.

5. Soothe your baby by patting or rubbing them on their back for about a minute or until they are calmer.

6. Walk back out of the room. If your baby starts crying again, wait until a little longer than the first time. For example, if you waited two minutes the first time, you can wait three minutes the next time.

7. Follow this routine until your child falls asleep.

8. If your child wakes up during the night, repeat the routine until they are asleep.

Along with a routine, there are many tips that you can use when trying a cry it out method.

- **Realize there will be a few tough nights.** It will take time for your baby to adjust to their new routine, which means you will need to sit through a few difficult nights of listening to your baby cry and going into their room several times to soothe them. Some parents state it took them close to three weeks while other parents say it was about a week.

- **Know that you will lose some sleep.** The first night will be the hardest and you want to make sure that you start on a night where you can lose a good amount of sleep. For example, if you work Monday through Friday, you will want to start on a Friday night as you will be able to get more sleep come Sunday night.

- **Relapses will happen.** Even when your child has started to self-soothe themselves to sleep, they will relapse occasionally. This is bound to happen when you take a family vacation, they are sleeping in a different house, or they are not feeling well.

If you are comfortable with the cry it out method and you are consistent, it will work well for you, your baby, and everyone else involved. However, if you are at your wit's end and there is no sign of the crying lightening up, you will want to look at a different method.

One parent who tried the cry it out method stated that after trying several methods, she finally decided to try the cry it out method when her daughter turned seven months old. While it took nearly four weeks, her baby continues to sleep well and she credits this method.

Another mother supports the cry it out method and it worked within the first night. Not only did her baby sleep all night after self-soothing themselves to sleep, but they slept about 12 hours the following night.

The main reason why people are against the cry it out method is that they feel it is more stressful for their baby—and themselves. While it is hard for parent(s) to hear their baby cry and not try to soothe them immediately, it is not more stressful for the baby unless you leave them to cry for too long. Babies will become overwhelmed when they are crying and are not cared for by a certain period of time. They can become so upset that they vomit, which is why you want to set a time by following your baby's personality and stick with that time. You can slowly start to increase your time as your baby starts to calm down and begins to soothe themselves.

No Tears Method

There are many reasons why people look at the no tears method. One reason is that parents know they cannot stand to hear their baby cry alone. Another reason is that they tried another method, such as the cry it out method, and it did not work for them.

Most parents who follow the no tears method use bedtime as a way to bond with their baby. This method allows them to develop a bedtime routine that is quiet and calm as these factors will help your baby drift into a peaceful sleep. When your baby falls asleep in this manner, they are less likely to wake up during the night. When they do wake up or if they have a difficult time falling asleep, you respond to them. You feed them if they give you the cry of hunger and comfort them if they are not content with their environment.

The no tears method seems to be the opposite of the cry it out method. Many people feel if you support the no tears method, then you do not support the cry it out method. While this is not completely true, most experts will agree with either the cry it out or the no tears method.

Experts who support the no tears method state that it is more soothing for the baby. They are less likely to feel overwhelmed and will start to trust that their parent(s) will take care of them when they cry out. The no-cry method will help make babies feel well-adjusted. Experts who support the cry it out method state that the no tears method will make babies become overly dependent on their parent(s). They will not learn how to independently put themselves to sleep.

There are a number of experts who discuss the no tears method.

- William Sears is a pediatrician who supports the no tears method and often discusses this method with his patients. To help them through their sleep training phase, William uses his personal experiences guide parents through sleep training. He doesn't believe in a "one size fits all" sleep method. Instead, he says to focus on your family maintaining closeness with your baby by following their cues in order to develop the best sleep training approach for the whole family.

- Parent educator Elizabeth Pantly tells parents that they need to help soothe their baby to sleep so they can learn to self-soothe. For example, you can rock your baby and sing them a quiet and soothing lullaby until they are sleepy. Once they get to this point, you then gently lay them down in their bed and leave the room or back away. When your baby starts to fuss or cry, you tend to them immediately and continue to soothe them to a state of drowsiness.

- Tracy Hogg, a nurse, follows most aspects of the no tears method but does not agree with certain forms of soothing, such as patting or rubbing your baby's back. She believes that babies can become dependent on this type of soothing and it won't help them learn to self-soothe. Instead, they will feel the need to have you rub their backs when they are unable to fall asleep. Hogg states that parents should pick their baby up when they are crying and then place them back down. You should repeat these steps until your baby stops crying or falls asleep.

One of the factors about the no tears method is you can use your own soothing techniques and not follow a specific set of steps. For example, you might disagree with Hogg that you should not rub your baby's back until they fall asleep. Instead, you pick them up, hold them until they calm down, and then lay them back down. Even if you repeat these steps 20 times within an hour, it is what you believe is right for everyone involved.

Even though you do not need to follow every step, there are several practical tips that can help you develop your no tears method.

- **Ensure all changes to your baby's routine are gradual.** No matter what part of your baby's routine you are focusing on changing, you need to make sure they are not too sudden. Your baby can tell when their routine is changing so if you change the routines quickly, they won't feel comfortable and can become fussy. For example, if you are changing their feeding time because you don't want your baby to fall asleep as you feed them, you should move the time by five minutes every few days. If you normally feed your baby about 7:00 p.m. and they fall asleep by 7:10, you might decide to start feeding them at 6:55 p.m. After a couple of days, you can change the time to 6:50 and then finally 6:45 p.m., a time that ensures that your baby will still be awake when you finish feeding.

- **If your baby is sleepy, put them to bed a little early.** Your baby will have days where they are more tired than normal, just like you. On these days, you will start to notice your baby showing the cues that they are ready for bed, such as rubbing their eyes and face. Even if it is 30 minutes before your baby usually goes to bed, it is perfectly fine to start their bedtime routine sooner. If you don't do this, your baby can quickly become overtired, which can make it harder for them to fall and stay asleep.

- **Develop keywords to use during bedtime.** Even though your baby cannot verbally communicate words with you, you can still communicate verbally with them. To ensure they understand what you are telling them, you want to use keywords, such as "ssshhh" or "mommy's here." Using keywords during their bedtime routine will let them know that it is time to go to bed. Furthermore, it will allow you to bond with your baby is a specific way and give them the comfort that you are there with them.

- **Ensure your baby is comfortable in their sleeping area.** You will start to notice your baby's personality when you are in the hospital. In fact, some people begin to feel parts of their personality when they are still in the womb. You want to follow your baby's personality when creating their sleeping area so it's as comfortable and calming as possible for them. For example, if your baby likes to fall asleep by watching colorful lights, make sure that you have lights that your baby can look at during the night. When they wake up in the middle of the night, they will notice the lights and this will help them soothe themselves back to sleep. If your baby likes a stuffed bear, place the bear up on a shelf where they can see the toy as this can help soothe them to sleep as well.

- **Don't jump up at every sound you hear coming from your child's bedroom.** It is normal for your baby to make a little whimper sound now and then. They might make this sound when they are in a half asleep and half awake state or even when they are still sleeping. If you hear a noise coming from your baby, wait a minute to see if they actually start crying and need you to come in to help them fall back asleep.

While no tears method works in time, it will not work for every baby. If this method is to work for your baby, you need to have patience as it will take a while for your baby to learn to self-soothe themselves to sleep. It is true that the cry it out method does not take as long. However, many people believe that no tears method is less traumatic for your baby in the long run, which makes this method work better for some.

Parents who have tried the no tears approach and stated that it worked, give the following tips:

- **Be patient.** You will have nights where you feel like you are picking up your baby 100 times and it seemingly will never end. You will also have nights when they go down a little easier. The number of times you pick up your baby might gradually decrease before they learn to self-soothe themselves to sleep. You can also notice the number of times you need to pick up your baby increases after it decreased for a few nights. No matter what happens, you need to remain consistent and not give up.

- **Co-sleeping works.** Some mothers talk about how their babies learned to fall asleep within a couple of nights because they co-slept with their baby. Once the mothers felt their baby squirming in the bed or heard them make a noise, they fed their babies and noticed them falling back asleep quickly. In fact, many mothers agreed that their babies didn't even fully wake up to eat.

- **Soothe your baby to sleep without taking them out of the crib.** Many parents discuss how they will rock their babies to sleep but won't pick them up once they lay down. Instead, they will rub their stomach, arm, or hum gently. They feel taking their baby out of the crib can wake them up more. It is easier for your baby to learn it is time to sleep when they remain in the bed.

Chapter 8: Good Nights Start With Good Days

Why Is It So Hard to Get on a Schedule?

From the moment your baby comes into this world, you will want to start focusing on a schedule. It will take a while for your newborn to adapt to their schedule, but they will soon find peace.

The Order of Events in Your Baby's Day

Your newborn will have a different order of events than an older baby. For instance, when it comes to newborns, they have three major events that happen throughout their day:

1. Feeding

2. Changing their diaper

3. Sleeping

When you are developing a schedule with your newborn, you want to try to follow this sequence of events around the same time every day. For instance, your newborn eats every three hours, so you will start the routine by scheduling their feeding time every third hour. After feeding time, you burp them and interact with them a bit before changing their diaper. At this point, it is time for them to sleep.

You have probably heard about the eat-sleep-play routine. While most people will tell you it works like a charm, it does not work for everyone. One reason this routine does not work for every baby is that babies are individuals. One routine will work for one child but not the next. Another reason the routine does not work, specifically for breastfed babies is because they work on a supply and demand basis with you. Furthermore, breastfeeding gives your baby a special bond with you that is more important than placing them in a certain routine. The bottom line is you need to find a routine that works for you and your baby.

Nap Training

Some experts will tell you that you need to follow your bedtime routine when it comes to naptime. Other experts will tell you that you need to create a new routine for naptime so your baby understands the difference between bedtime and naptime. Of course, you need to do what is best for you and your baby. If this means you sing them a lullaby as you do when they go to bed, by all means, sing!

When it comes to nap training, you want to wait until your baby is about three to four months old. Whether you start nap training and bedtime training at the same time is up to you. You can do one at a time, which is a great idea if your baby is struggling with sleep training, or you can start them both at the same time.

You also should know the amount of sleep your child needs for their age when you are thinking about nap training. You need to follow the daily guide for routines and do your best to make sure your child gets enough sleep throughout their day.

If you have a baby who does not care for naps, the best step to take is to create a quiet routine before naptime. You will want to do this with all babies, but it is more important for babies who fight you when it comes to their naptime. Creating a calming routine will help them become sleepy.

Effective Ways to Train Your Baby for Self-Soothing

Self-soothing allows your baby to put themselves to sleep through their own comforting techniques. They might look around at a light in their room, play with their hands, or simply lay there until they fall asleep with their eyes closed. Other forms of self-soothing involve rubbing their eyes, sucking on a blanket, toy, or pacifier, and holding their hands together like they are in prayer.

While there is no specific age when it comes to teaching your baby to soothe themselves to sleep, babies are generally not able to do this before three months of age. Usually, parents start to teach their babies to self-soothe when they start sleep training.

Around four months of age, the brain can handle the baby's emotions a bit better and they start developing their sleep pattern, which helps them become drowsy enough to use self-soothing techniques to get to sleep.

Parents like to teach their children how to soothe themselves because it holds many benefits:

- Your baby will sleep better for longer periods of time.

- As a mother, you can have a bit more time for yourself.

- Your baby will become more self-reliant.

- Your baby will grow up and can manage their tantrums a little better.

After reading these benefits, it is no wonder why you want to teach your child to soothe themselves to sleep. To do this, there are a few steps you need to follow.

1. If you need to change your mindset to let go of the guilt of not comforting your baby every time they fuss or cry, this is the first step you need to take. It might take time but know that you are helping your baby by teaching them how to self-soothe.

2. Make sure you set a routine for your child's 24-hours. You can use the daily guides that are placed in chapter 10 to help you establish a routine depending on your baby's age.

3. Set a time limit that will tell you when you can go into the room and comfort your baby. You can start with one minute and slowly increase the time as they learn to self-soothe.

4. Always place your baby in bed when they are drowsy, but not sleeping.

5. Do not feed your baby to sleep.

There are a number of tips you can use to help your baby self-soothe.

- Place a musical toy next to their bed. Once they are old enough they will learn to push the button or you can turn it on and leave it for the night.

- Create a night routine that involves relaxation.

- Make sure you are consistent with their bedtime and routine.

There are many dos and don'ts that you want to follow as you help teach your baby to self-soothe.

- Always have patience. It will take time for your baby to learn their self-soothing techniques.

- While this might be difficult, you need to make sure you don't allow them to always be dependent on you putting them to sleep. This means you cannot rock them to sleep.

- Do not feed your baby to sleep. You want to separate feeding and sleeping times.

While you will not start sleep training your newborn, it is important to keep them on a schedule as this will help them develop their self-soothing skills, which are needed when it comes to sleep training. Some babies will catch on to self-soothing techniques a little quicker than others. As long as you have patience and remain consistent, your baby will gradually learn to self-soothe.

One of the biggest problems when it comes to struggling to self-soothe is babies are used to nursing before bed. If this is the case, you want to gradually push back the time you nurse your baby. You might do this by feeding them 10 minutes earlier once a week until you have separated feeding and bedtime.

To recap, here are some guidelines that you need to remember when you are self-soothing:

1. You always need to work with your baby when they are learning a new skill. This means you will practice with them until they start to understand the concept and they can do it on their own.

2. Your baby can only learn to soothe themselves to sleep when you place them in the bed while they are still awake but tired.

3. Always have patience and realize you need to go at your baby's pace and not your pace.

Chapter 9: The (Not So) Dreaded Night Training

Parents usually dread sleep training for many reasons. They may have heard that it works, but they have also heard that it means you will get less sleep for a couple of nights and that you might not find the best sleep training method right away. In other words, you might start to use one of the cry it out methods only to start on a no tears method a week later. It is true that sleep training can be exhausting. But, it is also true that when you find a method that works, it is 100% worth every moment.

What Is Sleeping Through the Night?

Sleep matures over your baby's first year, but this does not mean you need to wait a year to start sleeping through the night. But, it *does* mean you need to understand what sleeping through the night for your baby truly means.

First, your baby will not sleep through the night without waking up for a minute or a bit more. Even after you successfully sleep training your baby, they will most likely self-soothe themselves back to sleep. While they wake up, they might not fully wake up, which will allow them to easily drift back into a peaceful sleep. However, it is still important to

261

remember that not all babies can self-soothe by six to eight months old. About 30 to 40% of babies still need help getting back to sleep when they wake up (What 'sleeping through the night' actually means, 2018).

Bedtime

When your baby is ready to sleep through the night, they will give you the following clues.

1. Your baby can put themselves back to sleep when they wake up. They might make a little whining noise or fuss for a bit, but they will self-soothe themselves within a few minutes.

2. Your baby will sleep for longer periods of time without waking up. This usually happens around the three to the four-month mark.

3. Your baby can lay in their crib for six to eight hours without needing to call you to help them get back to sleep.

The following general guidelines vary by age group when it comes to your baby's first year.

- **Birth to six weeks.** Your baby will have between six to eight regularly occurring sleep periods. Each period will last about two to four hours. This is a 24-hour cycle, which is why it is important to get your baby on a daily schedule. Until about four weeks old, your baby does not have a day and night pattern.

- **Six weeks to three months.** Your baby's sleep time per period will increase to about four to five hours. They will continue to briefly wake up one to three times while they are sleeping during the night. This is around the time they start to learn to self-soothe themselves.

- **Three to six months.** The length of time your baby will sleep during the night in one stretch continues to increase. They are now between five to six-hour stretches, can self-soothe themselves, but might still need help getting back to sleep from time to time. Your baby will still wake up between one to three times during their nightly stretches.

- **Six to 12 months.** Your baby is still sleeping for about 12 hours during the night, but it is split into two stretches. With the proper guidance, they will self-soothe themselves to sleep during their one to three awakenings per stretch of sleep. While your baby can put themselves to sleep, they will need you to help them now and then.

- **From 12 months.** Around 12 months you will start to see your baby truly sleep through the night. They will no longer need two stretches to sleep 12 hours, but only one. They might still wake up from time to time, but it won't be an every night situation and if they do, they can usually self-soothe themselves back to sleep.

Dream feeding

Dream feeding happens when you decide to gently feed your baby before you go to bed so they will sleep longer. You do not fully wake your baby up. Instead, you just get them to eat while they are kind of in the half asleep and half awake mode. The best time to dream feed your baby is between 10:00 p.m. and midnight.

Dream feeding is a lot easier than it sounds. Many parents worry about dream feeding because they do not want to wake their babies. By following these three easy steps, you can quickly dream feed your baby without bringing them into a fully awake state.

1. Between 10:00 p.m. and midnight, around the time you are going to bed, you want to gently wake your baby from their crib.

2. Set your baby's bottle or your breast on your baby's lower lip. They should start automatically feeding without waking up.

3. Nurse for about five to 10 minutes on each side. You might have to encourage your baby to continue eating if they stop sucking.

There is a possibility that your baby will be really tired and not want to eat much, but you should still try to encourage it as much as possible. You can also tickle their toes a bit to change their diaper if they are too tired to rouse from their sleep during this time.

Remember you will want to burp your baby before you lay them back down after they dream feed. If you do not do this, you can cause them to have gas pains, which will keep your baby and you up most of the night.

Depending on your baby's age, the best step to take to get them back to sleep is to swaddle them. If your baby doesn't like swaddling, then you can simply play some low white noise or lullabies that usually put them back to sleep. If you are sleep training, you should follow your method as you always need to be consistent.

There are many benefits to dream feeding your infant:

- The meal is at a convenient time for you as it allows you to get more sleep during the night.

- Because your baby ate before she went to bed, they will not wake up due to hunger earlier in the night. They might wait two to three hours, depending on their age and their feeding schedule.

- The dream feeding gives your baby more calories, which is one reason they will sleep better.

- You do not respond to your baby's cries by feeding them. When your baby cries and you feed them, they tend to wake up and cry more during the night to eat.

If your baby wakes up around 3:00 a.m. on a regular schedule to eat, set your alarm clock for 2:30 a.m. and do another dream feed. The point of dream feeding is to feed your baby before they wake up.

When you dream feed for a second time, you want to make sure you do not give your baby the same amount of milk. For example, if you are nursing, let them eat on one side. Giving them the same amount of milk as before can cause them to have tummy trouble.

There is no specific age to stop dream feeding your baby. You want to get them to the point where they will not wake up to eat, which means you and your baby are sleeping through the night.

What if my baby wakes up during the night?

There are many steps you can take when your baby wakes up during the night. The key to remember is that you want to remain consistent with your sleep training and do what works best for you and your baby.

Your baby can wake up for many reasons during the night, such as teething, dreaming, hunger, feeling unwell, or a variety of other disturbances. Depending on why your baby wakes up might depend on how you get them back to sleep. For example, if your baby is hungry, you will give them a bottle. If your baby is teething, you will need to use another method to ease their pain, such as giving them teething medicine or a teething ring.

Another solution you can use is calm music such as lullabies or white noise. This is helpful if you live in a city where outside noise can wake your baby up. While babies can sleep deeply, their sleep cycles are very short, meaning your baby will sleep deeply for 45 minutes out of the 90 minutes they are sleeping. It's easier for your baby to wake up during the 45 minutes when they are not in a deep sleep.

Some parents like to place their hand on their baby's chest to help them fall asleep. This gives your baby the added comfort that you are still with them even when their eyes are closed.

Every baby will go through a period of separation anxiety, which usually happens around the age of six months. Separation anxiety is another reason for nightly wakings. Even if you have already successfully sleep trained your baby, they can wake up and worry because they do not see you, making it harder for them to self-soothe. If your baby is struggling with separation anxiety, go into their room and talk to them gently. Let them know that you are there, but try to refrain from picking them up. Do your best to limit the time that you are soothing them so they don't become too dependent on you to get back to sleep.

A bedtime that is too early or too late is another cause of nightly wakings. It's easy to tell when your baby's bedtime is too early because they will wake up in the mood to play. It's important to not play with your baby when they wake up in the middle of the night as they will think it's time to get up. Instead, try to rock them or caress their cheek to ease them back to sleep.

If sleep training is inconsistent, your baby is more likely to wake up during the night. They need a routine that follows the same timings every day for their body to get used to sleeping through the night. If the routine is inconsistent, your baby will learn bad sleeping habits and they will continue to wake up during the night.

The best way to reduce night wakings is to develop a calm and consistent bedtime routine that works for you and your family. Make sure you have identified the strategies that work to help get your baby to sleep during the night, such as turning on white noise or closing the blinds.

When it comes to your baby, you also need to follow your instincts. You need to be comfortable with the strategies you use to get your baby back to sleep. If you're uncomfortable with a certain strategy, chances are they are too.

Where should your baby sleep?

Truthfully, no one can tell you where the best place for your baby to sleep is. You can decide to co-sleep or you can place them in their own room. While it is always best for your baby to be in their own crib and room when they are sleep training, this is not always possible. Sometimes you have space issues and do not have enough room in another bedroom for your baby, so they remain in yours until you can find a bigger place. Other times it is better to keep your baby in your bedroom for other reasons, especially if your baby tends to get sick often or your older children could disrupt the baby's sleep. You can decide to place a crib or bassinet into your room. This allows your baby to be next to you but gives them their own space. It is important to remember that just because your baby is in your room, does not mean they need to sleep in your bed.

You might also feel that co-sleeping with your baby in your bed is simply your parenting style. You do not want to place your baby in their own bed or even their own room until they tell you that they are ready, which might be around two years old.

If you do decide to co-sleep with your baby, you might look into products such as DockATot. This product helps separate your baby by placing them in a spot on your bed that will keep them from any dangers, such as falling into cracks between the bed and wall or heavy blankets getting on top of them.

However, you should be aware that DockATot is not approved for safe sleeping because your baby can suffocate if they get too close to the padding during the night.

If you want the safest option for co-sleeping, you want to look at attaching a little crib right next to your bed. This gives you easy reach when you need to dream feed or your baby wakes up. It also gives them the sensation of being in their own bed, yet they are still co-sleeping.

Even though co-sleeping is a favorite for most parents, at least for a certain period of time, there is nothing safer than letting your baby sleep in their own crib. Even if the crib is in your room, it allows you to control their sleeping space the best and can eliminate as many risks as possible.

To give you a run down, here are the pros and cons of cribs:

Pros	Cons
As long as you have a crib that is recently made, it will meet all the safe sleeping standards for babies.	When your baby cries, you need to get out of bed to take care of them.
You can sleep without worrying about covers and pillows covering	You need to get up to check on your baby

up your baby or them falling between any cracks.	throughout the night.
Your baby will learn to sleep independently starting at a young age.	Your baby can try to climb out of the crib when they are older, which can cause them to harm themselves.

No matter what you decide, the most important factor that should influence your decision is your baby's safety. Over 3,500 babies die every year due to sleep-related deaths, such as SIDS, suffocating, and strangulation (Should Baby Sleep in a Crib or Co-Sleep with Mom and Dad, 2019). These statistics are not here to scare you, but to make you aware that it can happen.

To help you make your baby's sleeping space the safest for them, here are a few tips from the American Academy of Pediatrics:

- Place your baby's crib into your room as this is known to reduce SIDS by 50%.

- Lay your baby on their back when they sleep.

- Do not place blankets, pillows, and stuffed animals around your baby's sleeping surface. Their sleeping area needs to be firm and clear of anything that can cover their face or strangle them.

- Do not drink or smoke when you are caring for your baby. Do not allow other people to smoke around your baby.

- Do not share a sleeping surface with your baby.

- You can use pacifiers.

Chapter 10: Baby First Year and Beyond

Your baby's first year is full of milestones. There is nothing like watching your newborn develop into a toddler. You will have many milestones throughout your baby's day, some of which you will not even be aware of. For example, you will never truly know how much your baby takes in and learns throughout their day. You will notice when they start to grab on to their bottle while feeding or when they start to roll over. You will notice when they sit up by themselves and start to crawl. You will hear their coos develop into words, but you will not hear their thoughts. You will not know everything they are taking in mentally. When they become older, you will not fully be aware of how much their brain works every day—which is harder than ours because their brain is still developing.

Not every moment of parenthood will be its greatest, but you can take every moment as you wish. In a perfect world, every day will be full of perfectly huggable moments. But, we do not live in a perfect world and you will need to take the stressful and chaotic moments along with the huggable moments. This is okay as it is a part of parenthood and one factor you need to prepare yourself for. After all, every moment is what you make of it. There are parents who take the chaotic moments and use them as learning experiences. There are parents who take every moment and do their best to remain calm and smile through it because they realize one day these moments will be gone as well. Your child grows quickly, trust me. Before you know it, they will be ready for their first day of school. You will enroll them in the youth group at your local church. They will start going out with friends during Halloween. And soon, you will have a senior on your hands, and you are preparing their high school graduation and sending them off to college.

But, for now, it is time to focus on their first year and learn to enjoy every moment as much as possible.

Keys to Start Your Schedule

When it comes to your baby, their needs are not too difficult to understand, which is one reason you will have people telling you that the first year is the easiest during your parenting journey. There will be moments throughout your child's life where you do wish they were a baby again—at least I have had these moments. However, when you are in your child's first year, especially if this is your first baby, it seems like some of the hardest moments of your life. No matter how you feel, it is important to note that your baby loves you and they are dependent on you. They trust that you will feed them, clothe them, love them, and take care of them. They need the basics at this point and even when you feel the most overwhelmed, you are the best person for your child and you are an excellent mother.

The biggest struggle for most parents is knowing what your baby needs and when and how to balance your baby's needs and the needs of your other family members. On top of this, you still need time with your friends, alone time, and to attend to your other needs. There are times that you will feel that this balance is nearly impossible, but you will do your best and make it through every moment.

One of the reasons parents start a routine with their baby is because it does make life easier, especially during the first year. This not only helps you when it comes to finding a balance within your life, but you will know what your baby needs because they will learn what comes next. For example, they will know it is time to burp after they eat and then you will change their diaper. If you take a few minutes longer to change their diaper, they will start to inform you that they are waiting, and it is time to change their diaper. Tanya Remer Altmann states that babies like to know what is going to happen next because it helps them feel more secure. She also states schedules help you because when your baby is "not sleep-deprived or hungry, it makes for a much happier baby. By meeting your baby's basic needs, you put her in the best frame of mind – and body – to learn about and explore her new world" (Montgomery, 2019).

Starting a schedule with your baby will also help you continue the routine as they grow. You will find yourself changing parts of the routine, such as changing bedtime and the number of naps they take.

Another benefit of starting a routine with your baby is it will give them an easier transition when they are left with a babysitter or caregiver. For example, they will feel more comfortable at daycare because they know this is part of their routine. They will also establish a routine at daycare and begin to learn when you will pick them up. Leaving your baby with a babysitter can be a scary time for them because they do not always know the person. However, by talking to your babysitting about their routine and making sure they are on the same page, the transition will go a little more smoothly. Your baby might still cry when you leave, but they will quickly turn their attention to the next task with their babysitter.

When should you start your baby on a schedule?

Experts are quick to weigh in on when you should start your baby on a schedule. As you read through everything the experts say, you might become overwhelmed and wonder what the right step to take is. Similar to starting your baby on sleep training, you need to do what feels right. If you are trying to follow a schedule, but it is making you feel a little uneasy your baby will start to notice this feeling and think that something is wrong. This will cause them to feel uneasy and become upset.

Pediatrician Harvey Karp states that everyone is a creature of habit, even babies. They are their happiest when they are on a routine because they know what is coming next. Their routine becomes their habit and they are comfortable.

It is important for you to note that your baby will have a natural pattern to their day. If you want to work with your baby on developing the best routine, then you want to observe their daily structure. You can track the times they seem most alert and ready to interact and play, when they want to eat, sleep, and even when they need a diaper change. For example, a friend of mine once told me, "I know when it is almost time to leave the house because I will need to change my baby's messy diaper." It is true, babies will have a pooping schedule just like they have a feeding schedule. I had someone tell me once that they started to set their alarm for 1:00 a.m. because they knew their baby needed a diaper change.

As a busy mama, you probably wonder what the best way to track your baby's schedule is, as using a notepad might not work for you. Fortunately, there are a lot of apps that you can download on your smartphone, iPad, or find online using your computer. Some of these apps are Bundle Baby, Trixie Tracker, and Feed Baby.

To help you establish a routine with your little one, there are three main routine groups for you to focus on:

1. **Baby-led schedules.** This type of schedule does not have a strict definition or a lot of guidelines because you basically follow your baby when it comes to setting their routine. You will track what they need and when and start to find patterns. From this, you can get ahead and know that in 15 minutes your baby will want to eat. You will know that about an hour after they burp, they will need a diaper change. While this might make your days feel a little unpredictable in the first couple of weeks, once you start to find patterns, you will develop a strong routine with your baby. However, this type of scheduling can be tricky because your baby might have a different routine depending on the day. For instance, they might need a diaper change anytime between 3:00 p.m. and 4:30 p.m. They might get hungry anytime between 11:30 a.m. and 1:00 p.m. These are factors that you will need to deal with the best you can. For instance, you have a varied time your baby will be hungry, so you can focus on setting a target time for feeding. You might track your baby's routine for a few weeks and decide they ate most of the time around 12:15 p.m. and establish this as your target time.

2. **Parent-led schedules.** This type of schedule is very strict as it is up to you to set times for everything. For example, you will not only set a naptime, but you will also set a certain amount of time for how long your

baby naps. You might follow your baby's patterns through observation, but once you put everything in place, your schedule is set and you remain consistent, down to the minute. You might set a timer that will tell you that it is time to get your baby up from their nap. Of course, there are some factors, such as diaper changes, that you cannot control. You also might let them sleep longer when they are sick or simply overtired. Gina Ford is an advocate for this type of schedule and commonly writes about it.

3. **Combination schedule.** I know many parents who tend to follow a combination of parent-led and baby-led schedules. While they set some of the timeframes and when their baby lays down for a nap, they do not follow it down to the minute. They are consistent, but also take it day by day. For example, if their baby is teething, they might allow them to sleep a little longer throughout the day as this lets their baby catch up on sleep—sometimes them as well. Sometimes parents will push back the nap because their baby is not tired enough to sleep yet. This doesn't mean that they will skip the nap or wait a half an hour. Chances are your baby will get tired enough within a few minutes and then they will be ready for their nap.

You should also note that it is fine to lay your baby down for a few minutes if they are overtired and seem to need a little cat nap. It is important to make sure your baby can make it to their bedtime, which is the purpose of a cat nap. Most cat naps are about 20 to 45 minutes long, so they are usually a shorter length of time than their regular naps.

No matter when you decide to start the routine, the best option for you is to trust your instincts and listen to your baby. You will soon understand what they are trying to tell you and be able to know when they are hungry and when they are tired.

Newborn Days

When you have a newborn you often wonder if you will ever get a full night's sleep again. The answer to this question is yes! You will get a full night's sleep. In fact, sooner than you think if you start sleep training your baby. However, with a newborn, there are a few months to wait before you start sleep training. This does not mean that you cannot get a start on the routine as every baby, from the time they are born, should have a daily schedule that is consistently followed.

Zero to Six Weeks Newborn: Sleep Schedule

The sleep schedule for your newborn is rather erratic and does not seem to have a set pattern. This is typical for newborns as they will mainly sleep throughout the 24-hour period. They can easily sleep 16 hours a day but will normally not go over that amount of time. Newborns will often be awake when they are eating, and you can find their eyes looking all around their environment as they are trying to take in everything they can.

Brittney Stefanic from Brittney Stefanic Sleep Consulting states that newborns are unable to stay awake for over 40 minutes. This means that your newborn is pretty much awake for their feeding, getting cleaned up, and changing. Once they get to the point where you are ready to change their outfit, they are pretty much ready for another nap.

A typical day for your sleepy newborn looks a bit like this:

- The day for your newborn should start between 6:00 to 6:30 a.m.

- Your newborn should sleep a total of 14 to 16 hours in a 24-hour period.

- Your newborn should take about three to four naps per day. Each nap is usually between 30 minutes to 3 hours in length.

- Your newborn will be awake between 45 minutes to two hours between each sleep.

- The longest amount of time they will sleep at once is between three to six hours.

- Your newborn's bedtime should be between 8:00 to 10:00 p.m.

Parents and experts agree that the biggest challenge when it comes to the 0-6 week mark is you feel that you are in a sleep and poop cycle. You will wonder if your baby will ever become a bit more active. Trust me, they will. Before you know it, your baby will start to coo and demand your attention when they want it. Brittney Stefanic states to help your baby during this time with the day and night confusion, "One of the best ways to clear up the day/night confusion...is to expose baby to natural light during the daytime and keep them in a dark room during the night to allow their circadian rhythm and hormone levels to start to adjust to life outside the womb" (Baby Sleep Simplified: Newborn Sleep Schedules + Patterns, n.d.)

Do not worry about having a structured sleep schedule at this age because your newborn still has their days and nights confused. The fact is, they need to sleep when they need it and they need to eat when they are hungry.

Two to Three Months: Baby Sleep Schedule

During this period, your baby's sleep pattern will start to become noticeable. You might notice that they tend to be up for half an hour between their sleep sessions during the night and then about an hour and a half during the day. You are also starting to notice your baby's signs that tell you they are sleepy.

Brittney Stefanic states the most important factor to remember when your baby is between their sleep sessions is a full feeding. They are typically only up for a little over an hour, which means you do not want to wait too long to feed your baby.

A typical day for your two to three-month-old will look like this:

- You should start the day around 6:00 to 6:30 a.m.

- The total hours of sleep your baby should get in a 24-hr period is 14 to 16 hours.

- Your baby should take three to four naps every day. Each nap should be about 30 minutes to three hours long.

- The time awake between sleep for your baby is about 45 minutes to two hours.

- The longest amount of time your baby will sleep in one stretch during the night is three to six hours.

- Your baby's bedtime should be between 8:00 to 10:00 p.m.

The biggest challenge you will face during this time is the

amount of sleep you have been running on. You are tired, in fact, you are exhausted. You are coming off of the six week stretch of feeding your baby every few hours and you are praying that they will start to sleep for a longer period of time soon. Fortunately, you are over the hump and your baby will start to sleep for longer stretches.

One reason your baby will start to sleep a bit longer, and continue to increase this amount of time, is because their stomach is growing. They will stay full for a longer time frame, allowing you a longer break between feedings.

Another reason is that your baby is getting in a routine, which means you should start to take notes. You want to note what makes your baby soothe themselves to sleep. For example, does your baby like to be swaddled or do they enjoy having a little white noise playing in the background? Note all the times they eat, when they sleep, and for how long. When does your baby want to be a little more active and playful? You should note anything you feel can help you set a daily routine for your little one.

Four to Six Months: Baby Sleep Schedule

Between four to six months is when your baby's sleep schedule will start to change. This happens because they are starting to sleep longer duration and because you will start sleep training. The schedule for your four to six-month-old baby should hold these factors:

- Your baby's day should start between 7:00 to 8:00 a.m.

- In a 24-hour period, your baby should sleep a total of 12 to 15 hours.

- Your baby should not take more than three naps, with each nap between one to three hours long.

- The time awake between their periods of sleep should be between 1 ½ to 2 ½ hours long.

- The longest amount of time they will sleep in one setting is between four to eight hours. This length of time will become longer once they are sleep trained.

- You should put your baby to bed between 8:30 to 9:30 p.m.

The number of naps your baby takes during this time will depend on your baby. You might deal with a baby that simply does not want to take naps or you might have one that enjoys their two naps during the day. If you have a baby who is a bit tougher when it comes to their naps, here are a few tips to help you:

- Set your baby in their sleeping space once they start to tell you that they are tired. Remember, you want them to be drowsy, but not asleep.

- Does your baby have time to calm themselves from any chaos of the day or playing? A calm baby will be able to fall asleep easier.

- Look around at your baby's environment. Is there anything that might be scaring them or making them stay awake because they are interested in the object. For example, many parents like to place lights in their baby's room that shows stars or animals. Sometimes the colors change with these objects and this can keep your baby interested in the pattern. Even though it repeats, they will fight sleep because this is their favorite show to watch.

The biggest challenge you will face with your baby is their transitions. These are hard on your precious bundle of joy because babies do not like change. It makes them worry about what will happen next and they do not feel as secure as they once did. While they know that everything will be okay because you are there, they still worry. The biggest key to working with your baby through their transitions is to be patient and understand that they are dealing with a big change in their life. Their transition might seem small to you, but to them, it is the most important factor happening in their life right now.

Feeding has come down a little bit by this stage. While they will eat about five to six times throughout the day, they might only need one nighttime feeding. Through your sleep training and dream feeding, you might be able to eliminate this nighttime feeding within a week or so.

Six to 10 Months: Baby Sleep Schedule

Your baby is unique. Your baby is different from all the other babies in the world and you need to hold this uniqueness with pride. Their personality is starting to show and with this comes the way they handle their sleep training and schedule. While your baby might have a bit of a different schedule, the basics are as follows:

- Your baby's day should begin at about 7:00 in the morning.

- Your baby should sleep about 11 to 15 hours in a 24-hour period.

- Your baby should have two or three naps, each at a length of one to three hours.

- Your baby should be awake two to three hours between each of their periods of sleep.

- The longest stretch of sleep your baby will have during the night is five to 10 hours.

- You should put your baby to bed between 8:30 to 9:30 p.m.

Unless you have already mastered the art of sleep training, your biggest challenge is getting your baby to sleep through the night. Because most parents start to sleep train at the beginning of this stage, it does not seem like a challenge for long. However, you need to remember that your little one will wake up a couple of times throughout the night and this is normal. They might self-soothe themselves to sleep or they might need you to come in and help them.

This is around the time you will start adding solid foods to your baby's diet. This can mess with their diaper changing schedule if they have one. It can also cause them to feel a little fussier from time to time as their body starts to adjust to the solid foods. Usually, the first step is adding rice to their formula. Another way people start introducing their baby to solid foods is baby food, such as Gerber. One nice factor about bringing in solid foods is your baby will start sleeping a little longer during the night, especially if you give them rice milk before they fall asleep. At the same time, they will still drink breast milk or formula about five times throughout the 24-

hour period.

10 to 12 Months: Baby Sleep Schedule

Starting about the 10-month mark is when you will start to notice your baby is following your sleep schedule a little more closely. They are awake more during the day, though still on at least one nap, if not two, and sleeping for a longer period at night. If you have sleep trained, your baby could easily be sleeping through the night with brief wake times where they are typically able to soothe themselves back to sleep. However, this is also the time of teething, which can definitely disrupt their sleep for your baby and you.

The biggest challenge you will have at this age is the possibility of setbacks. Your baby can fall into sleep regression and separation anxiety. For example, you leave your baby in their crib like normal. You have successfully sleep trained them, so you expect that they will fall asleep without a problem, especially because they are drowsy. You notice them watching you as you walk out of their bedroom, but you do not think much of this until you shut the door and they immediately start crying. This is not a soft whimper like they usually do or a little cry, it is almost their cry that they are scared and need you now. Of course, you head back in to calm your little one and notice that they quickly calm down. You lay them back down again, shut the door, and it repeats. If this happens, your baby might have hit the separation anxiety stage and they believe that once you leave their room and shut the door, you are gone. Because they can no longer see you, you are no longer there. Even if you are in the next room, they believe that you are gone.

This is a frustrating time for you, but it is normal for your baby. Whether you are experiencing separation anxiety or a sleep setback, Brittney Stefanic gives the following advice:

> "Responding with consistency and holding your baby to their personal best is a great way to overcome sleep setbacks as quickly as possible. It is important to minimize the confusion that our children experience by staying consistent in the messages we send them, in sleep and beyond!" (Baby Sleep Simplified: Newborn Sleep Schedules + Patterns, n.d.).

A typical day for this age looks as follows:

- Your baby's day should start between 6:00 to 7:30 a.m.

- In a 24-hour period, your baby will sleep a total of 11 to 14 hours.

- Your baby might be down to one longer two-hour nap after lunch, or they might take two one hour naps during the day. Either way, naps are normally between one to two hours in length.

- Your baby will start to stay away between 2 ½ to 3 ½ hours between their sleep sessions. They can stay up a little longer.

- Your baby's longest stretch of sleep at night should be between seven to 12 hours.

- Your baby's bedtime should be between 8:00 and 9:00 p.m.

When it comes to feeding, your baby should only bottle feed about three to four times every day. You will start to alternate between the bottle and solid foods. About 10 months old, you might start to notice your baby becoming hungrier. This is because your baby is also become a bit more active, such as crawling around wherever they can go or even starting to pull themselves up on furniture and walk along with the furniture. You might also help them walk around your home or set them in a walk so they can carry on as they wish. Their increase in activity means they will need more calories. Follow your baby's need to eat and feed them when they are hungry. They will help you develop a new feeding schedule.

12 to 18 Months: Schedule and Transitions

Between the ages of 12 to 18 months, your baby will amaze you with everything they are picking up. They are starting to talk, walk, and reaching so many other milestones that it is hard to keep up with them. Sometimes you will take this rather literally as while they have little legs, they can definitely run once they have learned.

This is another major transition time for your baby because they continue to grow and learn so much. However, this also means that they can struggle when it comes to sleep. To make sure your growing baby turning toddler is transitioning well, you want to make sure that they are continuing to get the sleep they need. This might mean that you will change their sleeping routine a bit. For instance, because they are attached to you and still struggling with separation anxiety, they will want to hold your hand or have you lay with them until they fall asleep. While this is sometimes a challenge for you as you have work you want to get done after they go to bed or want to take your time to be alone and relax (this is more important than housework), you need to tend to your child. Fortunately, you will help your baby through their sleep regressions and transitions the best way you can simply by being there for them.

If your baby did not go through a sleep regression between 10 and 12 months, they will most likely hit one at this stage. This is also the stage where they will change from two naps, if they are still on two naps, to one nap.

12 to 18 months of sleep schedule

Your baby's sleep schedule will depend on whether they have one or two naps during the day. Before we break down the schedule depending on the number of naps, let's take a look at the basics of the sleep schedule.

- The average time your baby will be awake in between their sleep sessions is four to six hours.

- The total number of hours they will nap during the day is two to three. It does not matter if your baby takes one nap or two, you want to make sure they sleep a total of two to three hours.

- They should sleep a total of 11 to 14 hours a day. The amount of sleep your baby will need will depend on them. You might also note that they sleep closer to 14 hours in a 24 hour period when they are 12 and 13 months, but when they start to reach 14 to 15 months, they start decreasing how much they sleep and do not need a second nap.

If your baby takes one nap during the day, their daily schedule will look similar to this:

- Your baby should start their day at about 7 to 7:30 a.m. They should stay awake for about 4 ½ to 5 hours.

- Your baby should go down for a nap at about 12:00 p.m. They should nap for about two to three hours.

- Make sure to get your baby up about 2:00 p.m. or a little later. You might go by how tired they were, how well or poorly they slept the night before, or what their typical nap schedule is. They should stay awake for about five hours.

- You should put your baby to bed between 7:30 to 8:00 p.m. This will allow them to sleep about 11 or so hours, whether they wake up or not.

Following this schedule, even if your times are a little different, will allow your baby to get the amount of sleep they need. For example, if you need to get your baby up for daycare at 6:30 a.m., you will want to put them to bed between 6:30 and 7:00 p.m.

If your baby takes two naps during the day, their daily schedule will look similar to this:

- You should wake your baby up about 6:00 a.m., providing they are not already up and ready to eat and play. They should be up for about three hours.

- Your baby should lay down for their first nap at about 9:00 a.m. They should sleep for around 45 minutes.

- You should wake your baby up by 9:45 a.m. and allow them to be up for 3 to 3 ½ hours.

- Your baby should lay down for their second nap at 1:00 p.m. They should sleep for about one hour and 45 minutes.

- Make sure your baby is up by 3:45 p.m. and allow them to be up for 4 to 4 ½ hours.

- Your baby should go to bed around 8:00 p.m. They should sleep about 10 hours or more with or without waking up during the night.

This schedule will give your baby a total sleep time of 11 to 14 hours during a 24 hour period.

12 to 18 months of feeding schedule

The feeding schedule for your 12 to 18 months old baby will also change. For instance, you might decrease or stop breastfeeding altogether because they are getting the nutrients they need from other foods. Therefore, your nutrients are not necessary anymore. You can follow the breastfeeding schedule of what is best for your family or you can choose to continue breastfeeding to provide your baby with more nutrients and bonding time. While there is debate on how long you should breastfeed your baby, there are mothers who breastfeed until their children are two or three and some who will stop a few months after their baby is born. Sometimes your baby will tell you when they are ready to be done with breast milk.

Around one year old is when your baby will start switching to cow's milk, providing you drink this type of milk. When you make the switch, it is best to discuss it with your baby's pediatrician as some babies will not drink straight cow's milk as they are not used to it (other babies will love it and not get enough!) To help ease your baby into drinking cow's milk, you want to purchase whole milk and mix it in with your baby's formula. You can start by mixing a bottle of ¾ formula and ¼ whole milk. Once your baby enjoys that, go half and half and then add more whole milk than formula. Soon, your baby will be strictly on whole milk. If you do not drink cow's milk because you follow a vegan diet, talk to your baby's doctor to see what the best substitute is for them.

18 Months to 3 Years: Schedule and Transitions

Though you will always consider your baby a baby, they are technically now a toddler and seem to be getting into *everything.* Their curiosity is more than you can handle from time to time, but they are still the most adorable child you have ever seen in your life and watching them grow is one of life's greatest treasures. One of my favorite parts about this age is you can start to notice when they are observing and learning. You will catch on to their facial expressions as they stop to smell the flowers. They are a little slow to walk and move around at this age, for the most part anyway, because their minds are constantly going as they are taking everything that is new to them. Always remember, even when you are in a rush, to allow your child to stop and learn. While we have seen a bee inside a flower several times, this is the first time for them and it is an exciting moment.

Your child's schedule will continue to change as they grow. You will also learn that you will change their bedtime routine up a little as they become more interactive. For example, one of my friends sang a lullaby to her baby until about the age of two. During this time, their toddler began to ask them to read a story. Therefore, my friend decided to read instead of sing and she continues to read to her toddler every night.

From the age of 18 months until three years old, the amount of sleep your toddler needs will change. A one-year-old, which includes an 18-month-old, needs 11 to 14 hours of sleep. A two-year-old needs 12 to 12 ½ hours every 24-hours. A three-year-old might still sleep about the same amount of time, but they will also start to drop their nap. However, some toddlers will continue to nap, at least for an hour every day, until the age of four.

Unless your toddler has a medical problem, wakes up from a dream, is sick, or starts teething again (they do start getting their molars between 18 months and 2 years old), they should sleep well throughout the night. Part of this is your sleep training while another part is because of their age.

Just because your toddler is most likely to sleep through the night does not mean they will not ever wake up during the night. Other than the reasons above, there are several reasons your toddler might find themselves awake. For example, you might have a new addition to the family and the baby wakes up your toddler. While you try to stop this, it is bound to happen and it is best you accept it and help your toddler understand the difference between a baby and themselves. If your toddler gets out of bed and wants to help you with the baby, you can allow this. Giving them a job to do is more likely to calm their minds and prepare them to fall back asleep quickly when they lay down. Your toddler might also wake up because it happens. It happens to adults and it will happen to toddlers too.

Because every toddler is different, it is hard to give you one schedule that your toddler should follow. Therefore, there are three different schedules below. You want to use one of these schedules as a guideline for your toddler. For example, you might put your toddler to bed half an hour earlier because they need to get up earlier. If this happens, it means that your time will always be a half of an hour ahead.

Toddler schedule number one: two naps

Your 18-month-old can easily be on the two nap schedule. By the time your child turns two, they should go down to one nap during the day. Until this point, here is a guideline for their sleep and feeding schedule.

- You will want to wake your child up by 7:00 a.m.

- Feed your child right away as they will be hungry from a full night's sleep. Breakfast should be no later than 7:30 a.m.

- Your toddler is growing, and they will get hungry making 9:30 a.m. a great time to give your child a light snack. You do not need to give them a snack if they are not hungry. For instance, if they are not in a growth spurt, they might not care for a snack. Yet, they might want a snack every day because they feel it is part of their routine.

- Lay your child down for their morning nap at 10:00 a.m. They should sleep for no more than one hour.

- Feed your child lunch between 11:30 a.m. and 12:00 p.m.

- Lay your toddler down for their afternoon nap at 2:00 p.m. Again, they should not sleep longer than one hour.

- Around 3:30 p.m. is a great time to give your little one an afternoon snack as they will be hungry by this time.

- You should feed your child supper around 5:30 p.m. This will allow them to have a little quiet playtime before the bedtime routine begins.

- Start your toddler's bedtime routine around 6:30 p.m.

- Your toddler should go to bed at about 7:00 p.m.

Toddler schedule number two: one nap

This schedule is similar to the first schedule, but it only has one nap during the day.

- Your toddler should get up by 7:00 a.m.

- You want to feed your toddler breakfast by 7:30 a.m.

- If your toddler needs a light snack, a great time to feed them is 9:00 a.m.

- Your baby should eat lunch at 11:00 a.m.

- Lay your little one down or a nap by 12:00 p.m. They should sleep for at least one hour. Because they only have one nap during the day, they might sleep closer to two hours, but should not go beyond that as it will be harder for them to fall asleep at night.

- Feed your toddler an afternoon snack about 3:30 p.m.

- Have dinner ready for your child at 5:30 p.m.

- Let your toddler quietly play until you begin their bedtime routine at 6:30 p.m.

- Shut off the lights and make sure your toddler knows it is time to go to bed at 7:00 p.m.

Toddler schedule number three: no nap

Your toddler will eventually stop taking naps altogether. This might come on gradually when you begin to notice that it is harder for your little one to fall asleep at night or because your child's pediatrician believes it is time to cut out naps completely so your child sleeps better at night. It is always best to follow your child's direction when it comes to taking away their nap. If you take it away too soon, your baby won't get the amount of sleep they need in a 24-hour period and this can cause them to become irritable, moody, and lead to other consequences.

- Wake up time for your toddler should be at 7:00 a.m.

- Similar to the other schedules, you want to feed your little one by 7:30 a.m.

- The best time to feed your child a light snack, if they are hungry, is at 9:30 a.m.

- Have lunchtime with your child at 12:00 p.m.

- Instead of giving them a nap at 1:00 p.m. you should instead have quiet or rest time. This is not a time for them to fall asleep, though they might from time to time. It allows them to transition better from a nap to no naps. It can also give you a much-needed break after a busy morning. This time should not last longer than an hour.

- The best time for an afternoon snack is 3:30 p.m.

- Sit down to have dinner with your little one at 5:30 p.m.

- You should start their bedtime routine at 6:30 p.m.

- Make sure your toddler knows that it is time for them to go to bed at 7:00 p.m.

Chapter 11: The Secret Sauce and Fine Tuning

So, what is the secret sauce when it comes to sleep training your baby? From one mom to another who has used her experience and research to help you, it is consistency. There is no escaping this fact. The more consistent you are with your methods, no matter what method you choose, the easier your baby will catch on to sleep training, self-soothing, and before you know it everyone will sleep well throughout the night.

Along with consistency, there are other ingredients that go into the secret sauce:

- You can wake a sleeping baby. It is okay to do this, especially when they are sleeping too long during their naptime. You want them to stay on their schedule.

- Set a bedtime that will allow your baby to get enough sleep during the night. This means you need to consider the time you need to wake them up if you have to bring them to daycare.

- Establish a naptime routine that is different from a bedtime routine, so your baby learns it is time to nap and not bedtime.

- Be comfortable with your sleep training method and follow your instincts. Let your baby guide you if this is what you prefer.

"But I Have Tried Everything!" (Training Tools for the Exhausted Parent)

I have been there and I know many other parents who have felt the same way—you have tried everything and absolutely nothing has worked.

I understand exactly what you are saying. Take a deep breath and know that I am here to help.

You have tried several methods and your child is still waking up. You are consistent, patient, and still, nothing works. What else can you do?

- **Bedtime fading** means you will move your child's bedtime to a later time. For example, you notice that your baby cries for about an hour before they fall asleep. Therefore, you decide to push bedtime back 45 minutes. If this still does not work, you push it back another 15 minutes to make up for that whole hour. When your child starts to fall asleep within 10 to 15 minutes, you can start moving the bedtime up to an early time by 10 to 15 minutes.

- **Avoid the late sleep.** Babies can be a bit sneaky and try to get in a nap later in the day when you think they are playing quietly in the corner. If you notice your baby falling asleep, try to keep them up to their bedtime. If this is impossible, you can try to let them sleep for a few minutes, like a cat nap, but not much longer.

- **Camp out in your child's room.** When you camp out, you remain in your child's room until they fall asleep, but you slowly move closer to their doorway. You might move a little closer every night or decide to move closer as they are falling asleep. You need to watch them because if they start to get fussy, you want to move closer to them.

- **Bedtime chart.** If your child is older, it might work to have a bedtime chart where they can see their progress. Children love to play with stickers and allowing them to put a sticker on their chart in the morning can become a helpful tool.

10 Steps to Sleep Training Success

1. **Sleep is a priority.** Sleep training is a lifestyle, and this means that sleep becomes a priority. Always remember that your baby needs their sleep because

their brain needs it. Without enough sleep, they will struggle to pay attention to what they need to learn.

2. **Get everyone on board.** Make an appointment with your baby's doctor, talk to anyone who cares for your baby and make sure that everyone understands the sleep training plan.

3. **Know the amount of sleep your baby needs.** You always want to watch your baby's age to make sure they are getting the right amount of sleep.

4. **Keep a journal.** You will not remember all the times your baby woke up, fell asleep, or when they ate, etc. So to help you track their progress and note any patterns, you want to keep a journal. You can also use this to describe how well your baby handled sleep training.

5. **Ensure you have a routine.** You should create your routine before you start sleep training so you have everything in place for your start date.

6. **Have a start date.** Don't get up one morning and tell yourself that you will start sleep training your baby. The more planning you put into sleep training, the more successful it will be. This includes having a start date as this will allow you to prepare your baby's sleeping space, allow them to get used to anything you changed, and prepare yourself.

7. **Make sure you have the right environment for your baby.** You want to set the scene with a calming environment. This might include getting a white noise machine or a few gentle music playlists.

8. **Put your baby down when they are awake.** You should place your baby in bed when they are still awake, yet sleepy. This will help them focus on their self-soothing techniques.

9. **Sit in a chair but move it away.** One method to follow when your baby is first learning the bedtime routine and training is to place a chair next to their crib. Sit there for a bit and then move the chair back a bit. Repeat this process until they are sleeping or you are at their doorway.

10. **Do not continue to use crutches.** Crutches are the soothing techniques that you use to put your baby to sleep. While you might still use them when your baby is sick or when they wake up and are inconsolable, you do not want to use them every night. This will make your baby dependent on your soothing techniques and they will not learn to self-soothe.

Two main things you need to remember are that sleep training is a lifestyle and do not quit. I know you are stressed, and you feel that you have tried everything and *nothing* is working, but I will tell you something else—*you got this*. This is often easier to say than believe, but you will one day look back at your sleep training and realize all of the stress and realize that it is all worth it. You will be grateful that you did not quit, and you continued to work toward your goal.

The Reasons for Sleep Regression

There are times you thought you would never get a full night's sleep, but it finally happened. Your baby is successfully sleep trained. They are sleeping through the night, mostly self-soothing when they wake up and taking naps. They are happy and energetic. In fact, you believe they are more energetic now than they were before. However, so are you.

But then it happens. It is like your baby takes several steps back when it comes to sleeping. Your baby might be protesting their naps, or they might decide to wake up five times during the night and demand that you come and soothe them back to sleep. It is real. No matter what other people tell you, sleep regression is real.

First, you need to understand what the term means. Regression means that you go back to a previous state, such as your baby waking up five times throughout the night. When it comes to your baby and seemingly forgetting about self-soothing or their sleep training, it can be a blow to your system. But there is one factor that you need to keep in mind to understand why your child went into sleep regression mode—they are constantly growing, developing, and reaching milestones. This can have an effect on them that causes them to need you to soothe them for a period of time. They have not forgotten how to soothe themselves back to sleep, they simply need you during this time.

So what can you do to help your baby and yourself through sleep regression?

- Forget about the term regression.

- Start to call it "sleep transition" as this is what your baby is doing. They are transitioning to a new developmental stage.

- Realize this is normal. Every baby goes through sleep transitioning.

- Remember, this will pass. It is hard to remember this when you are on the sixth night of waking up four times with your baby at 10 months of age, but it is true. It will pass.

- Take a breather. If you need to ask someone to help you out, let them know. Just like when your baby was smaller, you can still reach out for help as you need to take care of yourself as well.

- Never forget—everything will fall into place for both you and your precious little one.

So now that we have talked a bit about sleep regression or transitioning, it is time to look at the causes.

1. **Physical developments.** It does not matter if your baby is learning or learned to sit, crawl, stand, or walk, they can all cause sleep regression. While there is little research done on it, some researchers believe the amount of time your baby is in sleep regression depends on when they learned the skill and if they learned early or later.

2. **Illness.** Your child getting sick, whether it is with a common cold or something more serious, has a lot to do with sleep regression. In reality, they simply need you to comfort them during this time.

3. **Traveling.** Babies are not like newborns. While newborns can sleep anywhere, babies struggle to sleep in a new place. If you are traveling, expect your baby to go into sleep regression mode.

4. **They are overtired.** It happens from time to time, your baby becomes overtired because of a long day or they simply haven't slept well lately.

5. **Stress or change within the family.** Most people think that their baby won't realize that there is a change within the family or when you are feeling stressed, but they can. They know when something is not the same

and this causes them to feel insecure about their environment, bringing on a sleep regression episode.

6. **Switching to a big kid bed.** Your toddler will have trouble when it comes to making the transition between the crib to a new bed and this can cause them to struggle with sleep.

7. **Old habits are coming back.** It happens to the best of us. We are on a roll of developing new habits and soon, we find ourselves struggling and we start to bring back our old habits. The fact is, we usually do not realize that this is happening. Old habits can cause your baby to go into sleep regression mode.

Stages of sleep regression

Sleep regression can happen more than once and for many reasons. To help you better prepare for sleep regression episodes, here are the stages you need to keep in mind.

- **Four months.** At this stage, your baby might or might not be sleep trained. Whether they are or not, they will know self-soothing techniques and not often wake you up during the night because they woke up, until they start to go through their sleep regression. This comes on because they are going through so many developmental changes. Their sleeping patterns are changing, and they are more hungry because of a growth spurt.

- **Six months.** While nearly every baby will go through a four-month sleep regression, some will not go through a six-month regression. If your baby does, it is because they are learning how to crawl, stand next to furniture, or focusing on other physical developments.

- **Eight months.** In reality, this sleep regression can happen between eight to ten months, but most state it happens at about eight months. If your baby didn't crawl at six months, this could be the reason for their eighth-month regression. Other reasons are because they are learning more mentally than you realize. There is a lot going on within the mind of your child and this can make it hard for them to calm down and sleep. Furthermore, separation anxiety starts around this age, which can also cause sleep regression.

- **One year.** At around one year of age, your baby will go through another sleep regression as they are learning how to walk. They might also start to nap less, which can also affect their regression.

- **18 months.** Your baby might not go through this stage, but if they do it is because of all their developmental changes. They are learning more skills, starting to talk, and their mind is becoming even more active. Furthermore, they are becoming more active physically, which can make them overtired.

While you may not completely stop all the sleep regression stages, there are a few tips that you can follow to help your baby and yourself through a sleep regression.

1. Continue to keep their sleep schedule. Yes, you might need to go in and soothe them more, but you want to continue to remain consistent when it comes to their daily schedule. The only time you will change their schedule is when they are dropping a nap.

2. Be patient and give your baby the comfort they need. Sleep regression is temporary, and they will work through it and continue on their sleep schedule in time.

3. Do not fall back into old habits. Do not allow your child to stay up later because they are highly active as this is also a sign of overstimulation. When this happens, it will be harder for your baby to fall asleep.

4. If you feel that you are at the end of your rope and you are in need of help, ask for help. You can use the same people who helped you when your baby was little or find different friends and family members. You might even contact a sleep consultant. Of course, you can always find support through social media groups on Facebook.

Conclusion

I understand where you are now. You feel like you have tried everything, and you still cannot get your baby to sleep through the night. You are exhausted and you do not know where to turn. As a mother, I have the experience that can guide you in finding the best sleep training method for your baby, you, and your whole family. It does not matter if you are living with your partner or are a single parent, you have the skills and tools within this book to help your baby self-soothe themselves to sleep through your chosen sleep training method.

Throughout this book, we discussed several topics that pertain to sleep training. You know what sleep training is and you can prepare yourself for establishing a sleep training plan that will work for you and your baby. You know sleep training is a lifestyle and while it is hard, your baby will adjust as long as you are consistent and patient.

You now understand the harmful effects that sleep deprivation can have on your little one. It can affect them psychologically, emotionally, and physically. Sleep deprivation causes you to lose focus and patience. It can also lead to fatal consequences.

The contents of this book discussed how to sleep train with multiples, which inevitably brings a little more difficulty in the situation. But sleep training is still 100% doable with your twins as long as you continue to follow the golden rule of consistency along with the many other steps associated with sleep training.

You now know the seven types of cries and that there are many reasons why your child might be crying. There might be a reason that your child doesn't even understand or they simply just need a good cry. You know that while it seems daunting at first, you will learn your child's cries and communicate effectively with them.

You know that there is no reason to feel guilty or fear to try a sleep training technique. It is actually a helpful tool to help your child develop skills that they can continue to use throughout their life, such as self-discipline and soothing themselves.

There are no big secrets as to why sleep training fails. You know what to look out for and what you should avoid so you do not make some of the same mistakes parents before you have made.

You received information about two main methods when it comes to sleep training: the cry it out method and the no tears method. You should choose the method that best suits you and your baby. You need to be comfortable with the method as this will make your baby more comfortable as they learn the method.

There needs to be a difference between your child's naptime

and their bedtime routine. You also want to make sure that you do not combine their feeding time with bedtime. All of these pieces of their day should remain separate as it will allow them to keep their schedules more easily.

You learned about the secret sauce that you need to make sure that your sleep training is successful. As long as you carry this secret sauce with you through the sleep training journey, your baby will get the sleep they need to begin to thrive even more throughout their day.

There is a lot of information that I want you to remember through this book, but the most important factor is that you need to know that you can do this. You are not alone and even though you feel like you have tried everything, you will become successful in your sleep training efforts. You are an amazing person and all of the tension you feel from a lack of sleep will pass. Believe in yourself because I believe in you. When you need to take a step back, do this. When you need to ask for help, do this. When you need to let out a good cry because you are so overwhelmed, this is okay too. But know that at the end of your day, you are doing your best and you should be proud.

Part 3: Baby's First-Year Milestones

How to Take Care of Your Baby Effectively, Track their Monthly Progress and Ensure their Physical, Mental and Brain Development are on the Right Track

Introduction

Expecting a newborn is simultaneously one of the most exciting, yet most terrifying, moments of life as parents. Get ready! Your life is about to change in all the best ways. After the pregnancy is over and the delivery has happened, you are then catapulted into the role of being a parent to this being that is brand new to the world. From here, you need to teach this baby everything that they need in order to become a successful adult. A lot of expecting parents feel that they do not have enough information in order to feel confident in their abilities as parents – this is a problem. With all that you can discover through reading this guide, you will be more prepared than ever when it comes to welcoming your newborn into your life. Instead of questioning your ability to raise a baby, you will be excited and happy to teach your little one everything there is to know about the world.

After the delivery, it will feel as time is going to speed up. After being pregnant for so many months, holding your baby in your arms for the first time is a surreal experience. You might have to turn to your partner in disbelief at the fact that you two were responsible for the joy that is now your newborn. Your baby will be measured and cleaned, and any additional testing or aftercare will be performed. A short stay in the hospital will likely occur, and then you are sent home to begin life as parents. Not only do you have to get used to being a caretaker, but your baby is also getting used to a new environment. After spending so many months inside the womb, you can imagine how foreign everything looks and feels to the baby as they are brought into their home for the first time.

You will go through many sleepless nights, listen to crying that can't seem to be soothed by any solution that you can think of, and panic at the thought that you are doing something wrong. These are all normal aspects of parenthood, and you shouldn't feel ashamed or guilty if you go through any of these things. Though you won't always have all of the answers, you will figure out the solutions as you go. Guides like this one exist so that you can take the guesswork out of parenting. Instead of feeling clueless and helpless, you will be able to use your knowledge as power in order to take care of your new baby. The information that you receive will act as the foundation for how you wish to shape your child.

A lot of what you hear about doing the "right" thing for your baby is going to come from other people in your life or what society views as the "norm." While these opinions and the advice given to you might be helpful, it can also be hindering and confusing. Instead of letting other people tell you how to take care of your child, you can inform yourself in order to make the best decisions possible on your own terms. This is a confidence boost in itself! You will be able to navigate parenting with ease, and not to mention, you will also have fun while doing so. At the end of the day, parenting should be taken in a lighthearted manner. Enjoy all of the milestones and learn from the mistakes that are made – no one is a perfect parent, but an involved parent will raise a wonderful child.

You cannot redo the first year of your baby's life. This is the groundwork that you are responsible for putting down in order for your baby to grow up to be a thriving and independent child. It is a lot of pressure to think about the bigger picture, but don't let this scare you. With the knowledge that you have already, plus the knowledge that you will gain from reading this book, you will be able to approach parenting with ease by being able to have faith in yourself. You should *know* that your decisions are the right decisions.

Practical Solutions

This guide is meant to teach you everything that you really need to know about being a great parent. There are no gimmicks or promises with no proof to back them up; all you will find here are real tips and methods that are meant to make your life easier and your baby happier and healthier. As you learn this useful information, you will be taught exactly how to take care of your child as soon as the delivery takes place. This is a time when most parents are filled with a rush of adrenaline. Everyone is going to want to meet your new baby, and it will be a joy to show them off. You will be filled with happiness because of all the excitement. Once this socialization period has ended and you are left alone to care for your baby for the very first time, this can admittedly be a scary time for a lot of people. Thus begins the feeling of wondering, "What do I do now?"

A lot of parents agree that the nurse placing your baby in your arms for the first time is both overwhelmingly emotional and utterly terrifying. Many mothers, at this moment, realize that they are now responsible for the life that they are holding. While your baby grew and developed inside of your stomach for all of those months, you had little control over what happened. While you took care of yourself and ate a proper diet, your baby did the rest. Now, the tables have turned. It is your chance to lead your baby toward the best developmental decisions. You can show your baby what to do and how to behave in this world.

As your baby grows, you will be guided through what you must know in order to effortlessly get them through their first year of life. From what vaccines and vitamins are essential to whether or not you should opt for diagnostic testing, these topics will be discussed in detail for you to make your own decisions. By taking this initiative, you are already being a great parent. You will also learn about the essentials, such as how to buy the right diapers, clothing, equipment, and more. It makes sense to start from the beginning because your baby will also be starting from the very beginning. You will be learning together, every step of the way.

One of the best things that you will learn by reading this guide is how to differentiate truths from myths during your baby's first year. There is a lot of information circulating around that pertains to what a child *should* be able to do at certain points in life. By actually realizing that each child is going to develop differently and that it is normal, it will help to put you at ease as you compare your baby's progress to that of the average child. A unique path of development means that milestones are going to be reached when the time is right. Know that your baby is born with certain instincts, so they also know what they are doing.

Learning what is true and important will keep you on track and, in turn, make you a better parent. Instead of getting stuck on the what-ifs, you will be able to recognize that childhood can be unpredictable. All you can do is your best, and that is how to be the best for your child. Remember that you and your partner are responsible for making the decisions. No matter what you read or what you hear, you both know your baby best. Starting from day one, you will learn about all of their habits and quirks. It will likely be impossible to put the camera down as you attempt to capture each of these nuances.

There is no such thing as a guide that contains all of the answers, this one included. Parenting has a lot to do with discovery, and this is something that you will need to do on your own. After reading this guide, you will have the essential tools that you can use to guide you in the right direction. You need to show your baby that you know what you are doing, even though you might be thinking that you actually don't — fake it till you make it! With these solutions, you will be less likely to make as many mistakes. Though mistakes are an important learning experience, you don't need to make hundreds of them in order to be considered an experienced parent.

My Story

I am Harley Carr, a proud mother of three. I have been a parent for 8 years now, starting with the birth of my son. He changed my entire life, an unexpected blessing at a time that I didn't exactly have a plan. Years later, I had more children. Though they were in my plan this time, they each made me a better mother in their own ways. My 5-year old and 3-year old do their best to keep me in check, teaching me new things every single day. Having many children can be difficult, especially with these age gaps, but being their mother is something that I truly enjoy. I can say, without a doubt, that being their mother is my greatest accomplishment in life thus far. My journey has not been all sunshine and rainbows. As a mother, I faced quite a few difficulties.

During the first year of each child's life, so many decisions needed to be made. Nobody warns you of exactly how many decisions you will have to make during this year. Will you bottle feed or breastfeed? Do you plan on practicing attachment parenting? Are you going to secure childcare after your maternity leave is over? One of the hardest decisions that I personally had to make was when to return to my job. I loved my job, but through giving birth to my first son, I realized that I wanted to give him all that I could. I ended up leaving my position as a psychologist and becoming a full-time mom instead. I stayed at home with him each day, getting to know him better than I ever thought I'd be able to.

My days went from sitting at a desk to sitting in a rocking chair. I held my baby, soothed my baby, and fed my baby at all hours of the day. I was able to regulate a schedule that we could both follow, making it easier for us to eat and sleep together. This was the majority of what happened in the first year of motherhood. I enjoyed this so much, and I was thankful that I had a partner who was willing to support me as I stayed at home with our newborn son. The memories that we made at home together were some that I will never forget.

For each of my children, I truly saw the value of breastfeeding. They were all breastfed, and as they began to grow up, I could see the benefits. All 3 of my children have been generally healthy with strong immune systems. It has been quite a journey, raising these three children, and I could not have done it without the help of my dedicated partner. In this guide, I hope to share all of my insights into what I have learned throughout the last 8 years. No matter how many difficulties you encounter, know that I also encountered some of the same things. You are not alone, and you are not an incapable parent. You can be great, as long as you embrace parenthood to its fullest potential.

The Benefits of Being Informed

- You Will Be Able to Deal with the Unexpected: Being a parent involves a lot of flexibility. While you can have the best parenting plan in the world, there will always be something that comes up that will challenge the way you think. Being able to think outside of the box is going to help you deal with the unexpected challenges that parenting throws your way.

- You will Get to Spend More Time with Your Baby: When you aren't burdened by the worries of not knowing what to do during your baby's first year, you will actually get to spend more time bonding with your baby. During pregnancy, you should be doing all of the research you can about parenting and what to expect. If you are already prepared by the time your delivery date comes around, your sole focus can be creating that irreplaceable bond with your child.

- You will Learn the Milestones: During each month, your baby is going to hit various milestones. These include eating solid foods, teething, walking, and potentially even talking. As mentioned, even if your baby isn't at a particular milestone at the given time that the average child experiences it, you will still have an idea of what is to come. This means that there is always something to look forward to!

- You Can Learn Coping Techniques: There will be times of frustration and stress – that's a given. You are only human, and just as your baby will, you will also feel like throwing the occasional temper tantrum. What matters is how you choose to deal with them. As a parent, you aren't going to have a lot of time to sit down and decompress. Being alone with your own thoughts for even 10 minutes can often be a challenge, so you must learn how to find solutions for your mistakes, pay attention to things that can ease your stress, and learn how to keep your baby from being fussy.

- Your Daily Routine Will Transform: A lot of parents struggle with altering their daily lifestyle in order to fit the new role of caring for a newborn. By juggling a career, managing a household, and ensuring that the baby is safe and happy, a lot of changes must be made. If you are educated before the delivery, you should not have a hard time transitioning from being in the hospital with your newborn to being at home with them. Each aspect of your life is going to change a little bit, and it is possible to make this seamless if you work on it during your pregnancy. Don't stress over this part; the transition is going to happen the way it needs to.

Do You Want to Be a Great Parent?

If you want to know if your baby is developing well, how to cope with the struggles of parenthood, deciding on whether a particular vaccine or vitamin is necessary to your child, and more, then you need to continue reading this guide. For every step of the way, this guide is going to provide you with helpful and important information that is not only meant to educate you, but it is also meant to show you that you are not alone. You are not the only parent in the world who feels this way, and that is a promise. The solutions and tips you will find are meant to be used right away. As soon as you begin to implement them, you will notice that parenting is going to feel more natural.

By reading this book right now, you are securing a great future for your baby. Be proud of yourself for this because it is definitely an accomplishment! Most new parents don't give themselves enough credit in the beginning. Certain things are going to catch you off guard, but you will realize that your parental instincts will kick in right away. As soon as you have your baby in your arms, you will know what to do and how to do it. If you ever come to a point where you do not, then believe in your ability to learn how.

Much like being a great adult, being a great parent involves a lot of trial and error. No one tends to mention this about parenting, but it is true. At certain times, you will feel as though you can't do anything right. Seeing that smile on your baby's face is what will turn everything around, though. It will make all of the hard moments worth the challenge. A little giggle can be enough to turn your whole day around and remind you that you are this child's entire life right now. The smallest things that adults take for granted are what feel magical to a newborn.

Having the confidence in knowing that you are being the best parent to your child is a feeling that cannot be duplicated. In this first year of your baby's life, prepare to learn more than you will ever learn about becoming a parent. It is arguably one of the most important moments in parenting that you will ever experience. Don't forget to have fun while doing so, as well. As long as you are having fun, then you are doing something right. You'll notice that your baby is going to pick up the habit of mirroring quickly. Having a happy parent as a caregiver will healthily influence your baby.

Chapter 1: Baby's First Days

The first few days of your baby's life are going to be fascinating to both your little one and yourself. As they begin to explore how they are able to move their body and look around at their surroundings, you will begin to fall in love with them more and more each day. This is the time when you will truly get to know your baby and learn about their temperament. The first few days are important for both the baby and the parents because it is a transitional period of time. Your baby is brought into a new environment, and then your new lifestyle begins. In this chapter, we are going to go over everything that you will need to know in order to make sure that your baby is comfortable and happy.

Baby's Looks

Your baby may or may not have hair on their head when they are born. Some babies have full heads of hair, while others take several months to grow any at all. It will start to grow eventually, so don't worry about the pace that it does grow. It is not imperative to your baby's overall health. Their skin might appear wrinkled, but this is normal. The wrinkles will smooth out as your baby grows bigger. At the top of your baby's head, there will be a spot known as the "soft spot." Be careful not to put any pressure on this spot because it is incredibly fragile. Having this spot is normal for all newborns, and it will usually stay there until your baby reaches at least 7-months old. This is when their head reaches full physical development.

Another thing about your baby's head that you might notice is that it isn't perfectly rounded or symmetrical. This is also normal, and this can change as your baby's brain develops. A lot of brain growth happens during the first year of your child's life, and this can definitely change the shape of their head along the way. Be very gentle when handling your baby's neck and head because, as you know, newborns cannot support the weight of their own head in the first few months of their lives. As they get stronger, their muscles get larger and fill in the spaces that appear indented.

Any birthmarks or unique facial features that your baby has should be celebrated. These make your child special, and though they can also change over time, they are going to be identifying characteristics. Some babies are born with birthmarks while others will have porcelain skin without blemishes. No matter what your baby's skin or birthmarks look like, it won't change anything about their rate of development. You will also love them the same! Think about how incredible it is that you and your partner created this newborn and that your DNA is directly responsible for their physical appearance.

Bonding

Skin-to-skin contact is the best way to bond with your baby. Most parenting guides will tell you the same thing. This contact is exactly as it sounds — holding your baby directly onto your skin. Even if it is just an exposed shoulder, your baby having access to the touch and feel of your skin will allow them to form a stronger bond with you by allowing them to get to know you more. Plus, this contact can feel soothing for both the parent and the child. Another benefit of having this skin-to-skin contact is knowing that your baby's temperature is regular. A feverish baby is going to be hot to the touch with clammy skin. If you are in frequent physical contact with your child, you will be able to detect this sooner and potentially save your baby from having to experience illnesses.

Hold your baby all the time, not only when they are crying. This will show them that they can receive this type of physical love from you at any time, not only while they are in distress. Fussy babies tend to cry more because they are led to believe that they can only receive this type of affection when something is wrong. By showing your baby that you are going to hold them and give them physical affection frequently, they will get used to growing up this way. Instead of fighting for your love, they will realize that you are giving it to them willingly. This creates a great sense of security for your little one.

Weighing and Measuring

Immediately after your baby is born, the hospital is going to provide you with their weight and measurements. A lot of parents like to include this information on the birth announcement. While it is not necessary to do so, there is not much else that you need this information for other than to satisfy your own curiosity. Don't become too involved in believing that your baby is going to become sick or unhealthy because they are smaller or larger than the average newborn. Babies come in all shapes and sizes. Also, genetic factors play a large role in the size of the baby that you give birth to.

During your baby's first check-up, they will be weighed and measured again. The measurements that were taken after delivery can be compared to these updated measurements in order to chart their growth. The doctor will give you an accurate account of how well your baby is developing and growing. If you have any questions or concerns about your baby's size, or if you believe that your baby's size is preventing them from getting proper nutrition, this would be the time to bring these questions up with your doctor. Try not to do too much detective work on your own because this could end up scaring you into thinking something is wrong with your baby when everything is actually just fine.

Vitamin K

Vitamin K is super important for your newborn because it helps blood clot quickly. If your baby gets a small scratch, their fragile skin will likely bleed a lot. Blood that clots quickly is important because it will prevent infections. After your baby is born, at your request, they can be given a vitamin K injection at the hospital. Most of the time, this service will be free if you have health insurance and give birth at a public hospital. No matter how healthy the mother was during pregnancy, it is just not possible for the baby to have received enough vitamin K in the womb. This is why a lot of mothers opt for vitamin K injection after birth.

Your baby is not required to have vitamin K, but it is something that you should consider for their well-being. The ability to locate and stop the bleeding right away is useful for any parent, but especially a parent with a newborn since they are so tiny. If you do decide to get your baby the vitamin K injection, they will usually receive one dose after birth, one 3-5 days later, and one four weeks later.

With decades of testing, there have been no links to any side effects that have been seen in babies who have been given the vitamin K injection. While it is essential for all newborns, premature babies might need it in smaller doses. The decision is a big one to make, and it will likely be one of your first big decisions as a parent. If you do not opt for the injection, look out for any bleeding or bruising in the first few days of your baby being at home. If you notice this, it might mean that you need to go back to get them the vitamin K injection after all. Consult your doctor if you are still undecided.

Cord Blood Collection

There are four different possible blood types that everybody is born with — A, B, AB, and O. Of these blood types, there can also be positive and negative variations. Blood types are inherited, and they allow you to know if you are either RH positive or RH negative. This stands for your Rhesus factor, and it indicates whether you have a protein called "D antigen" on the surface of your red blood cells. Your RH factor doesn't impact your body during your daily life, but when you are delivering a baby, it matters a lot.

What this means for your baby is that they are either going to be RH positive or RH negative, as well. If the two of you have different RH factors, you might face some complications if your baby's blood enters your bloodstream during birth. This can happen through the umbilical cord. Any remaining blood that is in the cord as your child is born can accidentally be transferred into your body (known as a "cord blood collection"). If you are RH negative, your body will begin to produce antibodies to ward off the positive cells; this can lead you to feel unwell. RH positive women typically don't experience any complications.

While it is nothing to be majorly concerned about, there are injections that can be given to the mother at the 28th and 34th weeks of her pregnancy to help prevent this potential complication. It will usually be offered to an RH negative mother with an RH positive partner. It is predicted that two partners who have opposing RH factors are going to likely conceive a baby that has a different RH factor than the mother. While this isn't always the case, receiving the injection is simply a precautionary measure. The injection is safe for both the mother and the baby, but know that it is not mandatory. You can ask your doctor if they recommend that you get it.

Feeding

The idea of feeding your baby might seem simple, but it has been the experience of many new mothers around the world that the baby just won't latch on or create a proper feeding schedule. Don't worry, you are going to get the hang of this all. Since you are still going to be in a transitional stage within the first few days of bringing your baby home, try not to let this stress you out. Both of you are going to be bonding and learning about one another. Through trial and error, you will learn what it takes to get your baby to latch on. You will also be able to identify what the different cries mean – not all of them are an indication of hunger.

Newborns must be fed every 2-3 hours, and it is up to you to regulate this because you will be the source of their nutrition. Know that it is normal in the beginning to need to feed your baby a little bit more frequently in order to soothe them. Once they realize that feeding, much like affection, will be given regularly, then they will start to settle into some type of a comfortable schedule. If your baby doesn't want to eat at first, don't worry because they will let you know when they are truly hungry. As they learn that you have their food, they will develop different ways to let you know.

Sleeping

Say goodbye to your sleep schedule as you know it. Every parent undergoes the big change of completely uprooting their sleep schedule in order to accommodate their child. In the first few days, you can expect sleep to be sporadic for both the parents and the newborn. Some people say that their baby sleeps great and often after the first few days of giving birth, while others will tell you the complete opposite. As you know, there are no standards for comparison. Your baby is either going to be a great sleeper, or they aren't.

Try to put your baby down for a nap after each feeding. This will provide them will a full stomach which can be soothing and encouraging. If you try to put a baby down who hasn't eaten in a few hours, you likely won't have much luck. Your baby either won't fall asleep or won't stay asleep long. Through many experiments, you will learn which toys, songs, and methods your baby will fall asleep best to.

If you need a nap, take a nap when your baby is asleep. This is part of parenting 101, and it can save you from being overcome by total exhaustion. The best time to rest is when you know that your baby is resting. Any other time, you are going to need to be alert and paying close attention to your baby and their needs.

Apgar Scores

Apgar scores sound intimidating but don't worry, they do not reflect on how well you delivered your baby. To figure out the scores, the baby is checked at the 1-minute mark, as well as the 5-minute mark to see if anything has changed. In order to come up with the number, the doctor will check the following on your baby: skin color, heart rate, reflexes/responsiveness, muscle tone, and breathing rate. An Apgar score is what the doctor uses to assess your newborn's health. This is what alerts the medical team as to whether or not your baby requires additional care after they are born.

The rating scale goes from 0-10, with 10 being the highest. A score of 7+ for a newborn is normal. Anything lower than this might trigger the need for extra care after they are born. If your baby scores 6 or less at the 1-minute mark, this is often taken into account and then compared to the 5-minute score before making any final decisions on additional care. By the time the second number is given, your baby should be scoring no less than 7. While it may sound complex, it is truly a simple system that medical professionals use to gauge your baby's overall health once out of the womb.

It can be scary to hear that your baby's Apgar scores are low, but know that this is simply a guide for doctors to follow in order to best know how to help your baby if they are in need of treatment. The first few minutes of a baby's life can change in the blink of an eye, so knowing how to proceed is crucial. This is why the scores are given so early. Being knowledgeable about the Apgar scoring system, you won't need to feel any confusion or concern when you hear the medical staff talking about your baby's scores immediately after you give birth. If you are curious, you can ask them about the scores and how they have or have not changed.

Senses

You might be curious as to what your baby can see, hear, feel, and taste in the first few days of their life. Their senses are in their earliest stage of development as they adjust to being outside of the womb. Since your baby has been hearing your voice for nearly a year now, they might become very responsive when they hear it in person. Your baby's strongest sense will probably be their hearing; this is normal for most newborns within the first few days of life. Their vision will be blurry, but they will be able to see things that are around 1-

foot away from them. In terms of smell and taste, your baby is likely going to be experiencing the amniotic fluid and your colostrum, both have been said to taste similar.

Your newborn is going to develop their senses very quickly after this. Within a week, they will be able to see more clearly and hear even better than before. They will have tasted breast milk and your skin if you intend on breastfeeding. They will also likely know what it feels like to put their toes and fingers in their mouth; babies can be very curious in this way! You can expect an improvement in their senses every single day. Introduce your baby to as many new sights and sounds as you can. This is the best way to help them further develop their senses. This is your chance to teach your baby something new for the very first time.

Urine and Meconium

During the first day of your newborn baby's life, it is normal for them to pass urine and meconium. Known as the black and sticky fecal matter that your baby will pass, meconium is a perfectly normal bodily function. If you aren't expecting it in the beginning, it can appear somewhat alarming to see it in your baby's diaper. Don't worry because the texture and consistency will change as your baby adjusts to the new eating schedule. The meconium will eventually turn into newborn baby poop that you are likely more familiar with, a soft and lighter-colored stool.

You can expect your newborn's poop to change a lot in the first few days, but again, this is perfectly normal. The poop is still going to be pretty soft until your baby begins to eat solid foods. On the first day, you can probably expect your newborn to only have one poop. On the second day, this will likely increase to two. The number will increase the more that your baby is breastfed (or bottle-fed). The first few poopy diapers will likely be filled with what is known as transitional stools. These can contain blood and mucus, but there is typically no need to be alarmed. These substances can still be in your baby's body from the time of delivery.

Newborn Issues

You are likely going to be very cautious within your baby's first few days of life, of course. Every little movement and action is going to be analyzed and observed. While health issues are possible for newborn babies, knowing the signs to look for will help you remain at ease. Skin conditions are a common concern for newborns. Jaundice is known as the yellowing of the skin and eyes, and it is very normal for newborns to develop. It happens due to too much bilirubin being present in the skin. It is typically not painful or too concerning, but you should contact your doctor if you notice this yellowing.

Your doctor should also be contacted if you notice any dehydration paired with fewer wet diapers. This means that your baby isn't getting enough milk in their system. Fevers are also another sign to look for. If your baby feels warmer than usual, this is typically an early sign of infection. Newborns can reach high temperatures very quickly, so make sure that you are checking your baby's temperature often. Contact your doctor right away, and make sure you are ready to bring your baby in if their fever reaches 100-degrees or higher.

Spitting up is going to happen a lot, especially after feeding. This is how your baby has to learn how to digest in the beginning. It might look like your baby is throwing up after each feeding, but this is normal in order to regulate their body and get used to the amount of food they are receiving. This will happen less and less as your baby gets older and gets used to eating. Know that throwing up happens with more force; spitting up can result from a simple burp that leads to a little bit of excess milk coming up with it. If you notice that your baby is actually vomiting and the coloration is dark green or other abnormal colors, a visit to the doctor might be necessary.

Test Screening

In the first few days of life, all babies are tested to ensure that they are of optimal health. This is known as test screening. These tests are meant to monitor your baby's development and to ensure that everything is on track. Test screening is required in every state, and it is performed before the baby leaves the hospital. It starts with a blood test in the first 24-48 hours of life. A second blood test is performed at your baby's first check-up to compare results when your baby is around 1-2 weeks old. If your baby is born outside of a hospital, a doula or midwife will typically collect the blood sample.

Your baby will also be tested for hearing loss and congenital heart disease. Both of these tests will be done shortly after birth. The first test involves a pair of earphones and sensors to monitor your baby's reactions. The second uses a sensor to measure how much oxygen is in your baby's blood. Low oxygen levels can be an indication of a problem.

When it comes to vaccines, the HepB vaccine is typically what a newborn baby will get if you consent to it. As your baby gets older, around 2-months old, you will have the option to provide them with a lot more vaccinations if you choose, as well as the second HepB shot. This can all be discussed with your doctor if you are unsure about what is best for your baby.

Chapter 2: Baby Essentials

Having knowledge about what your baby needs is the first step to being a great parent. The second step is having all of the proper equipment. Before your baby is born, you will likely purchase, or be gifted, many different clothing options, diapers, bottles, and more. These are all essentials for taking care of your baby, and knowing which items you would like to use during the newborn stage is important. Again, these first few weeks come with many decisions for you to make as a parent. This is why doing your research ahead of time will allow you to feel well-prepared for when your baby is actually in your arms and in need of care.

Breastfeeding vs. Bottle Feeding

A big decision to make is if you wish to breastfeed your child or go straight to bottle feeding. While there are many nutritional and developmental benefits to breastfeeding, some mothers choose not to and that is okay. No matter what your decision is, the following topics will allow you to decide what is going to work best for you and your baby.

Benefits

As mentioned, whether you breastfeed or not is a personal decision. A lot of women opt for breastfeeding because it allows the baby to receive the nutrition that is coming directly from your body that the baby is already used to receiving. It is thought to be easier to digest than formula, and your body is likely naturally going to produce the breast milk anyway. Overall, breastfeeding provides you with a healthy and convenient way to feed your child. While there are plenty of reasons why a mother cannot or will not breastfeed, you need to take into account your own child and your own health and desire to breastfeed. The choice is solely up to you to make.

OB-GYNs recommend that a newborn only consumes breast milk for the first 6 months of life. After this, solid foods can be introduced, but breastfeeding can still continue until the baby reaches 1-year old. Breast milk contains certain antibodies that are known to ward off illnesses that your baby could be exposed to. It lowers your baby's risk of developing asthma and allergies. Another benefit is that breastfed babies are typically less likely to develop ear infections, respiratory conditions, and diarrhea. Taking a look at the bigger picture, it is thought that babies who drink breast milk also end up having higher IQs as they get older.

When you are at the hospital, a nurse will assist you in getting your baby to latch for the first time. This part can be intimidating for a mother who is breastfeeding for the first time. You might be wondering what the best position for feeding is, and this can be entirely up to your comfort and your baby's responsiveness. Try different positions in order to show your baby that you are trying to feed them.

Pros and Cons

There is a lot for you to take into consideration before you fully commit to breastfeeding. While it does provide your baby with several nutrients, it can also be a lot for your body to handle. Considering your baby's health is one aspect of your decision-making process, but it is rightful that you also consider your own health. Breastfeeding can lead to painful, clogged nipples and soreness that can often be very hard to soothe. Not to mention, your breasts might leak if your milk production is heavy. There is also the opposite problem of not producing enough milk. These things all depend on your own unique biology.

If you begin to experience difficulties while breastfeeding, there are plenty of ways that you can physically help your body, while also ensuring that you are pumping enough milk and preparing as best as you possibly can for feeding times. Getting enough rest and staying healthy yourself is one of the key factors in producing a healthy amount of milk for your baby. If you are stressed out, this is going to impact your production levels. Also, consider incorporating pumping into your normal daily routine, especially if you are going back to work after having your baby. You will need to ensure that your baby has enough milk to last throughout the day. If you do not breastfeed, then you will need to measure the correct amount of formula.

No matter which one you choose, your baby is eventually going to drink from a bottle with the milk that you give them. You might find that your baby will start to naturally try to hold the bottle by themselves – this is a great sign. It is a natural instinct. Position your baby so that their head is propped up as you feed them with the bottle. Don't tilt it so much that the milk pours out quickly, but keep it tilted just enough so that there is a steady flow of milk. Your baby might grab the bottle or bite the nipple to indicate that they want more milk. As they develop, they will become more interactive during bottle-feeding.

The following are some comparative pros and cons for you to review:

<u>Breastfeeding</u>

Pros

- The nutrition that your baby needs
- Your body is naturally producing the milk
- A bottle won't always be necessary

Cons

- Your nipples can get sore
- Your milk production can get low
- Pumping can be painful

Bottle Feeding

Pros

- You can prepare many bottles ahead of time
- It can be easier for your baby to latch
- Bottle-fed babies are usually hungry less often

Cons

- There will be potential indigestion issues
- The formula will not have the same nutrients as breast milk
- Bowel movements might be more stinky and loose

Introducing Solids

As mentioned, solids can be introduced around 6-months old. As you begin to introduce your baby to certain foods, you can also begin the transition of weaning from being breastfed or bottle-fed. If you breastfeed, it is thought that breastfeeding for as long as you can is best for your baby. Most mothers find that they begin weaning at around 1-year old, though. This is a natural part of your baby's next chapter in life. You'll know that your baby is ready to begin eating solids and start drinking less milk when you notice the following signs:

- The ability to support their neck and head on their own
- Can hold the food in their mouth without pushing it out
- Opens their mouth when they see food coming
- Can refuse food by turning away or closing their mouth

- Starts getting hungry earlier than usual each day

Remember, weaning doesn't happen overnight. It can be a gradual process that happens in steps. Start by replacing one feeding at a time. Instead of breast milk or formula, allow your baby to eat something solid instead. This will seamlessly allow your baby to become ready for the transition without it seeming like they are getting fed less. Listen to their cues; your baby will be letting you know when they are hungry and when they've had enough to eat. If it is possible, avoid doing anything abruptly. This can confuse your baby and potentially even lessen their appetite. It is always better to wean in steps, no matter if you are breastfeeding or bottle-feeding.

Start off with simple, single ingredient foods to introduce your baby to. Make sure that you wait at least 3-5 days in between each new food introduction so you can monitor your baby for any allergies. Iron and zinc are very important for newborns, so ensure that you are selecting food with plenty of both. Baby cereal is great for this. It is typically what mothers decide to give their infant's as the first taste of solid food. Most baby cereal is prepared by mixing 1 tablespoon of cereal with 4 tablespoons of breast milk or formula. After the introduction of baby cereal, you can try giving your baby pureed fruits and vegetables, still waiting for a few days in between each food introduction.

When your baby is around 8-10 months old, you can introduce

finger foods. These include soft fruits (with no skin), vegetables, pasta, crackers, cheese, meat, and dry cereal. Make sure that there are no choking hazards by giving your baby tiny pieces of the food that you would like to introduce. Foods that melt in a baby's mouth, like crackers are also a great introduction to solids. You will find out very quickly what your baby's preferences are. A bad taste and your baby will be spitting the food out and possibly even redecorating your kitchen with it.

Clothing

While there are so many cute baby clothes available for you to purchase, what you buy does matter regarding your baby's health and comfort. Know that great baby clothes do not have to be expensive. There is nothing wrong with buying packs of onesies that are cheap or affordable. A lot of parents feel the pressure to only buy the very best clothing, but remember, your baby is going to get everything dirty! This is natural, and it is definitely going to happen. Whether it is a diaper mess or a stain from feeding, all of the clothing your baby wears will need to be washed frequently. For this reason, selecting a durable material is a smart decision.

Your baby's skin is going to be very sensitive as a newborn. Try not to opt for any synthetic fabrics. Those that are breathable are typically best, like cotton. Know that your baby won't be able to regulate their body temperature as well as you can. A cool breeze to you will feel a lot colder to them, so make sure that they are dressed weather-appropriate. Bundle up if necessary, and don't forget to layer clothing so that you can remove some; if the temperature warms up suddenly. Baby's grow extremely quickly, so don't get too carried away with the quantity of the clothing that you buy. Some items might only fit your baby for a week or two before you are already moving up a size.

Learning how to properly swaddle your baby is going to come in handy. Swaddling is the action of wrapping your baby up tightly so that they feel secure. Some clothing is actually made for this, allowing you to swaddle without the help of an additional cloth or blanket. Don't forget about bibs and burp cloths. After each feeding, your baby is going to need to burp and possibly spit-up. If you do not have anything to cover your baby's clothing, you can expect to be doing three times as much laundry as usual. Buy a lot of bibs, and make sure you have plenty of burp cloths nearby at all times. These are a few things that your baby will not grow out of quickly.

You might be wondering when would be an appropriate time to go baby clothes shopping is. A lot of women choose to do this after the 12-week mark. Much like making the pregnancy announcement, waiting until this point typically indicates that your pregnancy is going well so far. While it can be tempting to go out and buy onesies the instant you get your positive pregnancy test, it is usually better to wait until you are at least well into your first trimester, possibly into your second, before you go out and buy a wardrobe for your soon-to-be newborn. Another determining factor that matters to some parents is gender. If you decide to find out the gender of your baby, you usually have to wait until this point anyway. This can allow you to decide on what kind of clothing you wish to purchase.

The way that you wash this clothing is important. As you know, your baby's skin is going to be ultra-sensitive. You can't necessarily wash their clothing the same way you would wash your own. Harsh chemicals and scents can do a lot to irritate your baby's skin. Before you wash the clothing, have it pre-soak in hot water to kill any germs or bacteria. After the soak, do a load of laundry containing only your baby's clothing with a detergent that is unscented or labeled as safe for infants. If you decide to hand-wash the clothing, the same steps can be followed. Make sure that you properly disinfect your hands before you begin.

If you want a little bit of extra reassurance, you can run your rinse cycle twice on your washing machine before taking the clothing out to dry. This will ensure that there is absolutely no more soap or residue present on the material. Also, it is best to do your baby's laundry before you do any other household laundry. This will eliminate the chances of cross-contamination. A lot of this clothing is going to be stained, so make sure that you are properly treating these stains before you throw them into the wash. This part should happen before

355

the pre-soak, and this means that you must examine each piece of clothing before you put it in. Do some research on which natural stain removers you can use on your newborn's clothing.

Drying clothing is also very important. If you put your baby in wet or damp clothing, not only can bacteria gather, but your baby can also catch a cold or other illness. Dry your baby's clothes in the sunlight if you can. If not, make sure that you read all of the clothing labels to see which dryer settings to use. Since the clothing is so tiny, your dryer can be very powerful, potentially even ruining or shrinking the material. Each label and article of clothing might require different instructions, so make sure that you always read them.

When the clothing is brand new, it is a good idea to wash it before you put it on your baby. Since it came directly from the store, you never know who touched it and what kind of germs might still be lingering on the fabric. If you are being super careful with your baby's laundry, yet you notice that a skin allergy is still developing, consult your doctor for how to properly clean and dress your baby. You might have to take some extra steps in order to make sure that you are not further irritating your baby's skin. Typically, a lot of skin allergies can be grown out of, but it is best to be extra careful in the first few months of your baby's life.

Diapers

Much like feeding, there is a decision that you will have to make regarding your baby's diapers – disposable or cloth. At the beginning of this section, you can take a comparative look at the pros and cons of each decision:

<u>Disposable</u>

Pros

- Throw them away when they get dirty
- There are more size options
- They tend to be more breathable

Cons

- They are harsh on the environment
- Dyes and gels can cause irritation
- The pull tabs can rip easily

<u>Cloth</u>

Pros

- They are eco-friendly
- They are gentle for sensitive skin
- Waterproof bands can keep leaks in

Cons

- Cleaning them requires more effort
- You will have to do a lot more laundry

- They can be less absorbent

A lot of mothers wonder about the cost of each option, as well. It is no secret that diapers can become pretty expensive! They are essential, and you are going to need a lot of them every single day. Keeping your baby clean and changed frequently is what will prevent rashes from developing. This will also keep them soothed and relaxed. Sitting on a wet or dirty diaper for a long period of time is distressing to a newborn. In general comparison, the typical cost for a family to use disposable diapers for two years is around $2,000-$3,000. For cloth diapers, the cost is around $800-$1,000. Remember, cloth diapers do require the additional step of you cleaning them. If you opt for a cleaning service for cloth diapers, this can cost you an additional amount of money, placing you closer to the price range of using disposable diapers.

If you are considering the environmental perspective, it is clear that cloth diapers produce less waste. You are going to be contributing less to landfills, but don't forget that you are going to be using more water and electricity to clean the cloth diapers. This can be a toss-up for some parents, making the two options seem almost equal in the end. A lot of disposable diaper companies are becoming more eco-friendly at the request of their consumers. Some disposables are now actually up to 40% biodegradable, therefore producing less waste in landfills. Much like the decision to breastfeed or bottle-feed, this is solely up to you and your own personal preference.

While you know the benefits of each, it is your decision as a parent to make.

No matter which diapers you decide on, you need to make sure you have a proper changing station for your little one. This includes a changing table or pad, a diaper pail, wipes, and rash relief cream or powder. The height of your changing station does matter because if it is too low, you are going to be spending a lot of time hunched over and in pain. Your table should be anywhere from 36-43 inches above the floor, depending on what is comfortable for your height. The diaper pail should also be easily accessible so that you can quickly toss the dirty diaper without having to leave your child on the table unattended.

You will go through wipes very quickly, probably more quickly than diapers. Make sure that you buy refills in bulk. Naturally, you are also going to need easy access to them during your diaper changing duties. Anything that you are going to use while changing a diaper should be within arm's reach. This means that your diaper cream or powder should also be easily accessible. Irritation is unavoidable at times, so it is important that you have something around that you can put onto your baby to safely ease this pain. It might also be a good idea to keep a hypoallergenic moisturizer nearby because chafed skin can become an issue during the diaper-wearing age.

Bathing and Skin Care

Until your baby is actively crawling, a daily bath actually isn't necessary. At first, your newborn should only need a bath around 2-3 times per week. Start out by giving your baby a sponge bath until the umbilical cord stump has healed. This happens at around 1-4 weeks after birth. A sponge bath is exactly what it sounds like, and soap isn't even necessarily needed. In a baby bath, take a sponge and gently clean your baby with warm water. After the umbilical cord stump has healed, you can start giving your baby longer baths in the baby tub.

Your baby can get cold very quickly, so make sure that you keep track of the water temperature. While you don't want the water to be scalding, you do want to make sure that it stays around 75-80 degrees. If you find that the water is getting cold but the bath isn't quite finished, you can add more warm water to reheat the tub. Make sure that you have a soft washcloth nearby, as well as a plush towel. The great thing about baby shampoo is that it often serves a dual purpose. Most baby shampoos can also be used to wash the body, as well. This needs to be within easy reach, of course. Just like diaper changes, you wouldn't want to leave your baby alone in the tub to go grab something.

Create a bathing routine. As mentioned, you won't need to bathe your newborn every single day at first. It does help to decide on giving a morning bath or night bath, though. Some babies feel more awake after a bath, ready to play and stay alert. Others become sleepy afterward. See how your baby responds, and this will help you decide when you should be giving them a bath. If you do want a bath to be a precursor to sleep, make sure that you swaddle your baby once they are dry, and keep the room dimly lit. This will promote sleepiness. You should also make sure that your baby isn't hungry or too full before bath time. They won't be able to go straight to sleep after they bathe if they are either one of these things.

Putting your baby into the tub for the first time can be a nerve-wracking experience as a parent. Your baby might react suddenly to the water since this is a new sensation, so don't panic. Holding your baby in your arms, gently slide their feet into the water first. Allow them to become acclimated to the way that it feels. With one hand supporting your baby's bottom and the other wrapped around their torso under the arms, you can gently begin lowering them into the tub. For the first few baths, don't let them last for very long. As mentioned, your baby will get cold very quickly. Quick introductions are the best way for your baby to get used to bathing.

As they get older, they will likely begin to enjoy bath time more. This becomes a great bonding experience that you can share with your baby. Try to make baths seem fun and positive. Always guard your baby's face as you rinse out any shampoo, even if it is safe on the eyes. Getting water poured directly onto the face can be a very jarring experience, so do your best to avoid it. You can begin to incorporate bath toys as your baby gets old enough to enjoy them. You might notice your baby splashing and kicking in the water. This is typically a sign that they are enjoying the bath and having fun in the tub.

Your baby can get pimples, and this is normal. They can appear on your baby's cheeks, noses, and foreheads. This tends to happen during the first few months of life, and the bumps will go away on their own. Blotchy skin is something that can also happen to your baby; it will also typically go away on its own. Your baby's skin is adjusting to being outside of the womb, so certain things will irritate it very easily in the beginning. There should be no cause for alarm unless it is causing your baby discomfort. Know that any sort of blemish or pimple will go away within a few days. Breakouts that are getting worse or lasting for more than a few days can be brought up with your doctor.

Once you begin bathing your baby, you might notice that their scalp is getting flaky. This is known as cradle cap. This is a normal buildup of cells that a lot of infants experience. It will usually go away on its own by the time your baby reaches the age of 1. In order to help their scalp, you can wash the flakes away with their shampoo, ensuring that you rinse it all very carefully. Cradle cap is nothing to be concerned about. If there seems to be an excessive amount of flaking that does not improve, you can ask your doctor for other solutions. Certain mineral oils are safe to use on your baby's head, and your doctor can recommend which one would work best.

You might notice that your baby's skin is irritated because they keep scratching themselves. Usually, infant mittens will fix this problem and protect them. If a nail trimming is in order, there are special nail clippers that are safe for infants. Their nails will be softer than your own, so be very gentle with them. Clip them when your baby is asleep if you'd like to have the most fuss-free experience. When cutting fingernails, follow the curve of the finger, ensuring that you aren't cutting too short. For toenails, they can be cut straight across.

Chapter 3: Healthcare, Vaccinations, and Childcare

Knowing what to do when your baby is in need of a check-up, a vaccination, or childcare are all very important parts of their first year of life. Wellness check-ups are going to happen frequently for your baby. They are meant to ensure that everything is going well developmentally, and during these visits, your doctor can recommend which vaccines are typically given at the age your baby is. Another important decision to make is who will watch your baby when you are not available. Unfortunately, many parents must return to work shortly after their baby has been born. This decision is so important because you need to make sure that you have a trustworthy and safe option for your baby.

How to Choose Your Baby's Healthcare Provider

Your baby's healthcare does not end after birth; this is only the beginning. At around three months prior to your due date, it is a good idea for you to start the search for a doctor that you can begin seeing regularly after you deliver. While some continue seeing the doctor that they currently have, a lot of people like to take a look at their options. There are several necessary check-ups that will be needed throughout your baby's first year of life, so having a regular doctor is very important. Get recommendations from everyone you know. Your loved ones might be able to provide you with some insight. Along with this, you can read reviews online from verified clients who have experienced visits with each doctor.

Options

You have one of two options when making your decision – pediatrician or family physician. If you chose the former, you can typically keep your child with them until they turn 21. Those who are trained in pediatrics have a special focus on treating babies and children. It is common for a baby to see a pediatrician, but it isn't mandatory. If you choose a family physician, this is going to be someone your child can see for life if they want to. They see patients of all ages, babies included. While both have the same amount of medical experience, they specialize in different practices. Parents normally start their babies off at a pediatrician, and then they switch to a family physician or regular physician once the child reaches puberty.

There really isn't a "better" option when it comes to who you decide to take your baby to. Through research and potential recommendations that you receive, you will be able to make a well-informed decision. Also, consider where your doctor is located. If you need to drive very far away to take your baby to the doctor, this can become an inconvenience. It can also become dangerous if you are dealing with an emergency. Having a doctor that is close-by will make your life a lot easier since you will be taking your baby there a lot in the first few months of their life. Consider that your health insurance provider can help you locate a doctor in your area. Most have searches that you can utilize that will allow you to provide a zip code and a radius that you are comfortable with.

Factors to Consider

Does your baby have any preexisting conditions? Some babies are born with certain illnesses or defects, and these must be treated properly. You might have to seek out specialty treatment depending on how healthy your baby is after delivery. If your baby was born healthy, without any apparent medical conditions, then you are going to have a lot of options. Think about your current schedule. Do you work? Does your significant other work? You need to select a doctor that has office hours that work for you. It wouldn't make sense to select a doctor who has limited time to see your baby. Being a parent, you will realize that getting rid of inconveniences is going to ultimately help your life become easier.

With the doctor you choose, consider if they are working at a solo practice or as a group. If your doctor works solo, this isn't necessarily a downfall, just know that securing an appointment might be harder. Doctors that are a part of a group practice will have more staff available to treat your child, so you can make appointments that are both scheduled and more urgent with ease. If you need to call your doctor, is there someone who will answer your call 24/7 or do the calls go unanswered while the office is closed? Some offices have a service that allows trained staff to remain available at all hours in case you call with questions. This can be very beneficial, as a lot of things can happen in your baby's first year that you'll likely want to discuss with a professional. Having this option is like having a bit of extra reassurance.

Comparing Providers

The easiest way to compare different providers is by reading online reviews. This is something you can do from home, and it allows you to read about real, first-hand experiences that were had by clients. Take a look at these first, and then make a note of the doctors that you would consider taking your child to. Once you have some options, give each one a call. Is the receptionist polite and helpful? This is important because if you have a bad experience from simply calling the front desk, it is likely that you aren't going to feel comfortable once you are actually at the office. A friendly staff is a big factor that can either make or break your experience, and it definitely should be taken into consideration.

Schedule consultations with each doctor that you'd like to meet. When you are able to talk to the doctor in person, you will be able to voice your questions and concerns. A good doctor is going to listen to you, free of judgment. You will have to decide if you feel comfortable at the office, so use your best instincts. Having your significant other there with you will automatically provide you with another opinion, so consider going to these consultations together. If you both like the doctor and feel that you can trust them, then they are probably going to be a good fit for you and your baby. Ask your loved ones if they have ever heard of any of the doctors that you are considering. Those in your life, especially those who have kids, will likely know about the reputations of the local doctors in your area. Getting their input again can be a helpful tool for you to utilize. Cost is yet another factor that you might want to keep in mind. Have an idea of your healthcare budget before you go in for any consultations.

Your Baby's Vaccinations

Today, many parents are on the fence about vaccinating their children. Since vaccinations are not mandatory, this puts a big weight on your shoulders about what you believe your baby needs and what your baby could do without. Vaccinations work by training your baby's immune system to recognize and combat viruses or bacteria that enter the body. When given a vaccination, a small amount of this particular bacteria is injected so your baby has the chance to learn how to fight it off. What is injected are known as antigens, and these antigens are all individually present in all viruses and bacteria.

Through the injection of the antigens, your baby's body is going to recognize that they are foreign, and if all goes well, learn how to fight them by utilizing their immune system.

If you are undecided on whether or not you'd like to vaccinate your child, consider the following benefits:

- A Vaccination Can Be Life-Saving: In the US, 50,000 people die from vaccine-preventable diseases. These diseases can be very dangerous and they can spread quickly, so choosing not to vaccinate your baby can potentially be putting them at risk of a dire situation.
- They Won't Give You the Disease: A common myth is that getting a vaccine will actually give your baby the disease that it is designed to protect against. Just because you are being injected with the antigens does not mean you are actually taking on the disease, willingly. Vaccines are designed so that it is impossible to catch the disease from them because they use cells from a "killed" virus. Others contain live, but weakened, cells.
- Vaccines Can Help Those Around You: If you decide to vaccinate your child, you are providing them with protection that will also prevent them from becoming carriers. An unvaccinated baby, at risk of becoming ill, can actually spread the disease very quickly and put others at risk. It has been shown that a group of vaccinated people have fewer bouts of illness than a

group of unvaccinated people. Overall, healthier immune systems can be seen.

Common Concerns

With all of the benefits provided, you might be wondering why some parents steer clear of vaccinations for their children. One of the main reasons is the additives involved. Some vaccines contain additives known as adjuvants. They are added to the vaccines because they help them work better. They are meant to create a stronger response from the immune system, and though this can sound questionable, these same adjuvants have been used successfully in vaccines since the 1930s. One of the most common adjuvants used today is aluminum.

Though not all vaccines contain these additives, the ones that do can produce harmful effects such as pain, swelling, and redness at the injection site or even a fever and body aches. This is why a lot of people believe that getting vaccinated will automatically make you sick with the illness that you are trying to prevent. Thinking about your baby's fragile immune system, it makes sense why you might question this process and the determination if it is really worth it, in the end, to get them vaccinated.

Another concern that has popped up recently has been the idea that vaccines can lead to Autism. This is a myth that has spread like wildfire among parents, but according to the CDC, this is not true. There is thought to be no link with vaccinations (additive or additive-free) and the developmental disorder that is Autism. There have been many studies done that aim to find links between vaccination ingredients and Autism, and to this day, there have been no common links found.

Vaccination Schedule

Birth: HepB

1 Month: HepB

2 Months: HepB, RV, DTaP, Hib, PCV13, and IPV

4 Months: RV, DTaP, Hib, PCV13, and IPV

6 Months: Hep, RV, DTaP, Hib, PCV13, and IPV, and Influenza (yearly)

1 Year: HepB, Hib, PCV13, IPV, Influenza (yearly), MMR, Varicella, and HepA

Side Effects

While the vaccinations themselves might be safe and beneficial to your baby, you must also consider any side effects that are presented. Your baby might feel unsettled or sleepy after getting a vaccination, but this shouldn't last very long. It is common for your baby to need extra rest after a visit to the doctor. Dealing with the injection site is also going to be something that can be painful for your baby. This can come with some redness and tenderness in the area, but you should easily be able to manage this pain for your baby. As mentioned, fever is also a side effect. This one should be closely monitored. If your baby starts to become feverish, you need to ensure that it does not get dangerously high. Contact your doctor right away if the fever doesn't break.

With everything considered, these side effects are particularly easy to manage. Once you become educated on all of the vaccines listed above, you should have enough knowledge to make an informed decision on what you believe your baby needs or does not need. Whether you opt for all, some, or none of the vaccines, this does not make you a bad parent. The fact that you are putting thought and careful research into your decision shows that you care deeply for your baby's health and strengthening the immune system.

While every single vaccination has risks involved, you will find that the benefits are typically greater than the risks. Even knowing this information, a lot of parents still opt to go vaccine-free today because they believe that their babies actually develop stronger immune systems this way. Since the body is left to deal with any bacteria or virus that it encounters naturally, they believe that their babies develop unique ways to fight them that pertain to their individualized immune systems and functions.

Choosing Your Childcare Provider

Selecting the best healthcare provider for your baby isn't the only important care decision that you will make. An equally important topic to consider is childcare. After you and your partner have returned to work, you must make the decision – who is going to look after your child? While some parents are fortunate enough to be able to remain at home, most do not have this opportunity. This brings forth a wide array of options and a choice that can seem intimidating to make. How can you trust someone to take care of your baby and be certain that they will be safe? This section explores all of your options and the benefits of each one.

Daycare

On average, you can expect to pay $975 each month if you decide to bring your baby to daycare. This can be a costly option for some parents, especially those on an already-tight budget. When you bring your baby to daycare, you can have the peace of mind knowing that you will have someone to rely on. A daycare operates like any other business, with hours of operation and certain professional procedures. Your baby will also get to socialize with other children at a daycare center, which can be an added bonus. The staff is going to be licensed and trained in dealing with the care of infants and children, so you can be sure that they will be safe while you are away at work. At no time should your baby be unsupervised.

Home Daycare

A home daycare only differs from a traditional daycare in one way – it is operated outside of a person's home instead of a facility. This can provide a more nurturing approach to childcare, as your baby will feel that they are still in a home environment. The amount of children present at home daycare is also usually smaller since licensing requires home daycares to take on fewer children per staff member. They can also be less expensive than traditional daycare. Since a home daycare can be more relaxed, you might have the option of flexible pick up and drop off times. On average, you can expect to pay around $650 each month for your child to attend a home daycare. Since they are a little bit more exclusive due to their size restrictions, it can be hard to find home daycares that have the space for your baby.

Nanny

When you hire a nanny, your baby gets to stay in the comfort of your own home. Depending on whether your nanny is live-in, or only comes when needed, your price point will vary. You will need to pay around $2,000-$3,000 for nanny care each month, which is considerably more expensive than the previous daycare options. When your baby is cared for by a nanny, they are receiving personalized attention. This is a person that your baby is going to bond with, and the bond can become very strong. The best part is, you won't have to worry about picking up or dropping off your baby. They will already be in the comfort of your home.

Relative

If you know of a relative who can take care of your baby, this can be a great option for childcare. Of course, pricing is going to vary with this option. You will need to come to an agreement with the individual to decide on what salary is fair. Most people pay their relatives minimum wage when they care for their children. Naturally, this option is rich in advantages. Your baby is likely already going to be familiar with this person, and there is going to be a personal interest in the care of your child because of this. Your relatives can be briefed on your particular requests for your child, respecting your parenting style when a lot of daycares or nannies wouldn't be able to abide by the same modifications.

Stay-at-Home Parent

If you can afford to stay at home with your baby, this is going to be a great option for childcare. A lot of parents just can't stand the thought of leaving their little one with a stranger or even a loved one, so they opt to stay at home and care for their child themselves. You need to consider, if you had a job prior to having a baby, you are not going to be earning these wages any longer. For some couples, this is manageable, but it does require a thorough overview of all the finances. When you stay at home with your baby, you are going to be present for every single one of their milestones. A lot of parents are saddened by the fact that they miss these things when they have to put their babies in daycare or in the care of a nanny.

Preschool

Despite what you knew before about preschool, it can actually serve as a great option for childcare while your child is still in their first year of life. While a lot of preschools are designed to take children who are at least 4-years old, some accept babies. On average, a preschool is going to cost around $740 a month. What your child will get here is a structured curriculum, which none of the other childcare options offer. Teachers work at preschools who are trained in early childhood education, both reliable and reassuring to a working parent. This is a structured option that allows your child to have the earliest chance at learning. Lots of parents enjoy the fact that educational activities are the focus.

Chapter 4: Baby's Safety and Medical Emergency Concerns

Knowing how to keep your baby safe is something that you will instinctively learn as a parent. In the first year, it can feel like your baby is prone to all of the worst dangers out there. Thinking about all of the possibilities, you might send yourself into a panic considering all of these what-if situations. Knowing what signs to look for and what to do to keep your baby safe in various situations is going to help you stay one step ahead.

Home and Outdoor Safety

Nursery Safety

Your baby's nursery should be the safest space in the home. A safe haven for your baby to grow up in, the nursery can actually be a dangerous place if you aren't careful. The crib that you choose is essential to your baby's safety. An out-of-date crib might not have as many of the same safety features as a modern one, so saving up the money for a better crib is a good idea. Artwork can be very beautiful and a great way to engage your baby from the crib, but be careful where you hang it. There is always going to be a risk of the artwork falling onto your baby if you hang it right above or next to the crib.

In general, all other furniture needs to be anchored and baby-proof. Think about anything that might fall onto your baby while they reach their crawling stage. These things must be safely secured. The same can be said for the windows and blinds. You wouldn't want your baby accidentally getting access to the cord that controls the blinds, or worse, opening up the window. Make sure that both of these things are also baby-proofed. Anything that is loose on tables or surfaces needs to be big enough so that your baby will not choke on it. Babies love to put everything in their mouths, so choking hazards need to be taken very seriously.

Feeding Safety

Choking is a big problem for infants and babies due to their inability to fully master swallowing. They can choke on anything very easily, and this includes food. This happens because their physical development is trying to catch up with their ability to eat on their own. When you are feeding your baby, especially when they reach the solid food stage, you need to make sure that the pieces are cut up very small. Any fruit or vegetable skins can also become a choking hazard, so peel them when you can. Babies need extra safety when it comes to feeding because a bad case of choking can turn fatal. This is something that you must be very cautious about as a parent.

In terms of breastfeeding, there are also safety precautions to take. The ideal feeding situation is directly from your breast to your baby, but sometimes, you will have to pump milk so that you can have it on-hand for later. With any breast milk that you pump, make sure that the milk stays refrigerated for no longer than three days. Always sterilize your hands before you feed your baby or pump milk for your baby. The germs and bacteria on your hands can be ingested very easily. If you are warming a bottle of milk for your baby, always check the temperature by placing a drop on the inside of your own wrist first. Though it might not feel hot on the exterior, the internal temperature can burn your baby's mouth.

Bathroom Safety

The bathroom is likely one of the last places you would think to make baby-proof, but it is an important room in the house that your baby will soon be visiting frequently. Though you only have an infant at the moment, you need to ensure that you keep your baby away from any standing water. Not only are there drowning dangers but there are also electrocution dangers. It is simply best to never leave any standing water, whether it be in the sink or bathtub. You should also make sure you do your best to prevent any slippery surfaces. There are bath mats available for this purpose. If your baby slips and falls, they could get injured very easily. Make sure that none of your bathroom cabinets can be easily opened. Many people keep cleaning supplies underneath their bathroom sink, and this can be fatal if your child ingests any of these chemicals.

When you are giving your baby a bath, closely monitor the water temperature. While babies can get cold easily, they also feel very sensitive to heat. Ensure that the bathwater isn't too hot.

Yard Safety

The main way to baby-proof your yard is by making sure that you have a fenced-in area that is safe for your child. While your whole yard does not need to be fenced, the area in which your baby will be exploring and spending time in should be fenced. Within this area, make sure that you aren't putting your baby near any poisonous plants or small rocks that can be ingested. There should be enough space for you to set up a blanket or outdoor playpen so that your baby does not have direct contact with the ground. This is the easiest way to stay safe while being outside in the first year of life. And of course, constant supervision is always necessary. Turning your back for even a few minutes can result in an unfortunate accident.

General Safety

- Burns: Young babies are at a very high risk of getting burned. This has a lot to do with their mobility and curiosity. When you are cooking, always make sure that you keep the pot and pan handles inward to avoid an accidental grab by your baby. Any hot things should also be placed at the very middle of the table or counter and out of reach. Make sure that you plug all of your outlets, and don't let your child touch light bulbs or any other exposed lighting (Christmas tree lighting, for example).

- Falls: Your baby is going to fall a lot; this is normal in a child who is learning how to crawl, scoot, and walk. What you need to make sure is that they do not get hurt in the process. Use barriers, like indoor gates, to section off safe areas of your home for your baby to practice. Always use the straps and buckles in highchairs or other seats where your baby will be left. Make sure that you also pad any sharp corners of furniture in your home.

- Drowning: It does not take a lot of water for your baby to accidentally drown. In fact, it can happen when there is only 1 inch of water present. To avoid this, you need to make sure that you never take your eyes off your baby when there is water involved. If you have a pool, this should always remain fenced and locked. Your baby might see the water and want to go near it out of instinct, so it is better to be safe than sorry.

When to Seek Medical Attention

If you think that your baby is starting to get sick, this can be an awful feeling. While you want your baby to feel better, you might be wondering when to seek medical attention. It is normal that your baby catches an occasional cold or illness, but certain symptoms can be more dangerous than others. The following are some indications of when you should contact your doctor or make an appointment for your baby:

- Appetite Changes: If your baby refuses to eat for several meals in a row, then this is a sign that something could be wrong. Also, if your baby is eating poorly, you can take this as the same type of indication.

- Behavioral Changes: You know your baby better than anyone, so you can trust your maternal instinct. Your baby might become hard to wake up or feel unusually tired, and this is definitely a big behavioral change to watch out for. Inconsolable crying can also be a cause for concern. Get to your doctor right away if you notice that your baby appears to be floppy or less responsive to their reflexes.

- Tender navel or penis: There are times when your baby's navel might get irritated and even bloody. The same can happen to the penis if you have a baby boy. Understandably, these are very concerning symptoms, so you will want to have them evaluated right away.

- Fever: For infants under 3-months old, fevers can often be deadly if left untreated. While it might seem extra precautionary, you need to seek medical attention right away for any fever that develops. In infants that are 3-6 months, a temperature of 102 or higher is considered dangerous. You would want to consult a doctor at that point. As your baby gets a little bit older, the case of a fever becomes less dangerous. You can contact your doctor if a fever of 102 or higher lasts for longer than 1 day. Whether or not they show any other symptoms, a fever is definitely something to pay attention to.

- Diarrhea: If your baby is having constant diarrhea, this could mean that there is something wrong with your baby's digestion. While it can be normal for babies to experience diarrhea sometimes, regular diarrhea can indicate that there is a problem.

- Vomiting: You are going to get used to your baby spitting up after feedings. This is an indication of good health and digestion, but if your baby is vomiting, then this becomes more dangerous. Vomiting is different from spitting up because it is more forceful. Projectile vomiting can be very alarming, as well. Contact your doctor if your baby cannot keep liquids down, especially if this lasts for 8+ hours.

- Dehydration: When your baby cries with fewer tears, has a fever, and is not able to urinate as much, this could mean that they are dehydrated. Keep an eye on their soft spot, as well. If it appears sunken in any way, this is also a sign of dehydration.

- Constipation: Much like diarrhea, occasional constipation is normal for infants. If you notice that your baby does not use the bathroom for a few days or appears to be struggling while using the bathroom, this can be a cause for concern.

- Colds: As mentioned, the occasional cold is normal. This is automatically more dangerous for infants since their immune systems aren't as strong as adults'. The time to contact your doctor comes when you notice that your baby's breathing is labored in any way or if they have nasal mucus that lasts for longer than a week and a half. Ear pain and a cough that lasts for longer than a week is also an indication that your baby might need medicine in order to get better.

- Rashes: A rash is normally an indication of an allergic reaction, but it can potentially mean that your baby has an infection. Get in touch with your doctor if your baby seems to have developed a rash out of nowhere, and definitely if it comes along with a fever.

- Eye Discharge: Any time that you notice your baby's eyes are leaking mucus, you will need to contact your doctor. You will be able to tell the difference between tears and mucus because it is a lot thicker. It can also make your baby's eyes red.

Of course, with any medical concern, you need to use your best judgment and common sense as a parent to determine when your baby should be taken to the doctor. There are some things that are direr and will require emergency care, such as uncontrollable bleeding, poisoning, seizures, unconsciousness, deep cuts or burns, major mouth and facial injuries, or lips that look blue or purple.

The most important thing is that you do not panic. Any of the above symptoms or situations can be enough to send a parent into a panic over their baby, and that is understandable. However, if you can keep the energy calm, then you will be doing what is best for your baby. Try to stay as calm as you can, and work quickly to get your baby the care they need.

Again, you might feel like you are being overly cautious, but it is better to be safe than sorry. Since your baby cannot talk to you yet, it can be hard to know exactly what is wrong. Even if it is something that turns out to be minor, you will be able to rest assured that you did everything you could do to make sure that your baby is okay.

Traveling with an Infant

Another situation that can be slightly stressful is the idea of traveling with an infant. While the same stressors of travel will apply, you will now have to ensure that you have everything that you need while you are away from home with your baby. These are some of the top tips to follow if you do intend on taking your baby on a trip:

1. Book the Right Seats: If you plan on traveling by plane, you need to figure out if you will be required to

purchase a separate seat for your baby. Some airlines do not charge you for this, but others will require you to buy one, no matter how young they are. You need to have a proper car seat that is up to code and that can be taken on the plane. Know that not all car seats are designed for air travel, so ensure that you have the right kind. If you are planning on holding your baby, consider booking a window or an aisle seat – there are benefits to each one. The window seat can be a great distraction for your baby, while the aisle seat gives you easy access to the bathroom or space to move around if the baby gets fussy. A lot of airlines are very accommodating if you tell them that you are traveling with an infant, so let them know ahead of time.

2. Pack Properly: Not only do you need to remember to bring all of your belongings for the trip, but you must also think ahead for your baby. You will need to bring everything necessary for feeding, toys, and comforts from home, changes of clothes, diapers and wipes, plus any car seats or strollers. Overall, you are going to be packing a lot more than you usually would, so keep that in mind when you are selecting a suitcase to take along. Also, consider that you might have to pay additional fees if you intend on checking in these additional items that you need to pack for your baby.

3. Bring Entertainment: Though your baby is still likely too young to be able to sit still long enough to watch a movie while you are traveling, you should bring along some sort of distraction or entertainment to keep your baby occupied. Babies tend to get fussy very easily during any type of travel that requires long periods of sitting still, so make sure that you can bring some toys along to help you keep them engaged and happy.

4. Take Your Own Food: If possible, bring food that your baby is familiar with. If you are only breastfeeding, this becomes less of an issue. However, if your baby is already eating solids, then you need to prepare for the idea that the place you are traveling to might not have the kind of food that your baby is used to eating. In your checked luggage, you should be able to bring jars of baby food to keep the feeding schedule normal and familiar. Know that not all countries carry the same brands of baby foods, either. If you do intend on purchasing baby food when you arrive, especially if you are traveling to a foreign country, it doesn't hurt to bring some of your own food as a backup plan.

5. Select the Right Stroller: Much like cars, not all baby strollers offer the same features. If you are going on a short trip, a lightweight stroller is likely going to be just fine. It will also be easier to carry around with you. If your trip is longer, you might want to consider bringing

a stroller that has plenty of storage space. When you have a heavy-duty stroller that fully reclines and allows you to bring food and toys along easily, you are going to have a much easier time transporting your baby.

6. Consider the Hotel You Book: Most hotels are very accommodating, but not all of them offer sleeping arrangements for infants. If you have a very young baby, putting them to bed in a regular bed isn't going to work. Call the hotel ahead of time to make sure that they will have a crib for you to use. Keep in mind that this crib likely won't come with linens, so you should pack your own just in case. Another helpful tip is to book a corner room. At some point, your baby is probably going to cry. Being in a corner room limits the number of other guests you will disturb as you are trying to soothe your little one.

7. Get Vaccinations: Depending on where you are going, you should contact your doctor to double-check that your baby is properly vaccinated for the trip. Whether or not you regularly vaccinate your baby, it can be worth it to check on area-specific vaccinations because some countries are carriers for illnesses and diseases that can greatly impact your baby. Any foreign contact with these germs can cause a lot of problems, and a potential overseas emergency. To avoid this, getting

vaccinated is the easiest way to make sure that they stay protected.

8. Consider How You Will Get Around: Once you reach your destination, you will likely need additional transportation as you explore. Are you going to be taking taxis or ride-sharing? Will you rent your own car? This is why bringing a car seat is very important because you never know if your mode of transportation is going to have one available for your baby. A lot of parents prefer to rent their own car, if possible. This allows for a lot more freedom during the trip and a safer way to get around for your baby.

Chapter 5: First Trimester Milestones (1-3 Months)

As you watch your baby grow you will be amazed by not only their physical development but also their emotional development. So much growth happens on both levels as your child is in what is considered the "first trimester" of life. This is the period between 1-3 months of age, and it is filled with many notable milestones to look out for. In this section, you will become familiarized with what to expect and how to recognize any potential issues.

First Month

Milestones Chart

- Eyes tracking objects
- Gripping objects placed into the hand
- Noticing people and faces within range
- Making throaty noises
- Crying subsiding when held by a caregiver
- Displays of reflexes
- Lifting head during tummy time
- Moving limbs symmetrically
- Recognition of mother's breast

Developmental Milestones

Cognitive:

1. Expecting Feedings: In the beginning, your newborn is going to eat when you feed them. You are initially the one who is setting the intervals between feedings. By the time your baby reaches 1 month, you should start to notice that their inner body clock kicks in. They will begin to cry at certain times, indicating that they are hungry.

2. Distinguishing Tastes: Your baby will know the difference between the taste of the breast milk after you have eaten certain foods. For example, when you eat something that alters the taste of the milk, your baby will react by either refusing to feed or making different faces.

3. Acknowledging Presence: If you hold an object up to your baby, they should be able to lock their eyes on it and focus on it. The same can be said for when a person stands within view.

4. Memory of Sensations: Your baby should now notice the difference between soft textures and rough textures. They will also respond to sweet smells differently than harsh smells.

Physical:

Your baby should be able to thrust their arms at their own

will. Though the movement is jerky at this point, it is intentional. Maybe your baby will begin to make strong fists. This does not necessarily indicate any type of distress, but it means that your baby is exploring exactly what can be done with their hands.

You will also notice an improvement in their reach and aim. When you place an object near them, they will likely try to grab or hold onto it. A baby who is physically healthy will enjoy reaching for things that they find enticing. Your baby might start lifting their head slightly on their own, but still won't be able to fully support its weight. This is why tummy time is important because that is how to quickly build up their muscles so that they can hold their head up on their own.

Social:

Crying is going to be the main form of communication. A cry can indicate hunger, being uncomfortable, and needing affection. They will likely respond well to familiar voices, such as your own, and can express joy at hearing it. If you are too rough while picking your baby up, they will likely be startled by this movement, sensing the roughness.

When to Be Concerned

You do not have much reason to be concerned during the first three months of development, but there are a few indicators that you need to be aware of. This is going to be a time of great exploration for your baby, and not all babies experience the same things at the same time. Some examples of when to become concerned are: feeding poorly, not blinking in response to bright lighting, stiff muscles, limp muscles, not responding to sound when fully awake, and not being able to focus on an object in close proximity.

Tips to Improve Development

Give your baby plenty of tummy time. This is going to allow them to gain enough muscle to eventually hold their head up on their own. Choose a fixed time each day to have tummy time, and stick to this regular schedule. Your baby will become familiar with the activity, and it will help strengthen nearly every muscle in their body. You can do this around 3-5 times a day if you want to. Each session should last a few minutes at a time to start out with. Keeping your baby on their tummy for too long can cause them to feel strained or fatigued. In order to capture their interest, place a toy in front of them that they can fixate on. It becomes the motivation to reach and grasp for the object while simultaneously focusing on it and using their muscles to stay upright.

Select stimulating activities that will engage your baby. This means choosing games and toys that are bright and colorful, make interesting noises, and involve some interactivity. You should also set aside some time daily for this kind of stimulation. When your baby gets to practice with this kind of interaction, they become better able to develop quickly on both a cognitive and a physical level. Social interactions are also important. Allow your baby to meet all of your loved ones, and get them used to be held by others. You need to show them that there is safety, even when they are socializing with people other than yourself. Of course, you will want to make sure that each person who handles your baby is a positive influence with a caring nature.

Mental Leaps

At around 5 weeks, your baby will be maturing rapidly. Everything from their internal organs to their perception of the world around them will be evolving on a daily basis. They will now be able to see at a distance of around 20-30 centimeters, so you can expect a lot more curiosity to shine through. You might also notice that your baby can produce more tears than they were able to before. At the 8-week mark, your baby will have a better concept of the patterns going on around them. Everything appears to be a jumbled mess at first, but as the maturity continues, your baby will be able to pick up on the repetition that goes on around them. They should have a fairly regular feeding schedule and sleep schedule at this point.

When your baby is 12-weeks old, your baby's movements will start to change. This happens as their muscles get stronger and they realize that they have control over their body. Instead of robotic, jerking movements, your baby will likely be able to make more purposeful movements. They are also likely going to be playing with their vocal sounds a lot more. Don't be surprised if you hear noises that are already beginning to sound like words. Remember, what you say around your baby is how they are going to learn how to speak. What you expose them to at this age is very crucial. Getting to see the world from different physical perspectives becomes exciting to your baby during this stage. "Flying" your baby around the room at your arm's length can often result in plenty of giggles and amazement.

What to Expect During a Check-Up

At 1-month old, your baby is already due for their first check-up. At this first visit, you can expect a general examination. The doctor is going to take a look at your baby to make sure that all of their systems are functioning correctly and that they are responding to certain stimuli. Measurements will then be taken. The length, weight, and head circumference are recorded so that the doctor can view your baby's numbers on a growth chart to make sure everything is on track. The doctor will also monitor your baby's developmental milestones. Since you are going to have to speak for them, you need to tell your doctor what your baby has accomplished since the last visit (or since birth).

Your doctor is also going to ask you a series of questions about your baby's typical behavior. This is to rule out any behavioral disorders or any abnormal patterns of behavior. There is nothing to worry about here, and it is best to just be honest with the doctor. Mention anything that you find noteworthy. Next, the physical examination will take place. The doctor will check your baby's eyes, ears, nose, mouth, lungs, heart, abdomen, skin, genitalia, and hips/legs. While your baby still has a soft spot, this will also be examined on the head. You might be given the option to get your baby tested for tuberculosis, and if you are vaccinating, they will receive their second round of the HepB vaccine.

Second Month

Milestones Chart

- Can raise head 45-degrees when on tummy
- Holds head straight while in a supported seated position
- Places partial weight on elbows
- Can visually follow objects moving in a small arch
- Can search for sounds by turning head
- Recognize faces
- Cooing and gurgling
- Will smile at familiar faces
- Becomes fussy when bored

- Responds to voices with cooing

Developmental Milestones

Cognitive:

1. Paying Attention to Faces: When your little one looks at your face, you should experience periods of eye contact. This happens as your baby's vision continues to develop.
2. Location of Sound Source: Your baby's brain and hearing should be pretty coordinated by this point. They will likely be looking directly at whatever is causing a sound that has caught their attention.
3. Unique Crying Tones: When your baby is hungry, you will know it. The same can be said for when your baby needs a new diaper. These cries should now sound different.

Physical: Lifting the head and being able to hold the head up is one of the biggest physical milestones that your baby will experience this month. They will also begin to partially push up onto their elbows during tummy time, but likely won't be able to hold the position for a long time yet. Their vision and eye coordination should be improving daily as well. Your baby can now track slow-moving objects without a problem.

Social: Smiling is a significant social milestone that can be seen from your 2-month old. If they see a happy face smiling at them, they are likely to smile back. They might also respond to questions with cooing or gurgling. If any self-soothing behavior is beginning, you might notice that your baby is a thumb-sucker. This kind of behavior can keep your baby calm for short periods of time. Overall, your baby is starting to become more independent.

When to be Concerned

If your baby never smiles, an expressionless face can be something to worry about. This likely means that your baby cannot process what is going on around them. Not being able to hold their head up at all is also a warning sign. Though it is still going to be difficult for your 2-month old to hold the entire weight of their head up, they should be able to do it for short periods of time. If you notice these things, you definitely need to bring them up to your doctor.

Not bringing their hands to their mouth can also be a warning sign. While your baby does not need to do this frequently, it is normal for a baby at this age to want to explore moving their limbs more and chewing on their own hands and fingers. This might be an indication of possible developmental delays taking place.

At the doctor's office, bring up anything that you find to be abnormal about your baby's behavior. Even if it seems insignificant, you know your baby best. Bringing it up to the doctor and catching it early can often mean that the behavior can be corrected. This means that your baby might be able to catch up, developmentally. Of course, don't worry yourself over anything that you might think is abnormal. Your doctor will be able to confirm or deny these things for you.

Tips to Improve Development

Tummy time is a must, and you can place your baby on their tummy multiple times a day. Keep the sessions short, around 5 minutes each. You can do this 3-5 times a day, and by doing so, you are helping to strengthen virtually every muscle in your baby's body. It is a great way to allow your baby to exercise while also providing a fun playtime position. You can put one of your baby's favorite toys in front of them to encourage them to look up and hold themselves up.

Play games that are going to stimulate as many senses as possible. A great game to play is one where you stand across the room from your baby and make a noise until they are able to track you. This will help with their hearing, vision, ability to focus, and range of movement. Making these games a part of your daily routine will allow your baby to be learning while playing.

Don't be afraid to introduce your baby to new people. Believe it or not, their social skills have already started developing. Though it seems early, and you might want to keep your baby hidden away to yourself, you need to allow other people to hold and interact with your little one. This shows your baby how to build trust for other people, and it also shows them that they can trust you in return. When they are handled by others and then returned to you, it proves to them that they can be social while still remaining comfortable.

Mental Leaps

Your baby now has a better perception of what is going on in the world around them. Instead of one jumbled mess, your baby is beginning to understand what eating is, what sleep is, and so on. Babies are very keen on patterns, so maintaining a regular schedule is very important. Try to get your baby on a schedule of some sort as soon as you bring them home from the hospital. This will regulate them and allow them to better understand what is happening. Having the consciousness of what is actually going on around them is a great sign. You can expect your baby to experience more moments like this one as the month goes on.

This is the age when an infant is likely to discover their hands. You might find your little one looking at, or even chewing on their hands more than usual. In their brain, they are processing that this limb is an extension of their body. Each time they move their arms or legs and touch something beside them, they will be more likely to notice it. Movements that are made might appear a bit wooden. This hyper-awareness might cause them to temporarily lose control over their reflexes, but this is perfectly normal. They will return soon.

What to Expect During a Check-Up

The basics of measuring will take place, as usual. This is the time when you can discuss your baby's latest behaviors. Your doctor will be able to tell you if your baby is developmentally on track with where they should be, and you can express any concerns that you might be feeling. Check-ups are intended to make sure that your baby is healthy and happy, but they can also serve as a way to give you that peace of mind that you crave. Being a parent isn't an easy task, as there is a lot to worry about at any given time. Don't worry, though, because it will get easier.

This appointment, your baby will likely have to get a lot of shots. This can be somewhat upsetting, but know that it is for the sake of their health. If you do elect to vaccinate your child, you can expect a second HepB shot. They will also get an RV (rotavirus vaccine), DTaP (diphtheria and tetanus toxoids and acellular pertussis vaccine), Hib (Haemophilus influenza vaccine), PCV (pneumococcal vaccine), and IPV (invacinated poliovirus vaccine).

Your baby might surprise you at how well they do at the doctor's office. If they do cry during the shots, know that the pain is very quick and temporary. If your energy is nervous and upset, they are going to sense this. Try to put on a brave face for them, and know that they will be back in your arms soon for that comfort that you both crave.

Third Month

Milestones Chart

- Regularly lifts head 45-degrees during tummy time
- Pushes legs down when held against a flat surface
- Brings hands to mouth a lot
- Grasps objects nearby
- Can shake an object in the grasp
- Tracks moving objects within the field of vision
- Can be quiet or more reserved around strangers
- Back muscles getting stronger from tummy time
- Beginning to imitate some actions
- Supports body weight on arms

Developmental Milestones

Cognitive:

1. Recognizes Familiar Faces at a Distance: Your baby might express joy from seeing you across the room. They might do this by cooing or gurgling to let them know that they see you.
2. Locates Sounds: Frequent head-turning to locate a sound is considered a norm. Your baby should be very curious about different noises.
3. Will "Talk" Back: If you say something to your baby, you can expect a reply. Though they cannot talk just yet, speech is coming just around the corner.

405

Physical: Head movements are going to be the biggest milestone during the third month. Your baby will be lifting their head more and supporting it for longer periods of time. They will be able to track objects at 180-degrees, and they should be super interested in what is going on around them. If your baby pushes their legs down a lot, this is a sign they want to stand. After standing, walking is going to come quickly! It can be very exciting to notice this.

Social: Your baby is going to be laughing a lot more, and it will be so nice to hear. It is a sign that something is amusing or pleasant to your little one. You can also expect a lot more smiling, especially at familiar faces. Your baby should regularly smile at those they interact with on a daily basis. They might become interested in other infants if given the chance to socialize with children around the same age.

When to Be Concerned

If your baby is unusually quiet, you might think that this is a great sign at first. A soothed baby will remain quiet and calm, but it won't take long for something to trigger a verbal response. When your baby seems as though they cannot gurgle or make any type of noise, then this can be an indication that something isn't right. While it can be a very slight developmental delay, it is a good thing to let your doctor know about this right away. An average 3-month old is going to be very noisy during their most active hours. They should also be expressing their delight by using their voice.

Head control is also something that you need to pay attention to. A 3-month old should have no problem with head control and preventing the head from wobbling or flopping forward. It is definitely an indication of some kind of developmental delay when your baby cannot keep their head up on their own, even for a few seconds at a time. In the meantime, make sure that you are always properly giving them support and then bring the issue up to your doctor. The same can be said if your baby is unable to hold an object. While they might drop it eventually, a 3-month old's grip should be fairly strong by now. When your baby plays, they should be holding onto their toys, maybe even bringing them to their mouth or throwing them around in delight.

Tips to Improve Development

You can help your baby by interacting with them all the time. No matter what you are doing, even if it does not directly involve your little one, practice narrating everything. When you explain things to your baby, this is going to pique their interest. Though they might not be able to understand all the concepts just yet, they are still going to be absorbing this information until it makes sense. Have regular conversations, and allow your baby the time to respond. You will find that they probably get excited when you reply back to them again.

Playing games that allow your baby to track objects will help to build this skill. For example, playing with toy cars that can move around will allow your baby to find something interesting, and this will then cause them to try to track the object. Don't go too fast, or this might seem overwhelming. You can play with moving toys with your little one every day and see how well they respond to them. Using sounds to get your baby's attention is also a great way to play.

Don't forget that tummy time is, by far, the best way to help your baby develop. Having enough tummy time each day will get your baby to the most advanced stage of development possible. This muscle-building activity is very fun for babies, and you can make it different each time by placing different toys out for your baby to reach for.

Mental Leaps

One of the biggest leaps that you will notice is how your baby begins to move. Instead of jerky or robotic movements of the limbs, the transitions will be a lot smoother. Your baby is still going to explore their range of motion by kicking or punching, but each action should feel more purposeful than it used to. Your baby will also be playing with their own vocal sounds a lot more. If you hear your baby yelling out in a shrill tone and then immediately giggling, there is no need to be alarmed. They are just testing out their vocal cords to see what they can do with them.

Play the "airplane" game with your baby. This involves flying them through the air, similar to the way that an airplane would fly, and allow them to see the room from this new point of view. Since your baby's vision and depth perception are both improving, this can be a mind-blowing experience. They will likely love this game, giggling and laughing as you make airplane sounds below them. You can fly them around different rooms of the house, changing elevation safely, as well. This is only one example of how you can mentally stimulate your little one. There are plenty of other games that you can play that will allow for the same results. Experiment and see which ones get the best reactions.

What to Expect During a Check-Up

There is actually no check-up scheduled for a 3-month old. The next time your baby will be seen by the doctor will be during their 4-month check-up. There is no need to worry because your baby is up-to-date on all of their vaccines and, as long as everything is going well developmentally, there should be no reason for you to take them to the doctor. Enjoy this month by letting your baby grow and explore as much as possible. Introduce them to new things, people, and environments. The more that you allow your baby to see, the more that they will have the chance to learn.

Of course, if you sense that something isn't right, you can call your doctor or make an appointment to take your child in. Use your best instincts to guide you through this month. This is kind of a test to the parents in terms of being able to read the signs that your baby is giving you. As long as you are paying attention and aware of what could be dangerous, then you should have no problems during this month.

This break from the doctor will give you a chance to think ahead about the next month's appointment. Are there any tests that you'd like your doctor to run on your baby? Do you want your baby to receive any particular vaccinations? Sometimes, this space between appointments gives you a great period of time to get grounded and confident in your parenting abilities.

Chapter 6: Second Trimester Milestones (4-6 Months)

You are now a parent to a baby who has reached the second trimester of their first year of life! Your little one probably has a big personality with plenty of cute traits that you are very proud of. Though you might be getting more sleep than when your child was a newborn, they still have a way of keeping you exhausted throughout the day. From tummy time to trying solid foods, this part of your baby's life is one that is going to be very memorable. A lot of milestones will be reached, and a lot of new information will be learned. Your baby is becoming a person that is an individual, and as a parent, that is one of the best feelings of accomplishment that you can imagine.

Fourth Month

Milestones Chart

- Responds to basic sounds and words
- Can support the body with arms during tummy time
- Smiles and laughs while looking at faces
- Can track nearby objects
- Can sit with support
- Makes basic movements during tummy time

- Can hold toys with both hands
- Cries differently when feeling certain emotions
- Can push legs downward when standing with support
- Watches new objects and people with curiosity

Developmental Milestones

Cognitive:

1. Understands Basic Cause and Effect: Your baby should now know that, when placed to your breast, this means it is feeding time. They should open their mouth in response.
2. Improved Memory: Your baby can now develop favorite toys, sounds, and colors. Their memory is improving daily, which gives them the ability to remember more things.
3. Purposeful Crying: A 4-month old can cry to tell you when they are hungry, fussy, sad, in need of a diaper change, or just uncomfortable. These cries will sound different.

Physical: Because of your baby's increased neck, shoulder, and back strength, they should be able to sit up straight when given assistance. Whether they are seated in a special chair or with the help of your hands, this should be fairly easy now. Their babble will also start to sound more purposeful, full of rhythmic sounds. You'll notice that they really take to words that start with the letters M, D, and B.

Social: They say imitation is the sincerest form of flattery, and this is especially true with a curious 4-month old. Your little one will now be imitating your gestures and sounds, perhaps even your facial expressions. They will also begin to display favoritism. This can apply to objects, toys, and people in their life. Though, this doesn't mean that they will ignore strangers. In fact, they might stare because they are curious. Your baby might try to get their attention to gauge their level of interest in interaction.

When to Be Concerned

If your baby displays absolutely no variety in facial expressions, this doesn't necessarily mean you have a little grumpy baby. It could mean that they actually are not able to make any facial expressions which are, of course, a sign of concern. Your baby should at least be regularly smiling, even if they have not yet mastered the other facial expressions that they can make. A lack of eye coordination is also a cause for concern at this stage in life. Your baby should be tracking objects with ease, especially if they are directly in front of them. If your baby isn't doing this, then there might be a developmental delay to blame.

The strength of your baby's neck and head should be closely monitored at all times. An average 4-month old will be regularly lifting and turning their head around. If your baby cannot do this and the head appears to be wobbly or floppy,

413

then a doctor's input is definitely going to be necessary. Their limbs should also be fairly flexible at this point. If you notice that they are stiff to the point where your baby is unable to use them properly, then you need to ensure that they are not causing them any pain. Sometimes, this symptom can be a precursor to autism-spectrum disorders, but only your doctor will be able to confirm if that is the case.

Tips to Improve Development

When you pick up your baby's toys, tell them what each one is by name. Even if your baby isn't talking in full sentences yet, they are still able to comprehend these things that you teach them. Do the same with food and people, too. The more familiar with these things that your baby can get before actually being able to talk, the easier time they will have with expressing themselves. Try to talk to your baby as much as possible. Think about them as your little side-kick, going everywhere with you and helping you along the way. Your baby is always going to be interested in what you have to say, especially if you make your tone higher-pitched and exciting.

As your baby is sitting in your lap and practicing the act of holding themselves up, read to them from picture books. Reading is a great way to keep your baby engaged, especially if the pages are colorful or textured. Your little one should be able to feel the book and know that the pages are meant to be read. Don't let them destroy the book or rip it while you are reading. This is how they will learn their first lesson in right from wrong. It will also keep them safer, as you will find that you are constantly going to be trying to do for your baby. Teaching them the difference between right and wrong is your responsibility; they have no one else to learn from.

Mental Leaps

This next mental leap is the concept of events taking place. To a baby, an event is likely going to be on a much smaller scale than what you would consider an event to symbolize. For example, feeding time is an event for a baby. Sleeping is also an event. They will notice when these events do not take place in their usual order, so be prepared for a tantrum if you do have to change up the routine or schedule. Your baby is going to become very accustomed to their set routine, so beware if you plan on changing it. You'll have to slowly transition out of it and into the new one.

Your baby's senses are developed to a point where they will likely be responsive in more than one way. This means that a hand gesture can be accompanied by a vocal sound. Children's songs typically encourage these behaviors, so play this kind of music for your child. Sing along and perform the appropriate action. Your baby will catch on quickly and might even begin to imitate you. This is a very fun and new way to see the world, so if you notice a look of fascination on your baby's face, this is a great reaction. They are starting to learn how certain behaviors and actions interact – the meaning of cause and effect. Try to keep them engaged at all times, frequently showing them how to involve all the senses.

What to Expect During a Check-Up

Your doctor will measure your baby, standard to past check-ups. There will also be some developmental, behavioral, and psychosocial evaluations done. After all of this, there will be a physical examination. Understandably, this can be a lot on your baby, even if they are normally not very fussy at all. Make sure that you bring them in for their 4-month appointment after they get a well-rested night of sleep. Your doctor is going to need as much patience from your little one as they can get as these various characteristics are tested and observed.

There is a potential screening that you can elect to have done on your child for help with indicating anemia. It might not be applicable to your baby, but a lot of 4-month olds do receive the hematocrit or hemoglobin screening at this check-up. Your baby is also going to receive several shots again. These shots will be the next rounds of RV, DTaP, Hib, PCV, and IPV like the ones given at the 2-month appointment. This is another reason why you don't want to enter the appointment with a fussy baby. If they are fussy, they likely won't stay still enough to receive their vaccinations. Much like any other appointment that you've had, your doctor will ask you if you've noticed anything noteworthy. Even if it is something very minor, if you have an instinct to mention it, then do so.

Fifth Month

Milestones Chart

- Sits upright with support
- Rolls over from back to tummy
- Responds to sounds
- Makes a few single consonant sounds
- Tongue grows more sensitive to tastes
- Shows curiosity toward non-moving objects
- Uses basic expressions to communicate
- Flexes legs when on tummy
- Tests basic cause and effect
- Can recognize familiar faces

Developmental Milestones

Cognitive:

1. Easily Distracted: You will find your baby staring off at shiny objects a lot during this time. They will love to look at bright or shiny things, hear interesting noises, and feel new textures.

2. Language Development: Your 5-month old should now have a mini vocabulary. These simple, yet effective, mono-consonant sounds are how your baby can communicate with you other than crying. You can

expect to hear things like "maa" and "gaa" coming from your baby's mouth.

3. Cause and Effect Testing: When a toy makes a noise, your baby will test this theory by either shaking it or banging it. This shows that they are putting together that the noise is coming from the toy. It's an excellent sign of healthy cognitive development.

Physical: You'll notice that your baby can fully grasp objects pretty well now. Your baby should be picking up toys and possibly even their bottle. They will also stretch their hands out far to try and reach things that are just beyond their grasp. Since their neck muscles are stronger, they are able to hold their chest up during tummy time now. They will also be able to sit up straight with minimal support. Your 5-month old should be very strong at this point in their life, and it will show how much more they try to move and reach for things that are beyond their range of motion. If you put your baby down for tummy time, you might find that they are rolling around a lot. This is normal, and this is a great sign that they have enough strength to do so.

Social: Your baby's favorite thing is likely going to be playing with you and your partner. Familiar faces are easily recognized at this point in their life. They might start showing slight apprehension toward strangers, but this will subside, as long as you teach them that they can trust the person. Lots of emotions will be expressed at the 5-month mark, and not all of them involve crying. Your baby will display bouts of joy and laughter, fear and confusion. They will even express boredom by losing interest in toys and switching to a new one. The more that you listen to your baby, the more expressive they will become. You need to show them that they are being heard.

When to Be Concerned

If your baby does not respond to sounds or voices, this might be an indication of hearing impairment. You can test your baby's hearing by making noises behind or beside them. See if they react to your voice from across the room. A 5-month old should be very responsive at this point in life. Another concern is poor hand control. This involves not having a strong grip. If your baby has ever grabbed your skin and pinched it hard, you know that their grip is developing very well. However, if you notice that they cannot seem to hold their toys or other objects for long periods of time, a developmental delay could be to blame.

If your baby's body is ever stiff or awkward, this could also be a cause for concern. Your baby should be more flexible than ever now, regularly reaching for objects and for you. This stiffness is especially alarming if your baby is getting plenty of tummy time, and it is advised that you visit the doctor right away. As mentioned, this is the precursor to many autism-spectrum disorders. But before you jump to any conclusions, you need to get your doctor's input. There is no need to worry about something unless your doctor tells you that something is wrong. From there, they will be able to guide you through a course of treatment.

It is abnormal if your baby does not display any affection toward you or your partner. Your baby should appear visibly happy to see you, if not audibly. If you notice that your baby does not elicit a response, then there might be a developmental delay occurring. Poor speech development is another thing to look for. If your baby isn't making mono-consonant sounds or even gurgling, then there is something wrong. A baby at this age should be at least making throaty sounds and plenty of noises. With all of these potential issues, it is very important to consult a doctor first. While the signs might alarm you, the prognosis could change very easily.

Tips to Improve Development

The very best thing you can do for your 5-month old is to allow plenty of tummy time each day. This is going to keep strengthening those necessary muscles in all parts of their body. Keep talking to your child, as well. As they develop, they are getting even closer to being able to say words and form sentences. You might see their facial expressions change as they try to imitate the words you are saying to them. By keeping up with the regular conversation, you are normalizing and encouraging speaking. Remember, what is so simple to adults is not such a simple concept to infants. You need to introduce them to these things that we have adopted as norms.

Make sure that you read to your baby frequently. Reading stimulates their mind while also encouraging the use of their imagination. While it is still early for them to be playing pretend, this phase is coming right around the corner. It all starts to happen a lot faster than you think. Brightly colored toys will also stimulate the mind and usually cause a visual expression of joy. Babies tend to favor certain colors by this age, so your little one is likely going to let you know which ones they prefer.

Try to put them in a seated position daily. This will further encourage the ability to sit on her own, without support. Much like tummy time, supported sitting helps them build up their core muscles so that they can eventually do it on their own. Continue with social development, as well. You should still be introducing your baby to as many new people as you can. This will allow them to have different experiences and develop their first few basic social skills. The most important thing is that you show your baby as many things as you can. The experiences that you give them are going to shape their outlook on life and on the world. It is a large job to take on, but it comes with many rewards. A lot of parents stress about doing enough for their children, but if you love your baby and teach them something new on a regular basis, then you are doing everything that it takes to be considered a great parent.

Mental Leaps

The mental leaps that your baby experiences this month will be relatively similar to the last. While there might not be any notable milestones reached, your baby is still learning something new every single day. When you compare your now 5-month old child to the tiny human they were when you brought them home for the first time, you will be surprised at all they have accomplished in such a short amount of time. Babies are like sponges; they crave knowledge, and they are able to absorb a lot of it. As much as you are willing to teach them, they will be willing to learn. In order to do this effectively, you need to find ways to keep them engaged and focused on what you are trying to show them.

What to Expect During a Check-Up

This is another month where a check-up isn't necessary unless you feel that your baby needs to see the doctor. The next check-up typically comes once your baby turns 6-months old. As long as you appear to have a happy and healthy baby, then you have nothing to worry about. If you feel that there are some concerning symptoms present, yet you do not want to make an appointment to see your doctor, you can always call them and see if they can provide you with some advice over the phone. Of course, in case of any emergency situations, you will need to get your baby help right away or take them to the hospital.

Sixth Month

Milestones Chart

- Can eat some fruits and vegetables
- Sitting up with no support
- Can use all fingers to hold objects
- Practices basic cause and effect
- Can recognize primary caregivers(s) face
- Makes simple vowel and consonant sounds
- Can roll in both directions
- Stretches to reach objects
- Can sleep for several consecutive hours through the night
- Has better vision and depth perception

Developmental Milestones

Cognitive:

1. More Curiosity: Your little one will be looking around a lot more and reaching for objects. You might notice some fascination in their eyes.
2. Cause and Effect: There will be more testing of cause and effect. For example, throwing toys on the ground and seeing that they can no longer reach their toys while seated.

3. Imitating Sounds: Since you are talking a lot, your baby will continue to imitate you. Some of these imitations might actually begin to sound like real words!

Physical: Your baby will now have better hand-eye coordination. They will be able to successfully and strongly grasp items that they want to reach. Their vision of color and depth perception is also greatly enhanced at this point. This is why 6-month olds are so easily distracted. One of the biggest milestones is sitting without support! Your baby should now have enough muscles to do so on their own.

Social: If you are feeling down, your baby will now be able to sense this. At around 6-months old, babies can feel empathy. The energy that you show your baby is often mirrored or an attempt to provide affection is made. It can be the sweetest thing when you have had a long day and your little one wants to keep giving you kisses. They learned from the best examples they were given!

When to Be Concerned

Though your baby might need some help sitting up every so often, especially if they accidentally fall to one side, they should definitely be very close to being able to sit up. Those with a delay in physical growth will not be able to accomplish this. A notable cause for concern is your baby's inability to hold themselves up, even despite all the tummy time given and other exercises from other supported sittings. In general, pay attention to your baby's muscle tone. Nothing on your baby's body should appear droopy or stiff. Either one of these signs can be an indication that there is something wrong.

Poor motor skills might lead you to realize that your baby has some sort of cognitive delay. Remember, a 6-month old should be able to hold onto their toys and purposefully move them around. If you see your little one struggling to do so, or not having any interest in playing with toys, you need to mention this to your doctor right away. Social skills are another thing to pay attention to. While your baby doesn't need to love strangers, it is important that they respond to new faces in some way or another. No response is a sign that they are not registering that the person in front of them is someone new.

Tips to Improve Development

Now is your time to mix play with conversations. Structured playtime activities are great for a little one's developing brain, and they are also very fun. Be interactive when you see that your baby is curious or excited about the games that you are playing. Explain what is happening, and continue to refer to objects and people by their names. If you can get the whole family involved during playtime, this is another great way to get some social interaction in with their playtime. Along with this kind of playtime, continue giving your baby plenty of tummy time. Make sure that you place several toys on the floor for your baby to interact with and reach for. They should be more interested than ever now to reach for these objects.

At this stage, your baby can try some finger foods. Make sure that you cut up any solid foods into tiny pieces to prevent choking. You will quickly learn your baby's preferences by what they seem to eat up and what they decide to spit out. It is an exciting milestone to reach and you will learn even more about your little one than you knew before. Though they are just starting out with solids, you still need to keep balance in mind. Even for a baby, a balanced diet is very important.

Mental Leaps

The biggest mental leap that your baby will experience this month is the concept of relationships. It is already well-established that you are the primary caregiver, but their ideas of other people in their lives will also be coming together. By acknowledging familiar people, you can know that your baby understands that these are loved ones. They should be able to clearly differentiate a loved one from a stranger. They will also begin to understand basic shapes. Toys that allow them to explore shapes that fit into certain holes will allow them to further explore this concept.

They will also have a better grasp of the concept of distance. This applies to both affection and playtime. If you are too far away to pick up your baby, they might become fussy until you come closer to pick them us. This is also another way that they can test out the basic concept of cause and effect. If they cannot reach a toy, they might become frustrated. You will notice this frustration by either a facial expression, grunts, or even crying. In their mind, your baby is starting to understand the way that things work and what their preferences are.

What to Expect During a Check-Up

The 6-month check-up is a milestone check-up. Along with all of the usual examinations, your baby is also due for another round of shots. These will include RV, DTaP, PCV, and potentially Hib. Your baby will also need a new dose of IPV sometime between the ages of 6-18 months. If you choose, your baby can now also receive the final dose of the HepB vaccine at some point between now and 18-months. If your appointment happens during the flu season, you can also consider getting your baby a flu shot. Though it isn't mandatory, babies can get hit with the flu very hard. It is difficult for any baby's immune system to fight off the flu, even the healthiest.

There are some screening options for you to choose from, as well. The doctor will give you the option to do a lead screening test. This will simply show you if your baby has been exposed to dangerous levels of lead at any point since birth, as this can greatly affect many factors of development. A tuberculosis test might also be offered. At this appointment, your baby might have their first tooth! In this case, your doctor will check on your baby's oral health as well.

Chapter 7: Third Trimester Milestones (7-9 Months)

You are very close to being the parent of a 1-year old. So many milestones will take place during this portion of your child's life. They are able to learn even faster than ever, and they are better able to communicate with you. Your baby should now have likes and dislikes, favorites, and things that they do not care for. Your little one is still little, but their mind is expanding to become bigger than ever.

Seventh Month

Milestones Chart

- Uses voice to express emotions
- Can understand the word "no"
- Can find partially hidden objects
- Develops a raking grasp
- Will respond to their name
- Tests out cause and effect
- Can identify tones in voices
- Has better depth perception
- Explores objects using hands and mouth

Developmental Milestones

Cognitive:

1. Finds Hidden Objects: A fun game that you can now play is hide-and-seek with toys! Hide your baby's toys under blankets and watch as their curiosity takes over

2. Exploring Objects with Hands and Mouth: This is a stage when you'll have to watch your baby extra closely. They will be putting just about anything they can into their mouth.

3. Understands Tones: When you speak sweetly to your baby, they will know that you mean this with affection. A harsher tone will be understood as something more firm.

Physical: While your baby still likely won't be able to stand up, more weight is able to be supported by their legs. If you assist your baby in a standing position, they should feel solid and balanced. When your baby is lying down, they should be able to roll around in any direction they choose. Your little one has reached a very mobile stage! Their vision is now fully developed, meaning they can see all of the same colors as you.

Social: As mentioned, the tone is normally understood by 6 months of age. If you say the word "no" in a stern voice, your baby will understand this as a negative thing. For example, if they put something in their mouth they aren't supposed to, they should freeze in place when you tell them no. They will also be very responsive to their own name, as they should know it well by now. Group play should be exciting for your baby. This social aspect adds more fun to the games.

When to Be Concerned

Much like the months prior, not having a response to certain sounds and sights is what you primarily need to be looking for. Your baby should be a better listener than ever before, and they should be great at spotting objects and people since their color vision has fully developed. If your baby still isn't showing a response to faces, colors, objects, and such, there is a big chance that a developmental delay of some sort is occurring. Notice how your baby looks at the floor when they are seated above. Most babies at 7 months will be very curious. A lost expression or blank gaze is a concerning sign.

Everything should be going into your baby's mouth at this stage, even things that aren't supposed to at times. If your baby shows no interest or ability to do so, this is another big sign of a delay. Aside from being unable to perform the task, this is naturally going to limit the amount of nutrition that your baby is going to be able to get. Unless you are the one who is feeding them, they will have to rely on you solely for their nourishment. A 7-month old should definitely be able to eat finger foods on their own by this point in time.

Tips to Improve Development

Do some play sit-ups. As you hold your baby in a vertical position, slowly lower them on the floor so they are flat on their back. With assistance, bring your baby back up into the vertical position. This is going to build muscle as well as curiosity. The next milestone will involve your baby being able to sit up on their own from a lying down position, and eventually, standing up. Encourage self-feeding as much as possible. Making sure that you offer your baby safe foods, place them on the feeding tray or plate in front of them and allow them to decide what they would like to eat.

Buying toys has never been more important than it is during this stage. Make sure that you are selecting age-appropriate toys that will offer stimulation and fun at the same time. Interactive toys will help your baby develop necessary motor skills. Social play is a great idea during this age. If possible, allow your baby to socialize with other children that are the same age. Keep it up with the family play sessions, as well. This is going to cut down any social anxiety your baby might still be feeling. Becoming a part of a playgroup that meets regularly can be a great way to maintain regular socialization.

Mental Leaps

Your baby should be very visually engaged at this point in their life. From the toys they play with to the images they see on TV or in picture books, they will show interest in many different activities. It might take you a long time to get your baby tired enough to sleep at night because of their undying curiosity for knowledge and discovery. Consider looking into some educational children's television. If you notice that your baby can focus on these, they are a great way to continue expanding the mind as the shows are typically interactive.

Being able to reach objects will require some effort – this should be very clear to your baby now. During tummy time, you might find them pulling on the floor or blanket below them in an effort to get closer to the toys they desire. Your baby might even be scooting or crawling by now! This is why having a fully baby-proofed home is important because your little one is going to want to take a look at everything they can. They might even want to explore these things by putting them into their mouth. When you set out toys for your baby to play with while they are on the ground, this will usually keep them away from things that are not toys.

What to Expect During a Check-Up

This is a month with no regular check-up scheduled. You should be very familiar with knowing that your baby is healthy, though. They should now be on a steady and balanced diet, paired with a regular sleep schedule. If anything changes in the routine, then you know that this can disturb your baby's health or make them feel off-balanced. Make sure that you are choosing foods that are nourishing to feed to your little one. Though it might be tempting to share sweet treats with them to get a nice reaction, it is best to stick to fruits, vegetables, and grains that will actually assist their growth and development in a more practical way.

There should be minimal fussing because you should be familiar with your baby's cues and desires. Certain patterns emerge as your baby gets older, and as a parent, you learn how to work with these things. While you can't give in to anything that your baby wants, you can learn how to soothe them and keep them happy. Sometimes, parenting involves compromise. You need to show your baby that you are the boss, but not in a mean or demanding way. It can be a hard thing to start showing disciplinary action, but your baby should understand this relationship dynamic by now.

Eighth Month

Milestones Chart

- Supports weight on both legs when in an assisted standing position
- Clearly tracks moving objects
- Can pass objects from hand to hand
- Speaks simple words
- Understands basic instructions
- Can typically say "mama" and "dada"

- Can grasp with a pincer motion
- Has separation anxiety
- Can easily get into a crawling position
- Understands the purpose of personal objects

Developmental Milestones

Cognitive:

1. Understanding Instructions: When you tell your baby to come to you, or when you tell them to put something down, it is likely they will be able to understand you. Though they might not be speaking full sentences yet, your baby has the ability to comprehend these simple requests.

2. Easily Tracks Paths: If you drop a bouncy ball, you can expect your baby to follow its path until it bounces out of view. Their vision should be sharp, and their comprehension should be at a high functioning level.

3. Pointing: Your baby might discover the ability to point at this age. If anything is exciting to your baby, you can expect pointing and some kind of verbal exclamation.

Physical: A pincer grasp is the ability to hold onto an object between the thumb and index finger. Your baby should have this mastered at 8-months old. You will likely notice them using it most during feeding times, carefully and deliberately picking up pieces of food that they want to enjoy. Whether your baby has many teeth yet or not, you will notice that a

435

chewing motion is starting to happen when they eat. This is practice for when they move up a stage in eating.

Social: Separation anxiety is a notable milestone at this age. If you leave your baby alone or with someone else for a long period of time, they might become fussy or difficult because they miss you. While it can be necessary at times, it is normal because your baby heavily relies on you. At this point, you have taught your baby all that they know, so their trust for you is very large. This can cause an increase in shyness around new people.

When to Be Concerned

Vision is important at this age. Your baby should have great eyesight, able to spot familiar faces as well as visually exciting objects from afar. Even when things are close to your baby, if it appears that they show no reaction at all, it is likely because they cannot see clearly. Some infants do need eyeglasses, and your doctor might need to do a vision test to determine if your little one does indeed need this kind of assistance as well. The inability to track objects can often mean that something is wrong cognitively. If your baby can see but cannot track, mention this to your doctor. It can be upsetting when your baby doesn't recognize loved ones or people who are always in their lives, but this does not mean that they do not have a love for these individuals. This can be caused by a developmental delay.

When you try to place your baby on the ground vertically, they should naturally put their feet flat on the floor in a standing position. If the legs curl up in response, this is a bad sign. The same can be said if your baby tries to put weight onto their arms, but cannot hold themselves up. Any muscle stiffness is definitely an issue to be discussed at your next doctor's visit. Try to assist your baby as much as you can if you notice that they are struggling. Your doctor will be able to provide you with additional recommendations.

Tips to Improve Development

Go to new places! Take your baby to markets, stores, shops, restaurants, and more. Each new place that you go, your baby will get a new experience. They will also get the chance to see and interact with new people. Normalize the idea that you are going to see plenty of new people when you go somewhere outside of the house. Make sure that your baby isn't becoming too reliant on you for comfort during social situations. While it is perfectly normal for an infant to become shy and bury their face in a parent's chest, they should also display a sense of curiosity sometimes. A healthy balance of new places and familiar places should be fairly easy for your baby to handle and comprehend.

Try to play games with your baby that will allow them to crawl. During tummy time, put all of the toys just outside of your baby's reach. While this might lead to frustration, it can also lead to crawling! If your baby becomes too frustrated and starts to cry, you can make the game a little bit easier by bringing the objects closer. Use your best judgment. If you always move the toys when you notice frustration, your baby can mistakenly get used to this concept and might begin to think that it takes tears to get what they want. Having a good balance of making your baby work hard to get what they want and also helping them when they are in need is important.

Mental Leaps

If your baby has mastered crawling, get ready for an exciting adventure of a stage! When your baby becomes fully mobile, this will really make the comparison of holding a newborn to watching your child move around on their own seem like it happened so quickly. Let your baby explore your home safely by providing designated areas in which they can crawl around. You can section off your home by using removable gates and other means of safety in order to teach them that certain areas are off-limits. Your baby will learn to understand where they belong and where they are allowed to go. If they pick up anything dangerous, they should also respond to your basic instruction to stop or put it down.

Having a larger appetite is also another huge leap that can be seen during this age. Eager to try anything that you provide them, your baby is going to be willing to eat a lot more than they used to. Being mindful of food allergies, try to let your baby experience as many different foods as you can. It is fairly easy to keep your baby on a balanced diet when you have been doing so from the beginning, but the occasional treat isn't a bad reward. Using infant utensils, offer them to your little one and show them that they can be used to assist them with eating. While they might not get the concept at first, an introduction will prepare them for any future eating that they do.

What to Expect During a Check-Up

There is typically no scheduled check-up for an 8-month old baby, but of course, you need to use your best judgment. Using the developmental milestones chart above, you can see how well your baby is developing and if they are on the right track. Remember, not every single baby is going to follow the same path of development, but your baby should be close to the indicated developments on the chart. Otherwise, keep feeding your little one nourishing foods and make sure that they are getting enough sleep throughout the day. If you notice a little bit of extra fussiness, you might need to include some more naps in order for them to recharge. Though they are growing quickly, they are still in need of a lot of sleep.

Their muscles should be strong and stable. Your baby should also have urges to stand and might be crawling all over the house by now. Don't be surprised if they are already able to pull themselves into a standing position from inside of the crib. These are all amazing milestones that you and your little one are going to enjoy together. Remember, stiffness or lack of muscular development are the two main indicators that something might be wrong. If you notice this, then a doctor's visit might be necessary. Otherwise, enjoy this time with your baby and keep encouraging them to learn more and do more every single day. You should be able to tell when something is wrong by the way they cry or fuss, or if they cannot be consoled.

Ninth Month

Milestones Chart

- Crawls for a little while and then sits down
- Can stand with support
- Says basic words
- Can understand the word "no"
- Copies simple gestures
- Has great depth perception
- Can hold and drop objects at will
- Has favorite toys
- Moves objects from one hand to the other
- Gets nervous around new people

Developmental Milestones

Cognitive:

1. Can Copy Sounds and Gestures: Your little one should be like a parrot now. If you make a noise or a gesture toward your baby, they might be able to mirror it back to you. They might even be saying new words on their own, which is an exciting stage to experience.

2. Understands the Word "No": The word no will now have a negative connotation behind it. Your baby should understand that when you tell them no, they need to stop what they are doing. This is their first understanding of what it means to be disciplined.

3. Loves Seeking Games: Peek-a-Boo and other hidden object games should send your baby into a frenzy of delight. These are the kind of games that should truly pique their curiosity at 9 months.

Physical: Crawling should be the biggest milestone at the 9-month mark. Your baby should easily be able to get into a crawling position and move all over the place. It might even be hard for you to keep up with them! When they need a rest, they will promptly return to a seated position without any assistance or support. Their leg muscles are also stronger than ever, allowing them into assisted standing positions. Your baby might test this by letting go of the support every so often, either resulting in a few seconds of standing up or falling back down onto their bottom. At this point, the parachute reflex has been developed. This happens when your baby's head is facing down and their arms automatically come forward to prevent injury to the head.

Social: This can be a very clingy time for the baby and the primary caregiver. They will be showing preference to you over anyone else at this stage. New people might make them nervous or even anxious. This is normal because they can also experience separation anxiety, even if they are only away from you for a few minutes at a time. You are their constant state of security and how they know to feel safe. On the same lines of favoritism, you will notice that your baby now has favorite toys and objects. They might ask for certain toys or whine until they get the desired toy. It is a very clear indication that your little one is developing their own interests and preferences. This peak is very standard at 9 months.

When to Be Concerned

Crawling and sitting are major milestones that should be achieved by this point. Even if your baby isn't doing much of it, a little desire to do so is a great sign. If you notice that your baby simply cannot do either one, then this can be concerning. Either their muscles are not strong enough, or something is cognitively wrong. This behavior can point to several medical issues, and it should be taken up with your doctor right away. The same concern can be made if your baby does not seem to put any support on their legs when placed into a standing position. Remember, if their legs just seem to curl underneath them, then this likely means that there aren't enough muscles built up to support their body weight. The grip is also very important. Your baby should be gripping onto you, their toys, and food. If they appear to have a weak grip, this can be another indication of a muscular problem. This problem might be made clear if your baby does have the urge to grip objects, but keeps dropping them accidentally.

Much like concerning issues in the past, a quiet baby at this stage is extremely abnormal. Most 9-month olds can say basic words and ask for certain objects. They will even be able to call you by name. A baby who is going through developmental issues will usually not be able to make any sounds at all, not even throaty noises or gurgling noises. If you notice that your baby can only make noise when they are crying, then this is something that needs to be mentioned to your doctor.

Your baby should be able to express delight when they see a familiar face walk into the room. Even if it is not the primary caregiver, such as yourself or your partner, your baby should still display some type of reaction toward loved ones or people who are in their lives daily. Cognitive developmental issues might be to blame if your baby seems to have no memory of people who should be considered familiar at this point. It can be an indication that there was a missed developmental milestone somewhere along the way. Your doctor will be able to officially diagnose a problem if there is one, or teach you ways in which you can help your child catch up.

Tips to Improve Development

When you set your baby up for playtime, let them play how they want to play. Whether this means banging toys together or trying to solve basic puzzles, allowing your baby to do their own exploration at this stage is a great way to promote independence. While you must always remember to keep a close eye on your little one, letting them experience their toys in a self-guided manner is going to be the best thing for them developmentally. If you are playing interactively with your baby, try to provide basic instructions. A great game you can play together is rolling a ball back and forth. Encourage your baby to roll a ball to you after you have rolled it to them. You can say something like "roll the ball to mama" to get your baby to understand what you are asking them to do.

Outdoor exploration is a must at this age! Your baby needs to know that there is a whole world that exists outside of your home. Take your baby on walks, and watch as their eyes light up at various findings in nature. As always, narrate the experience and explain what you are seeing. You can teach your baby about animals, people, plants, and trees. Spending a lot of time outdoors, if the weather permits, is a great way for your baby to gain new experiences and learn new things. This will also help to further stimulate their vision and depth perception.

As much as you probably enjoy feeding your little one, the time has come to let them take the lead. When it comes to feeding time, unless you are still breastfeeding, let your baby feed themselves. Cut up food into small pieces, and place them in front of your baby. This will teach them that they need to pick up the food and place it into their mouth if they want to eat it because you aren't always going to be there to do it for them. A lot of parents struggle to let this happen but know that it is best for the baby to learn a little bit of independence at this age. Of course, if your baby is fussy or struggling too much, you can offer a little bit of assistance. For the most part, your baby should be eating on their own though.

Mental Leaps

Your baby should know about the basic concepts of categorization. For example, they will know that animals are cats, dogs, horses, and cows, but they should now that these are all individually very different animals. The same can be said for colors and shapes. Keep encouraging your baby to play games that allow for some exploration with categorization. There are many games and toys that are designed for babies this age to sort objects or place them in the correct category. One of the best toys to further develop this skill is the kind that allows for your baby to place blocks into holes of the appropriate shape. Previously, your baby would likely just pick up the pieces and bang them together or chew on them. Now, their mind is more developed. You will be able to watch in amazement as your 9-month old is able to sort through all of the shapes by placing them in the correct spots.

As mentioned, taking your baby out into the world is very important. A lot of parents do want to take a more sheltered approach to parenting in order to keep their children safe but know when you keep your baby too sheltered, you are also preventing them from developing a healthy perception of the world. Small outings are great for your baby and great for mental stimulation. It is a big world out there, and the thought that one day your little one is going to be exploring it on their own might make you feel nervous, think about this as your chance to prepare them for what they can expect to see and experience.

Everywhere you go, take your baby along with you. This will give them the best chance of experiencing even more mental leaps. There are certain places that you might not be able to visit just yet, such as a movie theater, but most other places that you would commonly visit are going to be appropriate. If you notice that your baby appears curious about something, allow them to see it and experience it, if possible. Let them feel new textures and see different sights. The best thing that you can do as a parent at this point is to let your little one take the lead. Go where their curiosity takes you, and have fun while you do it.

What to Expect During a Check-Up

This is a milestone check-up, and you can expect the same procedures to take place in the beginning. Your baby will be weighed and measured, and they will also be given the usual exams that take place during typical doctor's appointments. There is one big development screening that will be offered to you. It is unlike the other screenings you have been offered in the past because it is meant to look at your baby's development overall instead of testing for one specific issue. It is a more formal test, and a lot of parents do opt for this in order to see if their little one is developing correctly and healthily.

The doctor will start by asking you a series of questions. These questions should revolve around your baby's growth and behavior. They might also ask you to play with your little one right there in the office to see how your baby responds to certain stimulation. Don't be nervous about this because it isn't a pass/fail test. This is simply a way for the doctor to see if your baby is where they should be on the developmental chart. Try to remain as calm and natural as possible because your nervous energy might end up making your baby nervous. You both know one another best, so stay strong for your baby. Depending on the results you get, you might have to put your baby through some additional screenings to rule out certain delays or impairments.

If your baby has yet to receive their final HepB vaccine, they will receive it at this appointment. Unlike past visits, your baby won't have to get many shots this time. The next shot they might receive is the final dose of IPV if they haven't had it already. It is likely that your baby has a mouth full of developing teeth by now, so your doctor will probably do a basic oral exam to ensure that their teeth are growing properly. Unless you request any other specific screening or vaccinations, this should be all that your baby needs to receive at this appointment. Your baby should be used to coming to the doctor by now. A little bit of anxiety is normal because they might associate getting shots with coming to the doctor, but you can calm their nerves by allowing them to bring their favorite toy along with them for the ride.

Chapter 8: Fourth Trimester Milestones (10-12 Months)

On the verge of turning 1-year old, your baby is probably going to start walking any day now. This is an exciting milestone that many parents wait on the edge of their seats for. Your little one isn't so little anymore, displaying favoritism and prioritization. You can tell that their mind is working extra hard to make sense of all that is happening around them as they try to figure out what their role is in this world. Your baby is likely going to be talking up a storm, as well. They will love to exercise their vocal cords, so be very vocal with them as well. Encourage them to use their voice as much as possible because this will prevent communication that stems from crying.

Tenth Month

Milestones Chart

- Crawls and pulls up to stand
- Understands the meanings of some words
- Can move from tummy to a sitting position
- Understands requests
- Searches for hidden objects

- Has some teeth

Developmental Milestones

Cognitive:

1. Understands Object Permanence: Your baby now understands that a hidden object continues to exist and that it can be found if searched for. This is a brand new milestone for this age.
2. Associates Meanings with Words: Simple words such as "no," "go," and "hi" will have a meaning to your baby. Instead of simply hearing sounds, your baby will have a deeper understanding of what you are saying.
3. Understands Requests: If you ask your baby to do something or to hand you something, this is a request that a 10-month old should be able to handle. Even if your little one can't repeat the request, there is still a sense of understanding the present.

Physical: Your little one should be crawling a lot by this point. There might even be some chance that your baby is pulling themselves up into a standing position. By taking a few wobbly steps, your baby might be experimenting with the idea of walking. Their muscle development should be very strong, and they will leave no space unexplored, no matter what it takes to get there. During tummy time, your baby will have a lot of independence because of their ability to not only rollover in any direction but to actually come back up into a sitting position on their own. Their two lower central incisor teeth should likely be present by now. This makes eating different finger foods very convenient. Depending on the rate of development, your baby could have quite a few teeth by now!

Social: Waving is a new social milestone that your 10-month old is likely capable of! When someone leaves the room, your little one might wave in an adorable manner. They can also likely wave hello at this point. Keep waving to your baby when you leave and enter rooms, and they will pick up on the same habit quickly. They are going to be much more reactional to specific situations at this time. For example, if you take a toy away before they are done playing, this might elicit a response that comes with tears and a full-blown meltdown. They have a very clear intention in mind of their purpose in this world and the things that they do now. You'll notice that your baby has a wider range of reactions than before, being able to break down and comprehend certain situations with ease.

When to Be Concerned

Crawling is something that should be absolutely effortless by now. If you notice that your baby is simply not capable of it, even if they show the urge to crawl, then there is likely a problem that is preventing them from doing so. You can test your baby's ability to crawl by assisting them in a crawling position. Most 10-month olds will start crawling right away, as it is natural for the average baby. Any sign of a struggle or simply no reaction can mean that there is a developmental delay that is hindering them.

Being unable to stand is normal for a 10-month old, but with the proper support, there should be no difficulty. As you have attempted in earlier months, when you place your baby in a standing position, their leg muscles should know exactly what to do. If you notice limp muscles or an unnatural stiffness that prohibits them from standing with assistance, you need to bring this up with your doctor. Make sure you take note of anything that seems to cause your baby pain or distress when you try to place them into a standing position.

As the months go on, a silent baby becomes more worrisome. No matter what noises your baby is making, there should be some sort of indication that your baby *can* make noise at this age. If they have not begun making consonant sounds or imitating words by this point, their speech development has likely fallen behind. This can often be corrected with speech therapy, but it also might be an indication that there is a cognitive issue to blame. Without a proper diagnosis from a doctor, it is hard to know exactly what is preventing your little one from using their voice to its fullest potential.

Since your baby should now be eating a wide array of finger foods, having teeth is essential to being able to properly eat them. While your baby won't have a full set of teeth just yet, their lower central incisors should have made their debut by now. If your baby does not have them, or any teeth at all, this can be an indication of a dental problem. Dental problems can cause infants to become fussy if you try to touch their gums, possibly even giving them headaches. It can also alter their ability to graduate to eating different types of foods.

Tips to Improve Development

Give your baby space! The best thing that you can do is to widen the amount of crawling space that they have available. Clear out your living room floor and make sure that everything dangerous is placed aside. The more room your baby has to crawl, the more they are going to do it. You will notice that your baby will have more fun when there are more space and fewer obstacles in their way. Put various toys on the floor so they can crawl over to each one for a more interactive approach to crawling time. Getting a temporary indoor barrier can be a great way to keep your baby contained in a safe space.

Toys that allow your baby to walk while pushing are essential during this developmental stage. There are many car toys that allow your baby to walk behind them in order to push them forward. This is a great exercise and will continue the growth of the necessary walking muscles that are continually emerging each day. One day, you might notice that your baby is feeling particularly brave and attempting to take some steps on their own, without the support of any toys or other surfaces. Encourage this if you notice it happening.

If your baby falls down when they are attempting to walk, it is likely in your natural reaction to run over to them and pick them up. As long as there are no injuries, try to avoid doing this. It will encourage them to get back up on their own and to try again. If they get used to you rushing over each time they fall, they will learn to expect this. Walking is a milestone that signifies independence, and whether you are ready for it or not, your baby is about to be walking around the house.

Have as many meaningful conversations as you can. Your baby is a small human, and they now have the ability to understand cause and effect, empathy, and emotions. Talk to your baby as if you were talking to any other loved one. This will give them practice for their necessary social skills in the future, and that isn't as far away as it might seem. Encourage your baby to express their feelings, and allow your baby to hear and feel yours.

Mental Leaps

The biggest mental leaps you will experience this month involve the way that your baby talks to you and the way that you respond in return. Since your baby is now understanding more than ever, it is a great time to introduce new words into their vocabulary. Show them new items, new places. Their minds are ready to receive this new information, so do your best to show them new things on a regular basis. Babies are going to be curious for a very long time, so while they are in this stage, it feels great to be able to allow them to continue on a curious path.

While your baby is probably very comfortable with you and speaking to you, encourage your baby to talk to other people, too. It can be hard to overcome shyness or separation anxiety, so be present when you encourage your baby to interact with others. In a group setting, do your best to involve your baby in the conversation and show them that it is normal and a positive thing to talk to other people. They should be fairly comfortable talking to those they see on a regular basis, but they might shy away from others that they aren't as familiar with. This is normal at this age, and as long as you keep working on it, your baby will outgrow this shy phase.

The days of banging toys around just to make noise are probably over now. Your baby takes deliberate action to express particular emotions. If your baby is mad, they will let you know. If they are happy, they will also let you know. Listen to them and be mindful of their feelings. Though they are still very young, their feelings should still be validated and acknowledged. This is a very healthy parent/child relationship to have that should continue well into the future of your parenting style. If you show them that you respect what they are feeling, they will grow accustomed to this idea. Remember, you are their teacher and everything that they will grow to know will come from the knowledge that you share with them. A lot of parents still baby talk or underestimate their baby at

10 months, but this is an impressionable little being that you have in front of you right now.

What to Expect During a Check-Up

There is no check-up scheduled for this month, typically. As always, you should be ensuring that your baby is getting enough to eat and trying new foods on a regular basis. You can introduce a little bit of what you are eating each day, as long as it is cut up into small enough pieces. When you are giving your baby a new food for the first time, always be mindful of any food allergies that you have yet to discover. Watch your baby closely for symptoms after they eat the new food, and if they seem to be having an allergic reaction, contact your doctor right away.

A few bumps and bruises are going to be common in the 10th month because of all the newfound mobility. If your baby is crawling a lot, you might need to get them some pants that provide extra support for the knees. It can be common for an infant to get bruises or sores on their knees from all of the crawlings that they will be doing. They might also experience having a sore bottom if they are trying to stand up and walk. These falls should be mainly broken by their diaper, so it is nothing to be too concerned about. Remember, babies are very accident-prone. Though they are becoming stronger every single day, you still need to be very careful when they are mobile and able to access various dangerous items around

456

the home.

Your baby should be sleeping pretty well at this point, during nighttime hours. While they will still need an afternoon nap, you should not have to be getting up in the middle of the night as much as you used to. Self-soothing will be mastered by now, meaning that your baby can console themselves if they wake in the night and start to cry a little bit. Give them time to explore this by not immediately rushing into the nursery. Usually, a baby will comfort themselves back to sleep unless something is truly wrong. You need to use your best judgment and keep in mind that you are trying to give your baby a chance to develop their independence by not rushing to them right away. Your baby is a lot more capable than they used to be, so have trust in them.

Eleventh Month

Milestones Chart

- Stands without support
- Walks with support
- Follows basic instructions
- Manipulates objects with nimble fingers
- Addresses parents with the correct noun
- Knows the names of personal objects (toys)
- Repeats easy/small words
- Can recognize familiar faces in a group of strangers

- Displays frustration through babbling

Developmental Milestones

Cognitive:

1. Learns Names: When you say someone's name, your baby should know who you are referring to now. Familiar people will have a name associated with them.
2. Obeys Instructions: If you give your baby specific instructions, they should listen to you. This obedience shows that they respect and understand you as the parent.
3. Experiments with Language: Your baby might be coming up with a whole new language! They will be more vocal than ever, testing out all kinds of words and sounds.

Physical: If your baby needs to change positions to reach an object, this should be done with ease. From crawling to standing to sitting, all of these positions should be possible for your little one. They will be standing more than ever now, and if you have stairs, don't be surprised if they have the desire to crawl up to see what is waiting at the top. Sectioning the house off into "safe zones" is very important during this stage of mobility.

Social: Your little one will be able to call for you by either saying "mama" or "dada" to the correct parent. They might even be able to call for their siblings and grandparents, depending on how regularly they see these familiar faces. Also, your baby will be able to spot known individuals in a crowd of other people. They will let you know by expressing excitement or delight at the discovery.

When to Be Concerned

Causes for concern are going to mirror those that you looked for last month. A lack of mobility is not a good sign, especially this far along in a baby's development. If there is a lack of standing, the desire to stand, crawling, or the desire to crawl, then you can probably gather that something is wrong. A lack of response to basic commands and a lack of vocal imitation can indicate some cognitive issues, so make sure that you are still paying attention to these things. Any problems that you will notice should be fairly obvious at this point, so do your best and use your best instinct to protect your child and contact your doctor when necessary.

Tips to Improve Development

Encourage independence as much as possible. If your baby cannot grasp a food item or cannot pick up a toy, give them a chance to experience this on their own before you jump in to help. Just like you should allow them the ability to self-soothe, they are getting older now, and it is useful to know how to do these things. Use positive reinforcement as your main tool.

When your baby does something great, celebrate it! To correct negative behavior, try not to jump straight into punishment. Instead, constructively lead them to better behavior that you expect from them. This will make it clear to them what your standards and expectations are.

Continue reading new books to them, and allow them to meet even more new people. As mentioned, playgroups are a great way for your baby to socialize. These groups typically meet once or twice a week, so it is a low-commitment way to allow your baby to meet other children who are around the same age. Plus, playgroups are normally filled with many interactive games that build essential skills that are necessary for development.

Mental Leaps

Your baby should now understand processes. For example, if they want to eat something, they know that it takes a few steps to make this possible. They must pick up their spoon, put food on it, and then put it into their mouth. There should be far fewer meltdowns about these things at the 11-month mark. Your baby, for the most part, should be feeding themselves. Though you might need to step in if it gets particularly messy, babies this age do enjoy eating and using their own hands to do so.

This series of mental leaps actually requires a lot of patience from the parents. It is going to be messy, and in some cases, frustrating. It will all be worth it when your baby finally succeeds at what they have been trying to accomplish, though. You need to let them figure it out on their own unless they express true signs of distress. Sure, they will become angry because they are not able to finish simple tasks, but this is how they are going to learn.

What to Expect During a Check-Up

With no scheduled check-up this month, you can simply enjoy the month of new developments. Celebrate all of the new milestones, and always make sure that your baby knows when they are doing something great. Your baby should be fairly healthy at this point unless the occasional cold happens to find them. There should be no need to visit the doctor unless of an emergency or developmental issues that you notice while you are at home. Remember, babies can be very accident-prone, so you still must be very careful as they are mobile around the house.

Twelfth Month

Milestones Chart

- Takes a few steps alone
- Pulls up to stand
- Speaks simple words
- Can imitate actions and gestures
- Responds to simple requests

- Remembers the last location of an object
- Can use fingers to poke and point
- Has good hand-eye coordination

Developmental Milestones

Cognitive:

1. Knows Where Objects are Located: Your baby should easily be able to find objects that are typically stored in certain places. Their memory will be developed enough to allow them to remember these things.

2. Object-Noun Association: If you tell your baby to pick up a certain piece of fruit, they will be able to do this. You can test them by placing a bowl of various fruits in front of them.

3. Uses Objects Correctly: There should be no more banging of items that aren't meant to be played with. For example, your baby will know that a comb is used for the hair now, and they might even begin combing through their own hair.

Physical: Walking should be the main milestone that you notice. Whether your child is walking with the support of your arms, the support of a toy, or all on their own, the desire to walk should be stronger than ever. They will also be able to use a wide variety of grips with nimble fingers that can point, poke, and prod. At this age, the average 1-year old should have three pairs of teeth. Even if your baby isn't quite there yet, you should be able to at least see a few pearly whites poking through their gums.

Social: If you ask your baby to pass you an object, they should be able to perform the task. The same can be said if you ask your baby to come to you or to stop doing something. Simple requests should be fairly easy to comprehend at this point. At 1-year old, your baby might start testing you. Even if they know what they are doing is wrong, they might try to push your buttons to see how you will react. Welcome to the beginning of toddlerhood!

When to Be Concerned

Nothing will have changed in what to look for as a concerning behavior by now. You can still keep an eye out on your child's muscle development, ability to stand, desire to walk, and eagerness to talk. Anything less than the above is considered abnormal for a 1-year old child. If you feel that your baby is behind in any way, you can bring this up to your doctor when you go in for your baby's 1-year check-up.

Tips to Improve Development

Let your baby play with blocks. This will stimulate them by showing them various colors and shapes. They will have to figure out which pieces fit together in order to build something. You can also give them a way to make music. A lot of parents opt for the traditional pot and wooden spoon. If you can stand the noise for a little while, let your baby go crazy on this makeshift drum. It is a fun and musical way to get your baby engaged. Another game you can play is "phone call." Pretend that you are talking on a toy phone and then pass it to your baby, this will encourage them to speak!

Mental Leaps

A series of actions will now be seen as a simple task. For example, when your baby watches you doing the dishes, they know that these dishes do not magically get cleaned; it takes a process. First, you scrub them in soapy water. Then, you dry them. Therefore, you are left with a pile of clean dishes. Let your child help you with chores as much as you can. This will get them to better understand how things work, and it will give them a sense of what it takes to make the series of events happen. When they play with toys, they should know where to locate them and how to put them back when they are finished playing. All the processes that are going on around them will make a lot more sense.

What to Expect During a Check-Up

This will be your baby's first official visit as a 1-year old! So much progress has been made. The typical procedures will be done, and then another big round of vaccinations will be given. You can expect your baby to receive the final HepB vaccine (unless they got it at the prior appointment), Hib,

PCV, MMR, and HepA. Make sure that you bring plenty of toys in the room as a distraction, and potentially a special treat for afterward. These are a lot of shots to get in one visit, but your baby can handle it and will usually put on a brave face if they see mommy doing the same.

Chapter 9: You After the Delivery

Becoming a parent changes you in ways you probably wouldn't expect. While you can prepare for the sleepless nights and endless attempts to get your baby to stop throwing their toys on the floor, it also comes with a personal adjustment that you will have to make as soon as you deliver. From this point on, you are now responsible for this little being. You also need to make sure that you are taking care of yourself and managing all of the changes that you are personally dealing with. This chapter explores self-care and what you can do as a new parent during the first year.

10 Truths About the First Year of Parenthood

1. You are going to have many successes, and many failures, at the same time.
2. Your postpartum body is going to be squishy.
3. Your baby is unique and might not follow the developmental path of an average baby.
4. Childbirth is not always easy and painless; it can often be unpredictable.
5. You will need to get very comfortable with cleaning poop.

6. Accept unwanted advice, even if you truly don't want to hear it.
7. Keep stretching in order to remain flexible; you'll need to be nimble to handle your baby.
8. The most important thing for your baby is a strong support system.
9. Become uplifted by other mothers who have been in the same position.
10. Success can be found when you are willing to grow as a person.

Living on Less Sleep

One of the first things you will notice is that your sleep schedule has been dismantled as soon as you bring your newborn baby home from the hospital. Frequent feedings have you getting up out of bed multiple times throughout the night. You might be wondering – how does any sane parent have the ability to do this and still live a life of their own? Sleep management is going to be your savior here. If you are home with your baby during the day, sleep when they are sleeping. This will be a peaceful time for you to both get the rest that you rightfully deserve. If you attempt to clean up around the house or perform other chores, you might be at risk of waking the sleeping baby. Also, once that baby wakes up, they are going to be renewed with energy and ready to take on the day again, leaving you more tired than ever.

Most babies do not start sleeping through the night until they reach the age of around 3-months old. This means, for the first 3 months of their life, you are going to need to make some major adjustments to your own sleep schedule. Learn how to let go of messes and chaos. This is going to allow you to relax when you have the opportunity. A lot of new moms make the mistake of thinking that they can take care of a newborn, lose several hours of sleep each night, and also keep the house in pristine condition – this isn't realistic. Learn how to be okay with leaving clutter out for a few hours (or days) at a time. You will be able to come back to it soon.

Though it might seem ineffective at first, put your newborn on a sleep schedule. Do your best to make sure that they take regular naps, but not too close to bedtime. Before bedtime, your baby should actually be the most active. When you are ready to have them settle down, get them fed, washed, and then the sleepiness should follow. If you ever put your baby to bed hungry or dirty, you can anticipate that they will be crying again in an hour or so. You need to make them feel as comfortable as possible. It might take a little while before they catch on to their sleep schedule, but starting early is worth it. Babies need structured routines.

Being a parent is full of stress. Not only are you worrying about your baby, but you are also worrying about your household and your other loved ones. How do you manage it all? By accepting the help that you are given, you will be able to lighten your load. Trust that your partner can cook and do the dishes. When you want to meet with your friends, have them come over for lunch while simultaneously meeting the new baby. All of your plans can be modified to include your baby. This will make everything seem a lot more manageable than trying to change everything all at once.

Know that there is no such thing as a perfect parent, so get that idea out of your head. Acknowledge your efforts and know that you are doing the best you can. Parenting actually comes with its fair share of trial and error. There will be times where you will have no idea what the best decision is, but your parenting instinct should guide you toward the best option. Listen to what your gut is trying to tell you because, for the most part, it is right.

Try not to load up on caffeine or other substances that will provide you with temporary energy. While this can give you a great boost at the moment, all good things must come to an end. When you experience your energy-crash, your little one isn't going to pause to give you the chance to take a nap. Try to work with the natural flow of your new schedule. If you need to have one cup of coffee in the morning to get your day going, this is okay, as long as you don't become reliant on it throughout your entire day. Your body will adjust, and things will get easier. You can think of these first 3 months as a test because the rest is going to be smooth sailing when you are able to get your 7-9 hours of sleep again.

Recovering from Labor and Childbirth

Recovering from a C-Section

After your c-section, your abdomen will be sore, but you will likely be in great spirits. You've just delivered a baby! This is something to be proud of. Unfortunately, a sense of nausea and grogginess can also follow. C-sections patients normally need to spend 2-4 days in the hospital before heading home just for precautionary measures. You will likely be given bandages that you have to change, as well as an ointment to put on the incision so that you can take care of it from home. Regardless of the kind of delivery you had, you should be able to breastfeed your baby right away, as long as your breasts are producing milk. You should also be able to walk just fine and potentially even perform moderate exercises – listen to your body.

After two to four days of having your c-section, you should be able to safely lift your baby without tearing any stitches. To manage any pain that you have after you leave the hospital, the doctor will prescribe you with around one-week's work of pain medicine. The human body heals surprisingly quickly, as long as you do not overdo it. Know that you can have sex after giving birth via c-section, but to avoid any pain, you should wait at least 6-8 weeks. Around this same time, you should also be able to get back to your normal exercise routine. Your incision should be nothing more than a scar at this point, and you should be proud to wear it. That scar is the reason why you have a happy, healthy baby.

If you need to wash your hair and body, try to avoid baths. Being submerged in water for long periods of time can actually make your healing scab soft, and potentially cause it to come off before it is ready. Making sure that your scar scabs up is important because this is an indication that your body is doing what it can to heal the incision quickly. It might not look very pretty, but you will thank yourself for being patient at the end when you are left with a clean and non-infected scar. You might feel a sense of sadness or disappointment because you didn't deliver vaginally, but each time you feel this, take a look at your baby. You are still a mother and you still gave birth to this bundle of joy. Not everyone can have a vaginal birth experience, but you still had a birth experience that was unique to yourself and your baby.

Recovering from a Vaginal Birth

One thing that most mothers aren't prepared for is the amount that they will have to pee after giving birth vaginally. This happens because your body has been storing these fluids in a compact way to make room for your baby. After your baby has been delivered, expect your frequency to use the bathroom to increase. It is normal to pee a little bit when you cough or laugh. Your pelvic floor muscles just need to be re-strengthened, and this can be done by performing Kegels. Don't be alarmed if you start to feel cramping in your stomach after giving birth; this is an indication that your uterus is shrinking back to its normal size. These cramps can last for around 2-3 days after giving birth. Remember, your belly has stretched for a 9-month period of time, so you might look like you are still pregnant after you give birth. A healthy diet and some gentle exercise will get your stomach back to what it used to look like.

A lot of mothers worry that they won't have enough milk to feed their newborns when breastfeeding. Even after giving birth, your body and hormones are still hard at work. From the very first feeding, your body is sending signals to tell these hormones to keep producing the milk. As long as your baby is eating, then more milk is being produced. In terms of your personal comfort, you might have some soreness while seated. This also depends if you tore during the delivery or not. If you tore, you will have stitches, but they should only be painful for a couple of days until they dissolve. Expect this to be an emotional rollercoaster. You might experience joy and sadness at the same time, but know that this is all normal. You will adjust, and your baby will adjust, too. Try to get as much rest as you can in the first few weeks – you will need it.

When to Have Another Child

Having another child is a very personal decision that needs to be discussed with your partner. As you are taking care of your newborn, keep in mind that a new child is going to involve this kind of care, plus the care of your firstborn. The work is doubled, but if you want to have a big family, then you know that the sleepless nights and stress are worth it. While your partner might be ready to have another child in a year, you might feel differently because of the delivery experience you had. You need to communicate openly with one another to decide on a proper timeline for the growth of your family. Try not to think about having another child in the first 6 months of your first baby's life. Not only are you still physically healing, but you and your partner both will be very busy handling your newborn.

A lot of couples want siblings who are close in age so that they can have a great bond. Most wait at least 1 ½-2 years before conceiving again, but this all comes down to your own personal preference. Families come in all shapes and sizes. You might want to wait 1 year to have another baby, or you might want to wait for 7. Consider your finances, as well. Having babies isn't cheap! Taking a new look at your budget, post-newborn, you will get an idea of how much additional money you will need if you were to add another family member to your home. It is always better to be over-prepared than struggling when the time comes. Having a healthy savings account for emergencies is a smart and responsible thing to do as parents.

You will also need to consider your current career path. It is likely that you took maternity leave if you currently have a job, so how soon will your job allows you to take this same kind of leave again? Is this something that you can successfully accomplish without putting your career at risk or cutting the family finances in half. This is very important to consider, and as much as you want to have more babies, you must think in these realistic terms. Without a job, there will be no steady income to feed your family or take care of your babies.

Don't allow any social pressures to allow you to believe that you *need* to conceive another baby by a certain time, or that you need to conceive another baby at all. Despite all the factors involved, it is still a very personal decision that is ultimately up to you to make. Even if your partner truly wants another child, yet you do not feel physically ready, then you shouldn't be afraid to express this to them. Pregnancy and childbirth are a lot for a woman to handle, and it is natural to need quite a long break in between pregnancies so your body can regroup and get back to normal.

When you do decide to have another baby, a visit to the doctor for a check-up is a good idea. Your doctor will be able to tell you if you are in the right health and state of being in order to carry another baby. No all women are, so don't assume that your body is just naturally going to ease into pregnancy as it did the first time. Sometimes, health issues can arise after having one pregnancy, so you will want to make sure that your body can withstand another one before you end up getting pregnant.

Conclusion

You should be proud of yourself for carrying your healthy baby for all those months, working hard to deliver them, and then doing whatever it takes to provide the proper care. Being a parent is a joyous feeling, but it can also be filled with many unexpected challenges that might make you question everything you thought you knew. As long as you are able to stay calm and provide your baby with love and care, then know that you are doing your very best.

The first year of your little one's life is going to be filled with so many milestones, and this guide is going to help you every step of the way. When you feel unsure about something, you have your parental instinct and your doctor's advice to guide you toward the best decision for your child. Know that these months go by quickly, and most parents often wish they had a remote so they can press the pause button.

I love to help mothers care for their babies because I remember so many of the joys that I experienced with my own children. This is why I compiled all the tips I learned into one easy-to-read guide. Know that you are strong enough to withstand any challenges that you face, and if you put in the effort, you are going to be able to give your child a great life. I know that things can seem uncertain at first, but you are going to get the hang of being a parent, even if you have to make adjustments to your personal life.

As you wait in anxious anticipation for your newborn baby to arrive, you should be well-prepared after reading this guide. For each month, you have a detailed outline of what you can expect, what you should be doing, and what you need to prepare for. This is what it takes to be a great parent – you should always be one step ahead of whatever is happening next.

Remember to enjoy your time with your infant because this stage does not last forever. A once-reliant little baby is soon going to develop into an independent child full of personality and their own interests. Get to know your baby and give them the same trust that they are going to give you in return. Parenting is not a one-sided job. Your baby is going to teach you just as many things as you will teach them.

It is normal to feel scared while also feeling excited to become a new parent. Both feelings are incredibly justified. Once you get into the swing of things, though, you will be able to build up your confidence and take every little smile and giggle as a sign that you are doing something right!

References

10 Reasons To Get Vaccinated. (2019, November 27). Retrieved December 9, 2019, from https://www.nfid.org/immunization/10-reasons-to-get-vaccinated/

AboutKidsHealth. (2019, January 7). AboutKidsHealth. Retrieved December 9, 2019, from https://www.aboutkidshealth.ca/Article?contentid=453&language=English

Adjuvants help vaccines work better. | Vaccine Safety | CDC. (2018). Retrieved December 9, 2019, from https://www.cdc.gov/vaccinesafety/concerns/adjuvants.html

Apgar Score. (2017). Retrieved December 9, 2019, from https://www.pregnancybirthbaby.org.au/apgar-score

BabyCentre UK Staff. (2003, May 14). Recovery after vaginal birth. Retrieved December 9, 2019, from https://www.babycentre.co.uk/a553491/recovery-after-vaginal-birth

Baby's First 24 Hours. (2018). Retrieved December 9, 2019, from https://www.pregnancybirthbaby.org.au/babys-first-24-hours

Boyd-Barrett, C. (2019, October 31). C-section healing and recovery time. Retrieved December 9, 2019, from https://www.babycenter.com/0_recovering-from-a-c-section_221.bc

Department of Health & Human Services. (2016, May 18). Immunisation – side effects. Retrieved December 9, 2019, from https://www.betterhealth.vic.gov.au/health/healthyliving/immunisation-side-effects

DiLaura, A. (2019, November 5). Creating a safe nursery: 10 mistakes to avoid. Retrieved December 9, 2019, from https://www.babycenter.com/101_creating-a-safe-nursery-10-mistakes-to-avoid_10414382.bc

Dorning, A. (2019, October 29). Childcare options: Pros, cons, and costs. Retrieved December 9, 2019, from https://www.babycenter.com/childcare-options

Easy-to-read Immunization Schedule by Vaccine for Ages Birth-6 Years | CDC. (2019, February 5). Retrieved December 9, 2019, from https://www.cdc.gov/vaccines/schedules/easy-to-read/child-easyread.html#table-child

Feeding babies and food safety. (2019). Retrieved December 10, 2019, from https://www.sahealth.sa.gov.au/wps/wcm/connect/55141580 47d940a7ac79adfc651ee2b2/Feeding+babies+and+food+safety+Fact+Sheet.pdf?MOD=AJPERES

Garoo, R. (2019a, September 10). 2-Month-Old's

Developmental Milestones: A Complete Guide. Retrieved December 10, 2019, from https://www.momjunction.com/articles/babys-second-month-development-guide_00101929/

Garoo, R. (2019b, September 10). 3-Month-Old Baby Developmental Milestones - A Complete Guide. Retrieved December 10, 2019, from https://www.momjunction.com/articles/babys-third-month-a-development-guide_00102426/

Garoo, R. (2019c, September 10). 4-Month-Old Baby Developmental Milestones - A Complete Guide. Retrieved December 10, 2019, from https://www.momjunction.com/articles/babys-4th-month-a-development-guide_00104153/

Garoo, R. (2019d, September 10). 5-Month-Old Baby's Developmental Milestones - A Complete Guide. Retrieved December 10, 2019, from https://www.momjunction.com/articles/babys-5th-month-a-development-guide_00103315/

Garoo, R. (2019e, September 10). 6-Month-Old's Developmental Milestones - A Complete Guide. Retrieved December 10, 2019, from https://www.momjunction.com/articles/babys-6th-month-a-development-guide_00103340/

Garoo, R. (2019f, September 10). 7-Month-Old's

Developmental Milestones: A Complete Guide. Retrieved December 10, 2019, from https://www.momjunction.com/articles/babys-7th-month-a-development-guide_00103344/

Garoo, R. (2019g, September 10). 8-Month-Old's Developmental Milestones: A Complete Guide. Retrieved December 10, 2019, from https://www.momjunction.com/articles/babys-8th-month-a-development-guide_00102825/

Garoo, R. (2019h, September 10). 9-Month-Old's Developmental Milestones - A Complete Guide. Retrieved December 10, 2019, from https://www.momjunction.com/articles/babys-9th-month-a-development-guide_00103235/

Garoo, R. (2019i, September 10). 10-Month-Old Baby Developmental Milestones - A Complete Guide. Retrieved December 10, 2019, from https://www.momjunction.com/articles/babys-10th-month-a-development-guide_00103241/

Garoo, R. (2019j, September 10). 11-Month-Old Baby's Developmental Milestones - A Complete Guide. Retrieved December 10, 2019, from https://www.momjunction.com/articles/babys-11th-month-a-development-guide_00103429/

Garoo, R. (2019k, September 10). 12-Month-Old's

Developmental Milestones: A Complete Guide. Retrieved December 10, 2019, from https://www.momjunction.com/articles/babys-12th-month-a-development-guide_00101960/

Garoo, R. (2019, September 10). A Guide to One-Month-Old Babies' Milestones. Retrieved December 10, 2019, from https://www.momjunction.com/articles/babys-first-month-development-guide_00101911/

How Vaccines Work. (2019, November 22). Retrieved December 9, 2019, from https://www.publichealth.org/public-awareness/understanding-vaccines/vaccines-work/

Khan, A. (2018a, June 20). Washing Your Baby's Clothes - How to do it Rightly. Retrieved December 9, 2019, from https://parenting.firstcry.com/articles/washing-your-babys-clothes-how-to-do-it-rightly/

Mayo Clinic Staff. (2019, August 13). Sick baby? When to seek medical attention. Retrieved December 9, 2019, from https://www.mayoclinic.org/healthy-lifestyle/infant-and-toddler-health/in-depth/healthy-baby/art-20047793

Montgomery, N. (2019, October 29). How to trim your baby's nails. Retrieved December 9, 2019, from https://www.babycenter.com/0_how-to-trim-your-babys-nails_10027.bc

Porter, L. (2018, November 6). When Should I Start Buying For Baby? Retrieved December 9, 2019, from https://www.everymum.ie/pregnancy/preparing-for-baby/when-should-i-start-buying-for-baby/

Rhesus D Negative in Pregnancy. (2018). Retrieved December 9, 2019, from https://www.pregnancybirthbaby.org.au/rhesus-d-negative-in-pregnancy

Safety at home. (2019). Retrieved December 9, 2019, from https://www.facs.nsw.gov.au/families/parenting/keeping-children-safe/around-the-house/chapters/at-home

Sheahan, K. (2019). Choosing a Pediatrician for Your New Baby (for Parents) - Nemours KidsHealth. Retrieved December 9, 2019, from https://kidshealth.org/en/parents/find-ped.html

Shopping Tips For Newborn Baby's Clothes. (2019). Retrieved December 9, 2019, from https://community.today.com/parentingteam/post/shopping-tips-for-newborn-babys-clothes

Solid foods: How to get your baby started. (2019, June 6). Retrieved December 9, 2019, from https://www.mayoclinic.org/healthy-lifestyle/infant-and-toddler-health/in-depth/healthy-baby/art-20046200

Taylor, R. (2008, October 28). Breastfeeding Overview.

Retrieved December 9, 2019, from https://www.webmd.com/parenting/baby/nursing-basics#1

The Bump Editors. (2014, August 19). Diaper Decisions: Cloth Diapers vs. Disposable. Retrieved December 9, 2019, from https://www.thebump.com/a/cloth-diapers-vs-disposable

Thurston, K. (2017). 10 True Things About the First Year of Parenthood. Retrieved December 9, 2019, from https://www.huffpost.com/entry/10-true-things-about-the-first-year-of-parenthood_b_4254464

Vaccines Do Not Cause Autism Concerns | Vaccine Safety | CDC. (2015). Retrieved December 9, 2019, from https://www.cdc.gov/vaccinesafety/concerns/autism.html

Vitamin K at Birth. (2018). Retrieved December 9, 2019, from https://www.pregnancybirthbaby.org.au/vitamin-k-at-birth

Weaning your child from breastfeeding - Caring for Kids. (2018). Retrieved December 9, 2019, from https://www.caringforkids.cps.ca/handouts/weaning_breastfeeding

Wears, C. (2018, February 9). Traveling With an Infant? 8 Things You Must Know Before You Go. Retrieved December 9, 2019, from https://www.flightnetwork.com/blog/traveling-with-an-infant-things-to-know-before-you-go/

WhattoExpect. (2019, January 9). Essentials for Diaper Changing Stations. Retrieved December 9, 2019, from https://www.whattoexpect.com/baby-products/diapering-potty/essentials-for-diaper-changing-stations/

What to Expect,Editors. (2019, March 30). Baby's First Bath. Retrieved December 9, 2019, from https://www.whattoexpect.com/first-year/first-bath/

Yang, S. (2014, August 19). Baby's Checkup Schedule. Retrieved December 9, 2019, from https://www.thebump.com/a/new-baby-doctor-visit-checklist

Your baby's mental leaps in the first year. (2019). Retrieved December 10, 2019, from https://www.thewonderweeks.com/babys-mental-leaps-first-year/#5weeks

12 Steps to Sleep-Training Success. Retrieved 25 November 2019, from https://www.parents.com/baby/sleep/tips/ten-steps-to-sleep-training-success/

15 Ways Lack of Sleep Is Harmful To The Baby. (2016). Retrieved 17 November 2019, from https://www.babygaga.com/15-ways-lack-of-sleep-is-harmful-to-the-baby/

Alexander, L. (2019). Decoding Baby Crying (8 Types of Crying You Might Hear). Retrieved 7 December 2019, from https://momlovesbest.com/decoding-baby-crying

Baby Sleep Simplified: Newborn Sleep Schedules + Patterns.

Retrieved 24 November 2019, from
https://www.nestedbean.com/pages/baby-and-newborn-
sleep-schedules-patterns

Begley, J. (2018). Top 10 Causes of Sleep Regressions.
Retrieved 25 November 2019, from
https://thebabysleepgeek.com/top-10-causes-of-sleep-
regressions/

Bryant, A. (2019). The complete guide to nap training your
baby. Retrieved 25 November 2019, from
https://momlikeyoumeanit.com/nap-training/

Canapari, C. (2015). The Top Ten Sleep Training Mistakes (&
How To Avoid Them). Retrieved 23 November 2019, from
https://drcraigcanapari.com/sleep-training-mistakes-and-
pitfalls/

Canapari, C. (2019). Sleep Training Tools and Methods for the
Exhausted Parent. Retrieved 25 November 2019, from
https://drcraigcanapari.com/at-long-last-sleep-training-
tools-for-the-exhausted-parent/

Chitnis, R. (2019). How to Teach Baby to Self Sooth - Effective
Tips & Benefits. Retrieved 25 November 2019, from
https://parenting.firstcry.com/articles/effective-ways-to-
train-your-baby-for-self-soothing/

Colic, reflux, flatulence, or allergy – Why is my baby crying?.
(2018). Retrieved 23 November 2019, from

https://www.lullame.com/blogs/blog/colic-reflux-flatulence-or-allergy-why-is-my-baby-crying

Decoding Baby Crying. (2019). Retrieved 22 November 2019, from https://www.whattoexpect.com/first-year/week-10/decoding-cries.aspx

DeJeu, E. (2014). 3 Steps to Help Your Partner Put Baby to Bed. Retrieved 6 December 2019, from https://www.babysleepsite.com/sleep-training/partner-put-baby-to-sleep-3-steps/

Ding, K. Baby sleep training: No tears methods. Retrieved 22 November 2019, from https://www.babycenter.com/0_baby-sleep-training-no-tears-methods_1497581.bc

Doucleff, M. (2019). Sleep Training Truths: What Science Can (And Can't) Tell Us About Crying It Out. Retrieved 25 November 2019, from https://www.npr.org/sections/health-shots/2019/07/15/730339536/sleep-training-truths-what-science-can-and-cant-tell-us-about-crying-it-out

Dubinsky, D. Baby sleep training: Cry it out methods. Retrieved 22 November 2019, from https://www.babycenter.com/0_baby-sleep-training-cry-it-out-methods_1497112.bc

Dubinsky, D. Baby sleep training: The basics. Retrieved 16 November 2019, from https://www.babycenter.com/0_baby-sleep-training-the-basics_1505715.bc

Elsevier. (2008, September 4). Loss Of Sleep, Even For A Single Night, Increases Inflammation In The Body. ScienceDaily. Retrieved December 1, 2019 from www.sciencedaily.com/releases/2008/09/080902075211.htm

Gorton, R. This expert wants you to know: Sleep regressions aren't real. Retrieved 25 November 2019, from https://www.mother.ly/child/what-a-sleep-expert-wants-tired-mamas-to-know-about-sleep-regressions

Harris, N. Baby Growth Charts: Birth to 36 Months. Retrieved 25 November 2019, from https://www.parents.com/baby/development/growth/baby-growth-charts-birth-to-36-months/

How to Deal With Crying Twin Babies. (2019). Retrieved 22 November 2019, from https://www.whattoexpect.com/first-year/baby-care/how-to-deal-with-crying-twin-babies/

How to Get Baby to Nap: Baby Nap Schedule During the 1st Year. Retrieved 24 November 2019, from https://www.nestedbean.com/blogs/zen-blog/how-to-get-baby-to-nap-baby-nap-schedule-during-the-1st-year?utm_source=page&utm_medium=intext&utm_campaign=newbornsleepschedules

Johnson, N. (2019). Toddler Sleep Schedules With Feedings. Retrieved 25 November 2019, from https://www.babysleepsite.com/schedules/toddler-schedule/

Karp, H. How to Handle Your Baby's Night Wakings. Retrieved 22 November 2019, from https://www.happiestbaby.com/blogs/baby/baby-night-wakings-help

Karp, H. What Is Dream Feeding? And How Do I Do It?. Retrieved 22 November 2019, from https://happiestbaby.com.au/blogs/baby/what-is-a-dream-feed-and-how-do-i-do-it

Martinelli, K. Finding a Sleep Training Method That Works for Your Family. Retrieved 22 November 2019, from https://childmind.org/article/choosing-a-sleep-training-method-that-works-for-your-family/

Michi, R. (2017). Gentle Sleep Training- The Role of Grandparents. Retrieved 14 November 2019, from https://childrenssleepconsultant.com/2017/07/24/gentle-sleep-training-the-role-of-grandparents/

Michi, R. (2017). Gentle Sleep Training: The Role of Dads. Retrieved 14 November 2019, from https://childrenssleepconsultant.com/2017/07/13/gentle-sleep-training-the-role-of-dads/

Montgomery, N. (2019). The basics of baby schedules: Why, when, and how to start a routine. Retrieved 24 November 2019, from https://www.babycenter.com/0_the-basics-of-baby-schedules-why-when-and-how-to-start-a-rou_3658352.bc

Moye, J. (2018). Sleep Training's Simple, Effective Secret Weapon. Retrieved 6 December 2019, from https://www.fatherly.com/parenting/how-to-share-sleep-training-with-your-partner/

Newborn Baby Routine. Retrieved 23 November 2019, from https://www.tresillian.org.au/advice-tips/daily-activities/0-3-months/

Our Guide to Understanding Childhood Sleep Regression. (2017). Retrieved 25 November 2019, from https://www.tuck.com/sleep-regression/

Pennington, C. (2016). Caring for newborn twins or multiples. Retrieved 18 November 2019, from https://www.babycenter.com/0_caring-for-newborn-twins-or-multiples_3590.bc

Pyanov, M. (2017). Why The Feed-Play-Sleep Routine Doesn't Work For Breastfed Babies. Retrieved 25 November 2019, from https://www.bellybelly.com.au/baby/feed-play-sleep-routine-breastfed-babies/

Ruiz, R. (2016). Why new parents shouldn't feel so guilty about sleep training. Retrieved 25 November 2019, from https://mashable.com/2016/05/25/sleep-training-guilt-study/

Schiedel, B. (2019). Sleep and feeding schedule for your 12- to 18-month-old baby. Retrieved 25 November 2019, from https://www.todaysparent.com/baby/baby-sleep/12-to-18-month-old-schedule/

Setting Up Your Twins' Sleep Schedule. (2019). Retrieved 23 November 2019, from https://www.whattoexpect.com/first-year/baby-care/setting-up-your-twins-sleep-schedule.aspx

Should Baby Sleep in a Crib or Co-Sleep with Mom and Dad?. (2019). Retrieved 24 November 2019, from https://lambsivy.com/blogs/news/should-baby-sleep-in-a-crib-or-co-sleep-with-mom-and-dad

Smart Solutions for Baby's Nighttime Waking. Retrieved 22 November 2019, from https://www.sleep.org/articles/smart-solutions-for-babys-nighttime-waking/

The Best Routines for Twin Babies. (2018). Retrieved 21 November 2019, from https://www.whattoexpect.com/first-year/baby-care/the-best-routines-for-twin-babies.aspx

The Secret Sauce for Sleep Training Babies. (2019). Retrieved 25 November 2019, from https://fortworth.citymomsblog.com/2019/08/15/the-secret-sauce-for-sleep-training-babies/

Thompson, A. (2019). Make Sleep Training Easier By Involving Your Partner. Retrieved 14 November 2019, from https://adelethompsonsleepconsulting.com/make-sleep-training-easier-by-involving-your-partner/

Thompson, A. (2019). Make Sleep Training Easier By

Involving Your Partner. Retrieved 21 November 2019, from https://adelethompsonsleepconsulting.com/make-sleep-training-easier-by-involving-your-partner/

Tweaking Your Toddler Twins' Routines. (2019). Retrieved 25 November 2019, from https://www.whattoexpect.com/first-year/baby-care/tweaking-your-toddler-twins-routines.aspx

Twins. (2019). Retrieved 22 November 2019, from https://www.basisonline.org.uk/twins/

What 'sleeping through the night' actually means. (2018). Retrieved 23 November 2019, from https://www.kidspot.com.au/baby/baby-care/baby-sleep-and-settling/what-sleeping-through-the-night-means/news-story/139696676cb12bb7459dba318decb95f

Your Twins' Bath Time. (2018). Retrieved 21 November 2019, from https://www.whattoexpect.com/first-year/baby-care/your-twins-bath-time.aspx

3 weeks pregnant - Pregnancy symptoms week 3. (2019, October 8). Retrieved November 13, 2019, from https://www.whattoexpect.com/pregnancy/week-by-week/week-3.aspx

Baby Centre Medical Advisory Board. (2005, April 21). What to pack in your hospital bag: Your complete checklist. Retrieved November 13, 2019, from https://www.babycentre.co.uk/what-to-pack-in-your-hospital-bag

Barllaro, M. (2019). 7 post-pregnancy feelings no one warns you about. Retrieved November 13, 2019, from https://www.parents.com/baby/new-parent/emotions/7-post-pregnancy-feelings-no-one-warns-you-about/

Bed Rest. (2019). Retrieved November 12, 2019, from https://americanpregnancy.org/pregnancy-complications/bed-rest/

Ben-Joseph, E. (2018). Breastfeeding FAQs: Getting started (for parents) - KidsHealth. Retrieved November 13, 2019, from https://kidshealth.org/en/parents/breastfeed-starting.html

Carey, E. (2015, August 5). Having twins? Here's what you need to know. Retrieved November 13, 2019, from https://www.healthline.com/health/pregnancy/having-twins-what-to-expect#Delivery

Cherney, K. (2019, April 5). Natural vs. Epidural: What to expect. Retrieved November 13, 2019, from https://www.healthline.com/health/pregnancy/natural-birth-vs-epidural#using-an-epidural

Daly, K., & Reece, T. (2019). Pregnancy weight gain: What to expect and why it's not as bad as you think. Retrieved November 13, 2019, from https://www.parents.com/pregnancy/my-body/weight-gain/why-pregnancy-weight-gain-isnt-as-bad-as-you-think/

Diet during pregnancy. (2019). Retrieved November 12, 2019, from https://americanpregnancy.org/pregnancy-health/diet-during-pregnancy

Ding, K. (2019, October 29). Expert sleep strategies for babies. Retrieved November 13, 2019, from https://www.babycenter.com/0_expert-sleep-strategies-for-babies_1445907.bc

Drelsbach, S. (2019). Top 14 pregnancy fears (and why you shouldn't worry). Retrieved November 13, 2019, from https://www.parents.com/pregnancy/complications/health-and-safety-issues/top-pregnancy-fears/

Eating seafood during pregnancy. (2019). Retrieved November 12, 2019, from https://americanpregnancy.org/pregnancy-health/eating-seafood-during-pregnancy

Fuentes, A. (2018). Prenatal tests: FAQs (for parents) - KidsHealth. Retrieved November 13, 2019, from https://kidshealth.org/en/parents/prenatal-tests.html

Getting sick while pregnant. (2019). Retrieved November 12, 2019, from https://americanpregnancy.org/pregnancy-complications/sick-while-pregnant

Johnson, T. (2018, July 2). How much vitamin B6 should you get when you're pregnant? Retrieved November 13, 2019, from https://www.webmd.com/baby/qa/how-much-vitamin-b6-should-you-get-when-youre-pregnant

Khan, A. (2018, September 19). 21 common pregnancy problems and their solutions. Retrieved November 13, 2019, from https://parenting.firstcry.com/articles/21-common-pregnancy-problems-and-their-solutions/

Lucla, C. A., Hartshorn, J. (n. d.) The benefits of breastfeeding. Retrieved November 12, 2019, from https://www.parents.com/baby/breastfeeding/basics/the-benefits-of-breastfeeding

Mann, D. (2008, June 3). 11 things you didn't know about twin pregnancies. Retrieved November 13, 2019, from https://www.webmd.com/baby/features/11-things-you-didnt-know-about-twin-pregnancies#4

Marcin, A. (2018, July 10). Waterbirth pros and cons: Is it right for you? Retrieved November 13, 2019, from https://www.healthline.com/health/pregnancy/water-birth#risks

Marcin, A. (2018, September 14). What medicines can I take while pregnant? Retrieved November 13, 2019, from https://www.healthline.com/health/pregnancy/what-medicines-are-safe-during-pregnancy

Marple, K. (2019, November 1). How to choose an obstetrician. Retrieved November 13, 2019, from https://www.babycenter.com/0_how-to-choose-an-obstetrician_1582.bc

National Sleep Foundation. (2019). Pregnancy & sleep - national sleep foundation. Retrieved November 13, 2019, from https://www.sleepfoundation.org/articles/pregnancy-and-sleep

Nierenberg, C. (2017, June 17). C-section: Procedure & recovery. Retrieved November 13, 2019, from https://www.livescience.com/44726-c-section.html

Nierenberg, C. (2018, March 27). Vaginal birth vs. C-section: Pros & cons. Retrieved November 13, 2019, from https://www.livescience.com/45681-vaginal-birth-vs-c-section.html

Pampers. (2018, July 5). Learn the signs of labour from Pampers PH. Retrieved November 13, 2019, from https://www.pampers.ph/pregnancy/pregnancy-symptoms/article/signs-of-labour-how-to-read-your-bodys-signals?gclid=CjwKCAjwlovtBRBrEiwAG3XJ-yagbXRHppq8WnF2VSZoP_vMpl-c5qyR0k7yoz5tgfDe9m336q2P-xoC-R0QAvD_BwE&gclsrc=aw.ds

Parents. (2019). 11 ways to ease contractions without drugs. Retrieved November 13, 2019, from https://www.parents.com/pregnancy/giving-birth/labor-and-delivery/10-ways-to-ease-contractions-without-drugs/

Pillai, S. (2014, December 19). 5 reasons why it is unsafe to have deli meats in pregnancy. Retrieved November 13, 2019, from https://www.momjunction.com/articles/is-it-safe-to-eat-deli-meats-during-pregnancy_00118527/#gref

Reading labels. (2015, December 2). Retrieved November 13, 2019, from https://www.allinahealth.org/health-conditions-and-treatments/health-library/patient-education/beginnings/diet-and-exercise/reading-labels

Smith, S. (2018, June 7). The important role of fathers during pregnancy. Retrieved November 13, 2019, from https://www.marriage.com/advice/pregnancy/the-important-role-of-fathers-during-pregnancy/

Surviving pregnancy without your favorite vices. (2017, December 15). Retrieved November 13, 2019, from https://carepointhealth.org/surviving-pregnancy-without-favorite-vices/

Symptoms of pregnancy: What happens first. (2019, May 11). Retrieved November 13, 2019, from https://www.mayoclinic.org/healthy-lifestyle/getting-pregnant/in-depth/symptoms-of-pregnancy/art-20043853

Three vices that need to be dropped pre, post, and during pregnancy. (2019). Retrieved November 12, 2019, from https://www.babyandme.com/three-vices-that-need-to-be-dropped-pre-post-and-during-pregnancy

Travel during pregnancy - ACOG. (2019). Retrieved November 12, 2019, from https://www.acog.org/Patients/FAQs/Travel-During-Pregnancy?IsMobileSet=falseWorking

Types of prenatal vitamins. (2019). Retrieved November 12, 2019, from https://americanpregnancy.org/pregnancy-health/types-prenatal-vitamins/

Vitamin D and pregnancy. (2019). Retrieved November 12, 2019, from https://americanpregnancy.org/pregnancy-health/vitamin-d-and-pregnancy/

Wikipedia contributors. (2019, October 14). Maternity leave in the United States. Retrieved November 13, 2019, from https://en.wikipedia.org/wiki/Maternity_leave_in_the_United_States

Woolston, C. (2019, January 1). Dad's role in the delivery room. Retrieved November 13, 2019, from https://consumer.healthday.com/encyclopedia/emotional-health-17/love-sex-and-relationship-health-news-452/dad-s-role-in-the-delivery-room-643267.html

Lightning Source UK Ltd.
Milton Keynes UK
UKHW020338060620
364543UK00017B/1019